BLOOD MINGLED WITH WINE:

THE LIFE OF THE EMPEROR HELIOGABALUS

By NIGEL BARNES

This book is dedicated to my wife Emma-Jane

He [Heliogabalus] was the last of the Antonines - a man so detestable for his life, his character, and his utter depravity that the senate wiped even his name from the records.

Lampridius, c 395 AD

Copyright Nigel Barnes 2018

CONTENTS

Introduction — 6
Note on the sources — 12

1. An Empty-Headed Young Idiot — 15
2. 'Mutilated by Many Wounds' — 27
3. The Rise of the False Antoninus — 64
4. Promises from the Sun-God — 93
5. The Boy in the Candy Shop — 119
6. 'Blood Mingled with Wine' — 160
7. God-Like Children — 204
8. Heliogabalus Heliogabala — 222
9. How the Assyrian became Tiberianus — 255
10. The Fall of the House of Bassianus — 300

Introduction

The Emperor Heliogabalus died a teenager and had been on the imperial throne for less than four years. In that time he had slowly but surely alienated just about every section of Roman society to such an extent that after his death he was, and still is, pilloried as a fool, an eccentric and a deviant. He was to become the template for the rottenness which ate the heart of the Roman Empire and led to its inevitable downfall.

Few people have made a serious attempt at unravelling the tortuous and sometimes bizarre events of his life. Most of who have were his contemporaries and ancient writers who had good reasons to hurl abuse at him, standing as he did against the mores of his time and the prevailing religious climate of the third to fifth centuries. His actions opposed both the contemporary mind-set as well as the Christian wind which would soon blow across the Empire.

While writing about Heliogabalus in the *Historia Augusta*, Lampridius wrote the following apology to its dedicatee, the Emperor Constantine:

> **It may perhaps seem strange to some, revered Constantine, that such a scourge as I have described should ever have sat on the imperial throne, and, moreover, for nearly three years. But at that time there was nobody who could depose him from the rule of Rome's majesty, whereas in the case of Nero, Vitellius, Caligula, and other such emperors, there had always been someone willing to free the state from them. But first of all I apologize for**

having written down the accounts I found in the work of various other authors, even though I have passed over in silence many vile details and those things which may not even be spoken of without the greatest shame. But whatever I have told, I have covered up as best I could by the use of veiled terms.

As Lampridius rarely shied away from unveiling the most obscene and revolting of sexual excesses, the above suggests that the subject of his writing was the most depraved of all the Emperors, at least on a par with the worst of those that came before him. But Lampridius was far from being reliable; so here is an extract from one of the Emperor's contemporaries, Herodian:

Observing his actions, Maesa [Heliogabalus's grandmother] suspected that the soldiers were outraged by his eccentricities... she tried to persuade the youth, who was in every way an empty-headed young idiot, to adopt his first cousin as his son and appoint him as 'Caesar'....

Who was this reviled man, this empty-headed idiot whose lewd behaviour rocked all of Rome and who committed acts so outrageous as to cause his name to be blackened for posterity? Surely, a man who manages to out-Caligula Caligula must have been a monster beyond description, a madman, a tyrant and a devil in human form? No good is written about him by any of the historians who take up their pens to describe his reign – all is muddied with the stain of depravity and debauchery. It must have been a very unique man to have earned such a reputation for disgust and scandal.

However, to write an honest account of the life of Heliogabalus, it is necessary to strip away the fabrications and the gossip and get to the true facts. It is desirable to deal with the prevailing thoughts and attitudes of the day, attitudes which might well colour an account when seen through too narrow a viewpoint. With this, a character emerges freed from aesthetic preference or the moral strictures of the times. It remains to be seen whether this figure is indeed a monster with depraved lusts or whether his memory has been overshadowed by the fog of prejudice which was settling over the Roman Empire in the third century AD.

All of the ancient histories dealing with the Emperor Heliogabalus are entrenched in the moral code of the day, and his reign judged by the standards of virtue prevalent at the time. A person's character, no less the Emperor's, was judged by its relation to the Roman way – the *via Romana* - and this 'way' was the culmination of qualities which made the Roman race great, great enough to conquer and to civilise the known world. High on the list of these qualities was *auctoritas*, a measure of one's social standing, and *dignitas*, a measure of worth which was of great importance in the pecking order of Roman politics. Other qualities – such as mercy, frugality, industriousness, self-control, prudence, forethought, honesty and tenacity were also greatly prized. Apart from these private qualities, others existed – Virtues – which aimed towards the common good. Many were deified and some stamped on the coins on the day. There were many of these, but they included courage, modesty, liberality, fair-dealing, clemency, nobility and piety. It was the aim of every Roman citizen to aspire to all of these qualities of character which added up to a complete and useful member of society. Persons lacking in the chiefest of these were looked down upon as base. From an early age, these good characteristics were thought of as distinctly Roman; eventually Italian; and outsiders could be assessed morally by their affiliation to these basic qualities. They gave no leeway for foreign attitudes, nor for psychological neuroses. A man should be whole in body and mind and strive for the good of himself and the god of the Roman state. Of all the virtues the most acclaimed was the Genius, or the acknowledgement of the combined 'spirit of Rome', which acted to preserve and maintain its spirit of greatness and nobility.

At the time of Heliogabalus, it was a highly unusual thing for a non-Italian to succeed to the imperial diadem, but they would be expected to step in line with the characteristics of Roman standards which, they believed, had made Rome great and which would continue to make Rome greater. But Rome had already begun its slow decline which would lead to its fall, and much of what happened had to do with a relaxation of these same ideals. The people were tiring of Roman government, and to an extent its religion. The changing times were caused by, or were instrumental in, a decline in imperial standards. The glory days of the great Caesars were over, and the Empire slowly sinking in a slackening of moral codes. In such an atmosphere, someone of the young Emperor's personality was bound to run into difficulties, and such a complicated character deserves a more detailed appraisal. To many in modern times, his name is still synonymous with debauchery and sadism, but that view is starting to be challenged. To the gay community, for example, he has become something of an icon. A boy who bravely flaunted his sexuality and stood alone against the prejudices of the macho regime of the time.

But Rome was still Rome; and when Heliogabalus entered the Roman arena he did succeed in one thing – uniting the people in the common cause of hating him. In many ways their inner dissatisfaction was deflected by a united disapproval of his actions and his sexual 'aberrations'. To outward appearances, Heliogabalus's downfall was the result of an unbending refusal to conform, although in reality he followed a predestined course from which it was impossible for him to extricate himself. In the end his life became a downward spiral from which there was no escape and no possibility of rescue. He was a martyr to his own fate, which had been decreed by his upbringing, and at the mercy of the headlong rush of forces over which he had no control.

Heliogabalus was a Syrian by birth, and he arrived into a world which was in a state of turmoil and upheaval. His family had become a material part of a short dynasty of Roman Emperors – the Severan dynasty – and the strange way in which he became embroiled in Roman politics has its origins in the way the family first rose to power in the form of his great-uncle, Severus. The brutal power-struggles and wars which created the vacuum he so awkwardly filled marked not only the beginnings of the Severan dynasty but, for much of the time, his early infancy.

The subject of this book is the Emperor himself and his reign. The aim is to present an unbiased and accurate portrait of the boy-Emperor, who took the reins of office aged only fourteen and was destined to rule for a mere four years. But it was a period of some activity during which the personality of Heliogabalus was the driving force. I have tried to gain insight into the youth's character and motives, from which the reader may decide whether indeed he was an ogre or whether he was more a victim of his own passions. I have also considered the question of how much blame can be attributed to the outrageous acts he committed. Most importantly, I have tried to reassess the life of Heliogabalus free from the contemporary prejudices and the works which were written about him during and after his lifetime.

It was not possible to delve into the character of Heliogabalus without some attention to his psychopathology. For this I am indebted to my good friend Peter Purvis, who brought me up to speed with modern psychoanalytic theories concerning gender issues and homosexuality; and psychotherapist Dorothy Hayden, who confidently led me through the misty maze of masochism.

The result is this biography of one of the most talked-about Emperors in the history of the Roman Empire. It is a life full of contradictions and occasional surprises and, whether one remains critical of it or in sympathy, it remains one of the most scandalous lives in Roman history.

Note On The Sources

There are three main sources for anyone wishing to study the life of one of Rome's most despised Emperors; one of these is the *Historia Augusta,* an extremely peculiar book which seeks to anthologise the lives of the Emperors from the years 117 to 284 AD. Its authors are supposed to be Aelius Spartianus, Iulius Capitolinus, Vulcacius Gallicanus, Aelius Lampridius, Trebellius Pollio, and Flavius Vopiscus of Syracuse; it follows that Lampridius is the author of the section purporting to tell Heliogabalus's story. Whether we can believe the assignation of authors to the work, we can hardly take its contents at face value, packed as they are with inventions, forgeries and often plain fiction. They did not even stoop at inventing an Emperor. It is impossible to be sure whether the work is a satire on previous studies or simply an entertainment for the pleasure of a public thirsting for gossip and scandal, but its worst feature is that hiding among the reams of invention lie jewels of undeniable fact. Faced with this dilemma, the only safe course is to accept or reject information in the light of revelations from more secure sources. The *Historia Augusta* remains a sideshow attraction, replete with amusing anecdotes but outstanding in its unreliability. It is also notable that it purports to have been inscribed for the benefit of Constantine, and the Christian antipathy to both the character and religion of Heliogabalus is striking.

The two contemporaries of Heliogabalus, Cassius Dio and Herodian, lead the reader to safer ground. Herodian was from Syria and his history was written in Greek. According to his own words, 'I have written a history of the events following the death of Marcus which I saw and heard in my lifetime. I had a personal share in some of these events during my imperial and public service.' These events cover the period from 180-238. Although the most unbiased account, his portrait of Heliogabalus reflects a man of perverse sexuality who alienated himself from the Roman world by his debased actions and his unsavoury sexual acts. There is much in the way of chronological confusion and the work is marred by some lies and occasional gossipmongering. However his 'History of the Empire From the Death of Marcus [Aurelius]' remains perhaps the most unprejudiced, if short, account available of the peculiarities of the Emperor's reign.

Cassius Dio Cocceianus was a prominent politician in the days of Heliogabalus, and subsequently wrote a massive history of Rome in 80 books, tracing its development from the founding of the Republic right up to the Death of Heliogabalus's successor. It is fortunate that he was around at the time, as this affords a fascinating insight into the corrupt world of the Emperors and of the political machinations of the day. Unfortunately not all of his work remains, and the last twenty books are almost completely lost – unfortunate, as these contain the life of Heliogabalus. However, an eleventh century monk named Johannes Xiphilinus of Trebizond made an abridgement of these works for ecclesiastical reasons, but much of his own Christian zeal appears to have crept into it and as such neither he nor Dio were appreciative of their subject.

This account of Heliogabalus paints the picture of a vicious youth who lived to follow his own debased appetites and does not flinch at revealing the depths to which the Emperor at times descended. The book describing his life gives a vivid depiction of what can happen if an Emperor places his personal 'perversions' before the claims of his Empire, but it is woefully prejudiced against its subject.

There was one other important Latin source – the histories of Marius Maximus, who was consul during the reign of the Emperor Septimius Severus, and at whose instigation he began to continue the history of Suetonius up to contemporary times. Apparently he went further and continued his annals up until the end of the reign of Heliogabalus. Unfortunately, nothing of his work survives, and debate still rages as to how much of his work was developed by later writers, especially Lampridius.

Chapter 1. An Empty-Headed Young Idiot

The Emperor Heliogabalus had to go. It was time to rid Rome of the most despicable, the most shameful emperor who had ever worn the purple, more disgraceful than even the crazed Caligula. In the days of the Caesars the people might have accepted much in the way of imperial eccentricity, but this was the third century and their shining example was beyond human memory. The great empire, the pride of the world, was rotten through and through and many eminent Roman citizens were tired of the embarrassment and failure that had dogged the nation and led to foreigners sniggering behind their backs. Some had gone further than moaning in private; they had made a stand against the tyranny of the imperial chair which was now a target for international scorn.

One such man was Pomponius Bassus. Bassus was a hardened politician with a shadowy history most of which has not been passed on to history. He reached the rank of suffect consul in Rome back in 193, and as such was at the hub of power when Rome was torn apart by civil strife. He would remember when the first of that accursed family, the Bassiani, marched on to Rome to snatch the diadem when the nation reeled after the death of the terrible Emperor Commodus. It was the Year of the Five Emperors and Bassus, along with most of Rome, approved of the new choice of Emperor, that old veteran Pertinax. The Praetorian Guard did not, and Pertinax was murdered, leaving Rome in a vacuum that muscle and money wedged forward to snatch. Bassus had watched in disdain as the empery was literally auctioned off in the Forum, and also waited in Rome while the bloodthirsty Severus marched his men to the outskirts of the capital to demand the Empire.

The consul Silius Messala had acted as go-between in the farcical proceedings and had mediated when Severus demanded that the Guard give up the soldiers who had assassinated their Emperor. Like many of the senators at this time, both Bassus and Messala looked back to the Golden Age of Marcus Aurelius (father of Commodus) with some nostalgia and hope. Often likened to the great Augustus, Aurelius had lifted the position back to its old standard of glory and put the imperial seat in the forefront of international renown. Neither man saw the upheavals of the time as likely to improve either the standing of the Empire in the eyes of her provinces or beneficial to the state itself. The buying of the Empire by Didius Julianus was the last straw and now a Syrian had simply marched into town and put the diadem in his pocket. Time would tell how the Syrians would deal with the nation.

It did. Severus proved a good soldier but a cruel and vindictive man. However, he was nothing compared to his crazy son Antoninus and it all ended up the way it was bound to sooner or later. Antoninus was murdered after a conspiracy in his army and the commander Macrinus took over. At least the hated Bassianus family had been rooted out. Not that the Syrian rule was unproductive for the Bassus family. His son, Pomponius Bassus, became consul under Severus and his star continued to rise as he became Legatus of Moesia and possibly even served as Governor of Mysia. Although Macrinus was accepted by the senate – whose hands were tied – he proved a poor military commander. In a Syrian coup the house of Bassianus regained power and then the teenage Heliogabalus took over.

Feelings were mixed when the young boy eventually marched into Rome in triumph, dressed as an all-conquering Caesar. To many it would be a case of wait and see. Meanwhile Bassus, marking his attachment to the house of Marcus Aurelius, married his granddaughter, one Annia Aurelia Faustina, a girl of renowned beauty. So that in the year 218 Bassus was a happy man. He had wealth, a lovely wife and an estate in Pisidia. The marriage was contented and Annia gave Bassus two children, a girl called Pomponia Immidia and a son called after his father, Pomponius Bassus. It had seemed that his life was settled.

Bassus watched the antics of the new boy Emperor with some distaste. Rumours of his eccentricities had reached his ears even before the boy had entered the capital. They said that he was more girl than boy and that he was a brainless puppet acting under the strings of his power-hungry grandmother Maesa. Maesa was no stranger to political Rome and had sat by her husband Severus throughout his reign, as well as that of her son Antoninus. Of all the Bassiani, she was the most devious and dangerous. Her forte was manipulation and while Heliogabalus remained as figurehead she was able to hatch her plots and intrigues. But without an emperor to steer she was impotent. Bassus would have had no doubt that the coup was her idea, or that the idea of claiming Heliogabalus as a true son of Antoninus came from her devious mind. It was common gossip that he was in fact his nephew, but the plot had succeeded and the boy had emerged victorious.

Some of the soldiers, particularly those based near Emesa, had had first hand knowledge of this new Bassianus. Far from being a man of war, such as his predecessors, it seems that he was in effect a boy-priest. He had been something of a tourist attraction. Tthe men would watch with some bemusement as the lad pranced about to the pipe and cymbal, tinkling his jewelry and singing. His face was made up like a girl, they say, and rumours suggested he was effeminate to an alarming degree. Moreover, he had taken his time in appearing before his people, prefering to hang about in Antioch and that god-forsaken Nicodemia, which was itself considered as a hotbed of homosexuality. Instead of putting a mature mind to the problems of the greatest nation on earth, he was playing in pagan temples and exulting in the fleshpots of Antioch. It boded no good.

Now this wretch, this prancing pagan, had elbowed his way as far as the Emperor's chair. It only proved how low the Empire had sunk in a gradual progression of rottennness which had begun with the death of Marcus Aurelius. Imperial glory depended on one thing and one thing only – the inclination of the army and the Praetorian Guard. The Empire could be grasped simply by buying them off. What credentials did this eastern youngster have to set himself up as Master of the World? By all accounts his mother was little better than a whore who had consorted with so many men she wasn't even certain who her son's father was. It was later said that that is precisely why she called him 'Varius', become he could have sprung from various men. Although the last Emperor, Macrinus, had left much to be desired as a military commander he had at least marched with his men and given battle on the field. The only thing the people knew about Heliogabalus was that he rode in the final charge against the Emperor's men in Immae - and that he would not let Macrinus go to the grave without turning aside to gloat over his severed head.

Bassus was not the only man in the Empire to be disgusted at this new leader. Messala was serving in the provinces and the intelligence he had heard of the crazy happenings in Rome animated him so much he wanted to do something about it and to witness the state of things at first hand. He badgered the senate with missives until he was at last recalled. As soon as he arrived he watched Heliogabalus and was soon convinced that the reports from Rome had not been exaggerated. Far from it.

Bassus and Messala had good reason to despise the new Emperor, as each had risen through the political ranks to the highest strata of Roman society. They would both have been aware that they were much more qualified to the job of Emperor than the fool they were burdened with at that time. In fact, Heliogabalus wasn't doing the job at all. The Empire was in the hands of women - Maesa and Mamaea especially - and that latter was little better than her lascivious sister Soaemias, the Emperor's mother. It would only be a matter of time before these harridans would sit in the senate and dictate duties to the Conscript Fathers! At least, such rumours had already begun. It would not be out of character. This mindless boy had already proven that he was going to live his life – and the life of

Rome – at a whim, and that the people and senate would have no choice but to obey his childish fancies.

At the Palace, Bassus and Messala had witnessed the bizarre grotesque follies for themselves. How the boy would torment and sadistically humiliate some of the leading figures in Rome for his pleasure. At the nod of his head huge temples were being erected to some eastern idol and the pair had been forced to sit and watch his priestly antics at his imperial decree. It was an eye-opener, all right – the head of the Empire mincing and prancing about, hopping around to the noise of flute and cymbal. The sight would have been laughable if it were not so disgraceful and if he were not stopped things might well get worse. They knew that those eastern orgies once upheld human sacrifice and stories of piling up human genitalia at the altar of the sun could become a reality if the boy decided so. The senators even had to pay obsequies to these outlandish cults at the door of the senate-house.

As if this were not bad enough, the little lunatic was squandering the privy purse at a rate which staggered belief. Throwing it away on undeservers and apes of idleness. His bizarre fancies were not only outlandish but time-wasting, expensive and idiotic. He had ordered a mountain of snow to be built by transporting it from the Alps. He had hired men to pile up a ton of cobwebs and he had sunk merchant fleets because it pleased him to do so. While, like a little girl, he danced into the *curia* simpering and tinkling feminine jewelry with a face painted like Cleopatra. What visiting dignatories thought of the young pervert - who looked more like a prostitute than an Emperor – did not bear thinking about.

An Emperor should exude dignity and authority. Not so this eastern whipper-snapper, who did not even baulk at prancing about like a girl dancer at the great amphitheatres beneath the gaze of the common people. His friends were not the wise old politicians of the senate, but fools and wastrels, whores of the street, pimps, dancing boys and theatrical acrobats and jugglers. Worse, he daily showered them with gifts and largesse from the coffers of the state. If these worthless wretches were to be the Emperor's guides and counsellors what was to become of Rome? Few politicians were fooled by the rare occasion on which he would don a garb of severity and sit as presiding judge. Everyone knew that his tastes lay in extravagance and pandering to his childish amusement despite the cost or impropriety. The attempts of the royal family to portray him as an imperial figurehead were threadbare and unconvincing. The Romans were stuck with a leader who was far more fitted for the stage or playpen than for the imperial chair.

It wasn't as if the young imbecile lacked advice. Even his own relatives had tried to persuade this Heliogabalus to curb his ways and they knew that he was courting disaster. But the young emperor was, it seems, so smitten with pleasures of the flesh that he had no time for sage counsel or wise words. He had even turned Maesa aside with a sweep of his hand and turned his life into a continual roundabout of licentious orgies If the young libertine was not prepared to listen to his grandmother, the Terror of Rome, there was little hope he would change his ways. The prostitute's whelp paid his bodyguards – the Praetorian Guard – handsomely, and it looked as though they were prepared to overlook his idiosyncrasies for a purse of gold. That was par for the military course as far as they went. For many decades they had proven that their love was not of their nation, or their home city, but of money only. Now they had forsaken their pride, their gods and their self-respect for a wage packet.

It was time to make a stand for the respect and sensibilities of Roman government. Now that these were being trampled underfoot, the precious precedents of the ancient Republic and the great caesars were under threat. It was more important even than a holy righteousness. The Empire was sliding down a slippery slope at such a speed that soon it would hit rock bottom. It was losing both its prestige and its pride. The Golden Age of Marcus Aurelius had changed into one of Iron and Rust with Commodus and now had been further eaten away by the putrescence of the Severan Dynasty. Bassus and Messala wanted to check its decline and resurrect the old values of the Roman people before it was too late.

It was unthinkable to make a military stand against Heliogabalus. His grandmother had made sure all opposition had been eliminated and a makeshift coup would be quashed as soon as it began. It had already been tried in various parts of the Empire and each time it had led to nothing but recriminations. As Heliogabalus was a stupid little child the only way to oust him was by guile. The Praetorian Guard could be bought, of course, but it was best to demonstrate a unanimous backing of any rebellion against the new regime. Bassus and Messala were important figures and as such had some say as to the protection of the city and the Emperor. Although it was obvious that, to the senate, Heliogabalus was a revolting character, they needed a dossier of facts to support their case. To this end they planted spies as near to the Emperor as they could manage. Messala even succeeded in infiltrating the Palace with men of his own. These brought back regular bulletins as to what was going on behind closed doors and these pieces of news convinced him more and more that Heliogabalus must be removed. What they had seen with their own eyes in the glare of publicity was nothing compared to the sickening debaucheries perpetrated by the boy in his own home. The catalogue of revolting perversions and lewd orgies made the conspirators shudder and would, they felt, have the same effect on the sage old counsellors of the senate. The great imperial palace had become little less than a homosexual brothel.

At this point Messala felt confident enough to state his opposition to the new Emperor publicly and as such must have been watched carefully by the Godmother of the Empire, Maesa. The situation was becoming tense, but the final confrontation was accelerated by new developments in Bassus's private life. His beautiful wife was attracting the attention of the mad Emperor and Bassus knew that steps had to be taken urgently. This crazed boy was more deadly than Caligula and might at any time have him assassinated to get his hands on the partner he loved so much. The conspiracy was speeded up, senators were approached, and the two men reached a point at which they were convinced that they could effect an uprising in Rome's political nerve centre. This is proven by the fact that Messala had the temerity to advertise the contents of his secret dossier in a formal meeting of the senate. As the two men passed through the doors of the *curia,* and past the enormous picture of

Heliogabalus sacrificing to the sun-god, they must have known that it was make or break time.

But no-one knows how Maesa or Heliogabalus himself might have reacted to the news that Messala was openly criticising the imperial house. Maesa had spies enough of her own, and it is surely probable that they were sent on counter-espionage missions. At any rate, it seems that not only did the gathered senators know that Messala was about to launch a direct attack on the Emperor, but that anyone who backed him would be in some danger. It was a battle of wills between the gifted orator and high-ranking ex-consul, and the might of the Bassiani.

One of the senators who sat listening in amazement at Messala's historic speech was the historian Cassius Dio. Dio argued that 'he resolutely laid bare many facts before the senate' and that Heliogabalus 'really feared that Messala might take the lead in bringing about a change of mind on the part of the senators.' Nothing of the speech remains, and it is left to speculation as to how many personal details he gave, but the fact that he read from the dossier suggests that he held back nothing in his attempt to prove what a worthless profligate Heliogabalus was. It must have been a stirring speech, as Messala was in effect fighting not only for the good of Rome but for his own life. When he finished, Bassus rose to back up his insinuations and add rhetoric of his own.

Both Messala and Bassus expressed opinions that they were displeased with what the Emperor was doing and must have had good reason to imagine that their attack would meet with little opposition. After all, the senate itself had good reasons to be suspicious and afraid of the change in emperor. But they had seriously miscalculated. Whatever assurances might have been made in private few people would stand up in the *curia* and be counted as enemies to the powerful royal family. Dio's comment suggests that, while many senators might have been swayed by Messala's plots, few would back him, and he translocates the general fear of the senate to Heliogabalus himself. Over the past few decades the senators had lived in constant fear and now they were a herd cowed down by the threat of punishments and reprisals.

Unfortunately for Messala and Bassus their plan backfired. Despite a spirited and vigorous attack on the imperial family they slowly found themselves completely isolated. It was time for the Bassiani to fight back, although the outcome was by now a foregone conclusion. Heliogabalus himself argued that both men were 'investigators of his life and censors of what went on in the palace'. There had been well-proven plots made by the two men against the Empire. The accusation was that the two men were therefore guilty of treason, and for that there was only one possible outcome. The senate, their hands tied, had no choice but to agree with their Emperor, and that done, condemn Bassus and Messala to be executed.

Once again the wilful boy had won the day by means of his powerful backers. Many senators were ashamed of their actions, even though they were left with no choice, and perhaps to assuage their wounded consciences they asked Heliogabalus to give them details of the plots and conspiracies Messala and Bassus had been guilty of. By this time the death sentences had already been carried out and, after their execution, Heliogabalus wrote to the senate:

I haven't sent you the proofs of their plots, because it would be a waste of time to read them. The men are already dead.

Hardly was the body of Bassus cold when the boy made overtures to his beautiful wife, still shocked and grieved by the death of her husband. Annia Aurelia was therefore forced to marry Heliogabalus in indecent haste, and was told by her new husband that she was forbidden to mourn for Bassus. There were many in the senate who brooded over this latest outrage, and some, like Dio, guessed that this marriage was merely a cover-up to disguise the Emperor's effeminacy. Bu, after the latest failed attempt at insurrection there was little they could do but vent their anger in secret and hope for a time when the opposition to the royal family would be stronger.

The marriage was not destined to last long, and Annia Aurelia was soon cast aside unceremoniously with little respect for her long and illustrious family background. In a spree which seemed to be calculated to stir up the maximum amount of animosity, Heliogabalus, true to form, chose and discarded a number of wives, including one which was so sacrilegious and blasphemous that it would shake Rome to its very core. Truly, one may say, an empty-headed young idiot.

Chapter 2. 'Mutilated By Many Wounds'

The Temple stood glistening in the rising Syrian sun on the banks of the Orontes, or Axius, River. Located in the town of Emesa, present-day Homs, it was the most magnificent temple to the national sun-god. Pilgrims travelled there far and wide, bringing with them both their religious zeal and their offerings. The river made Emesa a good location, as it flowed away through the mountains and the desert north towards the Lake of Antioch and south to Israel. Travellers would follow it by the waterside tracks. Once arrived in town, the pilgrims would admire the magnificent structure and participate in the rites, worshipping the temple's phallic-shaped meteorite, or holy stone, sent down from their god. They would offer the high priest the goods and sacrifices necessary to appease the solar deity.

On the days of worship Emesa was a town transformed. The shopkeepers no longer hung out their wares in the dusty streets and the small flat-roofed houses prepared themselves for the main event of the day. Animals were herded through the roads among the bustling crowds, meekly being led to the slaughter. When the time came, the masses moved back to the sound of hooves and a magnificent cavalcade of chariots rattled down towards the temple.

The highlight of which was the most exquisite jewel-encrusted royal carriage, carrying no other than the famed High Priest of the town, resplendent in his gorgeous robe of state. Even though the people had witnessed this spectacle so many times before, it never failed to excite feelings of awe and reverence. Newcomers simply watched breathless and open-jawed at the sheer magnitude of the spectacle.

Worship of the sun dates from the oldest records. It made sense. The great fiery ball in the sky was the creator and generator, from which food grew and people were nourished. It was the obvious choice for a godhead. The sun-god was probably born in ancient Peru, where the local Indians had a religion based on the solar system. They built observatories and sacrificed fruit and flowers – their Father Sun was called Yayta Inti.

Colonists brought the concept of solar worship to Egypt, where Inti became Ra, son of Ptah. Eventually Babylon was caught up in the sun craze, Sha-mash being their fiery deity, born of the Moon. *Baal* ('Lord', or 'God') appeared in many different guises, until he at last settled on Syria, where he took the title of El-Gabal ('The Mountain'), and so took his place among the various mountain gods of Syria, Palestine, and Anatolia. In Aramaic the god was known as Ilaha Gabal, in Latin, as Elagabalus; and the Greek version was Heliogabalus.

As with all religions, El Gabal needed His own high-priests and when Syria was freed from the bonds of the Seleucid Dynasty, in 64 BCE, the government of Emesa was taken over by the clergy. They now became all-powerful and wealthy, virtual demi-gods in their own right. The first of the priest-kings was Sampsiceramus and as succession was hereditary he was followed by his son Iamblichus, who was killed by Mark Antony for his political leanings. However, Antony was defeated by Augustus, and in 20 AD Augustus showed his gratitude to Emesa for its loyalty by re-establishing the line of priestly monarchs in favour of Iamblichus's son. For almost two centuries Emesa saw peace, and the royal family flourished.

One of the most eminent of these high priests towards the end of the second century was one Caius Julius Bassianus, meaning that Caius was of the old-established Julius family, belonging to the Bassianus clan. As in the west today, Romans had two names – the familiar name, analogous to our first names, and a surname, representing the family. In the case of a very large or distinguished family it was expedient to add the name of the particular family group, or clan. Things are further muddied by the fact that many eminent people liked to add adoptive names, and a fair rule of thumb is – the longer the name, the more eminent the ancestry. It is also a fact – and an awkward one – that daughters were invariably named after the family, and every daughter of a Julius was called Julia.

Caius Julius Bassianus, then, held an important office in the Temple of the Sun. As with most men of the day, Caius wanted a son and heir but to him this desire was even more important than usual. He was in a position of great authority which was hereditary, and as the high priests of Emesa were necessarily male he needed a son to continue the line. Both he and his people waited eagerly for the arrival of a new son and heir, and although he conceived two children, both turned out to be baby girls. While Caius was hale the problem seemed relatively unimportant; but as the years went by the cloud of a succession crisis must have often occupied his mind.

His two daughters were both called Julia, of course – Julia Maesa and Julia Domna. It would seem that, having no sons to carry on the family tradition, Bassianus concentrated his efforts on teaching and educating the girls, who developed traits which would, at that time, have been considered distinctly masculine. It was as if they compensated for the lack of a male heir in their determination to carry the Bassianus torch themselves. Of the two, Maesa seems to have been slightly the more assertive, and as the daughter of a local high priest her ambitions were boundless. Domna also had agendas of her own and, despite the disadvantage of their sex, the two women were determined to claw their way up in the world. Like dogs pulling on a leash, they were hungry for power, and any match in marriage would need to be a satisfactory stepping-stone to carry them upwards and onwards. This obsession with political muscle would increase as they grew in stature and in the end they would dictate much of the history of the next few decades.

The eldest daughter, Maesa, soon hooked an influential fish in the person of Julius Avitus. He was a local boy made good who had not only attained the rank of consul – the highest magisterial position in ancient Rome – but also been appointed Governor of Asia, Mesopotamia and Cyprus. This was a not insignificant connection for Caius's family. He was an ideal husband for Maesa, who now cast her nets not only in the provincial town of Emesa but also towards the Roman Empire itself. After the wedding, Julia Maesa bade farewell to the land of her birth and accompanied her husband to Rome. There she would learn all the nuts and bolts of its political machinery. Not for Maesa the life of a housewife, however honourable; her desires rose above the traditional woman's role and she was determined to involve herself in the business of government. She did, however, have two children to Avitus. Both were daughters and so called, confusingly enough, Julia. The 'second two Julias'. Even this was not necessarily due to maternal instinct. If the seed of the Bassianus family was to flower she needed heirs who could inherit the titles she wished to acquire for them – and of course rule them from backstage.

It only remained for Caius to find a suitable partner for Julia Domna – but that took care of itself. A wandering fortune-teller foretold that she would be a queen and that was enough to excite much curiosity. Astrology and superstition were rampant in ancient Rome and widely believed. After all, the gods had interacted with mortals before, such as during the siege of Troy. It was only to be expected that they should communicate with those down below, through signs in the sky or omens on the earth beneath. In any case, news of this portent found its way to the ears of an eminent statesman and soldier, Septimius Severus. Half Roman and half Berber Arab, he had been made consul and was now in charge of the Pannonian legions. He had been married before – to one Paccia Marciana – but even so he hurried to Emesa to follow up the signs, finding Domna and proposing almost before he had seen her. Having the right qualifications, Caius Julius Bassianus saw no impediment, so the couple were betrothed and subsequently married.

The story, however, has its inconsistencies. According to the histories, Severus heard of the oracle in 179, but Domna was only born in 170, making her nine years of age at the time. Besides, Severus was still married, and his wife was not to die for another eight years. But there is no reason why a betrothal should not have been thought appropriate and it is likely that Severus finally married Domna in 187, after the death of his wife. At the time he met the Bassianus family he commanded the Fourth Scythian Legion quartered in Syria (possibly in Emesa). Born in 146, Severus was twenty-four years older than Domna, not that it would have been an impediment in those days.

It was this union with Severus which would catapult the Bassianus family from local dignitaries to the centre of the world stage. Severus was a man of insatiable ambition and an attachment to a lady to whom the gods had decreed a regal title was an attraction too powerful to resist. Born in Leptis Magna, Libya, he became first a senator and after that a quaestor in Sardinia. Climbing further up the political ladder he was to be first a legate to Africa and then, on his return to Rome, a tribune. There seemed to be no stopping this ever-rising meteor, and before long he was serving as praetor and governing not only Upper Pannonia but also central France. Such was the triumphant blaze of glory carved out by a man whose father had held no distinguished office, although his family had achieved some measure of greatness in the form of his consular cousin.

For Domna, this was a match made in heaven, and it was in every way a marriage of like minds. Both she and Maesa had married high-ranking governors of the Roman Empire and both acted as spurs to prick on their respective spouses to better things. Of the two men, Severus was by far the most subtle and ambitious. A wily fox who would use any means to gain his ends and in his turn he would have surely appreciated the support and encouragement of his ambitious and enthusiastic wife. In no time at all he rose higher and soon after his marriage he was given the ultimate post of Roman consul. He and Julia Domna had two sons who would have an important influence on the events to come – Lucius Septimus Bassianus, better known as Antoninus or 'Caracalla', and Publius Septimus Geta, or 'Geta' for short.

So Severus was Governor of Pannonia, an ancient province comprising the western part of Hungary as well as parts of Austria, Bosnia, Croatia, Serbia, Slovakia and Slovenia. The young Julia Domna was there with him, and like Maesa she showed an avid interest in everything that went on. She was erudite, even at an early age, and gained a reputation for her learning in mathematics and astrology. She counted among her associates the famous Philostratus, who went on to write *The Life of Apollonius* and dedicating it to her. As well as Philostratus, she gathered to herself a *collegium* of physicians, historians, astrologers and philosophers. Including such illuminati as Ulpian, Papinian, Philo, Galen – even Heliogabalus's future biographer, Cassius Dio. There was a darker side to her too, at least according to rumour – she was thought, like most of her family, to have had a lascivious side. Tertullian mentions a number of intrigues. He also accuses her of plots against her husband, however, but that is most unlikely and casts doubt on the rest of his assertions.

More than anything else, she was intensely ambitious, possibly almost as much as Maesa. But whereas her energies were directed into action, Maesa excelled in plots. If Domna wanted something she would straightaway make an effort to grab it without considering any slower, more circuitous routes. It is said that she was the Lady Macbeth to Severus, but that is not likely. The idea of grasping the imperial purple was on his mind in any case, and her influence would have been a supportive one. Severus was crafty and ingenious enough to carve a path for himself, and had the daring and courage to do so.

So much for Julia Domna's fortunes. Her sister was busy watching the changes in fortune of the Roman Empire; then, in 193 AD, something happened which was to change her fortunes and to propel the house of Bassianus to undreamed-of heights. The good Emperor Marcus Aurelius has been dead for thirteen years and his slimy son Commodus had made himself so unpopular that he was assassinated by being poisoned and, afterwards, drowned in his bath.

The death of Commodus meant that Rome became a rudderless ship. Having left no heir, the state was left at the mercy of all the marauding pirates who had been watching enviously as she floundered under the mismanagement of her captain. Now that she had lost all protection she was easy prey. The Empire was in a crisis. It was obvious that sheer muscle was all that was required to snatch it, but no single party had enough clout to safely walk in and claim it. The subjugated provinces watched on with avid interest. Powerful commanders dithered as they made up their minds whether to strike or wait and see what would develop. Rome was now dying, and the vultures were quick to circle overhead. The powerful Praetorian Guard controlled the situation and when dissatisfied with the new Emperor Pertinax, an old and well-respected senator, they killed him and put the Empire up for a general auction, to be claimed by the highest bidder - which turned out to be one Didius Julianus.

While this farce was being acted out in the Roman senate-house, Julia Domna's star had finally begun to rise. The Bassianus family was always quick to exploit a volatile situation and Septimius Severus had been receiving reports from Rome in his Pannonian stronghold. He was not the only one. As Rome squirmed defencelessly, other commanders had been nursing ambition and there were another two strong candidates for the role of Emperor; the Governor of Syria, Pescennius the Black, and the Governor of Britain, Clodius the White. Because of the struggles between Pertinax, Julianus, Clodius, Pescennius and Severus, 193 AD became known as the Year of the Five Emperors.

The race for the imperial title would be won by the fastest mover, and that proved to be Severus. While Pescennius bided his time, Severus moved into Illyrica and gained the support of the people there. They had been ruled by Pertinax and were still enraged by his assassination. Afterwards he defeated both Pescennius and Clodius in battle to secure his position; these battles were so ferocious that historian Cassius Dio described the opposing forces as being 'mutilated by many wounds'. When the dust settled on the plains Severus had emerged as sole ruler of Rome.

When Julia Domna triumphantly entered Rome alongside her conquering husband, sweeping aside the weak and impotent Julianus, she would finally have met up with her sister. Julia Maesa had been living in a state of fear for the past weeks. Knowing that she had close ties with a man who was marching on Rome to claim the title of Emperor, if he failed, her situation would have been precarious. She and Julius Avitus had a home in a smart part of town, on the Aequiline Hill, and from the start her mind had turned to consolidating her position within Roman society. Patient and determined, she knew that wealth meant power, so now she had made a match with a wealthy servant of Rome she had a good grounding. But enough was never enough for Maesa, who assiduously gathered money and lands to her as a safeguard to her ambitions. As well as this, she watched the political arena with some astuteness, building up a store of knowledge and understanding which she kept to herself and nurtured.

The important lessons Maesa had learned in those earth-changing days were important in adapting her thoughts on power and how to use it. What Avitus really wanted was an heir and although Maesa had given him two children, they were both girls - both called Julia, of course. Mamaea and Soaemias were both well matched in marriage; Mamaea with a local pro-magistrate called Julius Gessius Marcianus and Soaemias with a senator by the name of Sextus Varius Marcellus. Mamaea had two children, a girl called Theoclia and a son called Alexianus; Soaemias had only the one child, Varius. His name has come through to posterity as the future Emperor Heliogabalus.

Varius was born in around 203. As Marcellus was a prominent Roman citizen, and a member of the senate, the couple had moved to a locality not far from the city. They moved to his estate at Velletri, some twenty-five miles south-east of Rome. This town, as now, was a well-to-do settlement in the Albian Hills which was a favourite haunt for the select and favoured citizens of the day. Augustus's family hailed from here, and it was inside this region of fruit-trees and lakes that he spent his youth. It was famed for its wines and its food, especially the fish from the nearby lakes. Originally it had been a pawn used in the struggles between the Romans of long ago and the Volscian troops, but those days had long gone and the town on its hill was littered with opulent villas owned by the rich of Rome.

Soaemias possessed an interesting character which had many aspects. She was loving, passionate, vivacious and sexually charged, but she was also deeply religious to the point of neurosis. She had no political knowledge or pretensions, and it was perhaps for this reason that a divide was to grow between herself and Maesa and Mamaea, to such an extent that it is said she was hated by her sister. Although she is only known to have had the one son, there are some doubts about this thanks to a single inscription which states: JULIA SOAEMIAS BASSIANA CUM FILIS ('Julia Soaemias Bassiana with sons'); the plural of the last word suggesting she may have had others. If she did, no mention of them has survived, and perhaps it was the case that he or they did not live long.

The future Emperor was born at home, to Julia Soaemias and Sextus Varius Marcellus. On the *dies lustricus*, the day of naming, he was given the *praenomen* Varius, after Sextus's family. So it was, that even at a tender age, Varius found himself at the centre of a conflict between the morals and religious beliefs of Italy and those of Syria. Although one of a line of high priests to the local god El-Gabal, his father, as a man of high Roman rank, wished his only son to follow in his footsteps. To do that he would have to be conversant with the ways of Roman politics. Consequently, his earliest education would have to follow the normal lines for any child of Rome.

He was born with the help of a professional midwife. Almost certainly he was suckled by a slave wet-nurse, as no Roman woman of breeding would perform the task herself. Despite Julia's obstinacy and single-mindedness, it is probable that the birth-rites would have been as his father wished, and as would become a prominent member of Roman society. These would include the celebratory bonfires, as well as the rite of purification at the age of nine days, during which he would be given a gold *bulla*, or charm, as well as other little trinkets called *crepundia*. The bulla was designed to safeguard the child and ward off evil presences, or *numina*. Whether Julia Soaemias performed any other rite as befitting a member of the high priesthood of El-Gabal is not known.

As to Varius's early education, he would have been taught the Roman and Greek language by appropriate Roman tutors, as well as the basics of Roman history and oratory. This was based on the semi-mythological accounts of the beginnings of Rome; Virgil, and his *Aeneid,* which depicted gods interacting with mortals, the sack of Troy and the subsequent flight of Aeneas, with his father Anchises, son of Venus, on his back. It was Aeneas who, after his flight, sailed towards Italy, and whose son, Julius, founded the dynasty which would eventually produce Romulus and Remus, the founders of Rome.

Historians being in short supply during those times, later Romans had to rely mainly on word of mouth and tales passed from generation to generation. Thus the first kings of Rome had no fixed basis in written fact and have become legendary, although at the time the stories about them would have been treated as the truest accounts of old history. Romulus became the first king, but the line ended with the seventh – Tarquin the Proud. Incensed when his son, Sextus Tarquin, raped the Lady Lucretia, the people (led by one Brutus) expelled the king and so began the Republic which would last until Augustus became Emperor in 27 BCE. These were the stories every respectable Roman citizen should know of and which every Roman child, including Varius, would be taught.

But religion, as the Romans knew it and which they treated with the gravest respect, represented the first of Varius's internal conflicts. As a follower of the local sun-god El-Gabal, Varius would later find it hard to reconcile his religious persuasion with that of the Romans. True, they did have their own sun-god, Apollo, but this was a deity stolen from the Greeks by Augustus Caesar and made to sit alongside the national pantheon. Apollo was the son of Zeus and Leto, had extraordinary beauty, and also became associated with a variety of subjects, from poetry and music to philosophy and the arts. Things may have been easier for Varius had Augustus chosen

Helios instead, which was the Greek equivalent of his own god El-Gabal.

Throughout Varius's childhood his abiding influence was that of his mother. To the Roman family the woman of the house was the mistress and her word was sacrosanct. Things had changed little since the historian Tacitus wrote:

> **The son of every citizen, the child of every honorable mother, was from the beginning brought up, not in the chamber of a professional nurse, but in that mother's breast and in her arms: it was her especial glory to give herself to her home and devote her life to her children. It was the usual custom to select an elderly kinswoman of approved and esteemed character to have complete authority over all the children of the household. In her presence it was the gravest offence to speak an unseemly word or to do anything disgraceful. With total piety and modesty she oversaw not only the boy's studies and occupations, but even his recreations and games.**

So it was that the earliest and most abiding influence of a child's home life was that of the mother, and as an only son the bonds between them were strong and enduring. As a Syrian it would have been inevitable that she would instil her child with the old tenets of religion and morals. Indeed, it would be necessary if he were to later gain his place among the line of priest-kings still so powerful in Emesa.

Like most children since time immemorial, Varius, the normal if comfortably-off child of Rome, was told that he was special. Soaemias, knowing the child's destiny, would have to prime him for his future at an early age and instil a reverence for the hidden sun-god to whom he was inexorably linked. What's more, as the sole surviving child, Soaemias pampered him and doted on him throughout his short life. It must have been pleasant to have been told that he was no ordinary boy, but a prince in disguise, an ugly duckling that one day would turn into a swan whom the people would adore and worship. Throughout his life Varius showed that he had a vivid imagination and it is not stretching possibility too much to suggest that he might easily have been carried away by such suggestions. Somewhere, over the mountains in the faraway East, El-Gabal was waiting for him, and his subjects eagerly awaiting the return of their prodigal high priest. Unlike other children, however, it was Varius's fate that the stories whispered in his ear were true, and that – sooner than he could have imagined – he would find that out.

So, as far as Varius's future prospects went, he was trapped between two mighty forces – the prospect of a sacerdotal situation in his native town or the prospect of an eminent career in Roman politics. The two were not compatible. On top of this, there is no doubt that he was spoiled by his mother as the only son and the one on which she pinned all her aspirations and ambitions. As his overbearing mother and educator, Julia Soaemias was the most important influence in the moulding of his mind, and her native beliefs and ancestry were stamped on his imagination with some power. El-Gabal towered over Apollo. At a young age, he was regaled with pagan instructions, of details of the symbolic and orgiastic rituals of the religion to which he was heir. He had been chosen from all other boys in his small milieu to be the religious leader and pedagogue. It was an education which stirred him deeply and he would never forget the sun-god of Emesa.

As Varius grew into boyhood, and as he reached puberty, these were the main influences on his little life. Another appeared in the person of one Gannys, a soldier and wily tactician who had ingratiated himself in the Bassianus family by being fostered by Maesa. It is known that he was very close to Soaemias, and that foremost of Varius's young life he acted as his tutor and even foster-father. For most of his early life Varius would be accustomed to seeing Gannys around the house, or scratching his lessons on a wax tablet during lesson times.

There is nothing to suggest that the childhood of Varius, up to this point, differed from that of any other contemporary Roman time of his time. Boys of his age would play the usual games of the day– war games, using wooden swords, or hide-and-seek, tic-tac-toe and leapfrog. Boys of that time would also delight in playing at see-saw, on swings or hobby-horses; they flew kites, played board-games and used yoyos. It was also popular for boys to play at charioteer using a small cart attached to some domestic animal, such as a dog, goat or even a pony, and it may be that this was how Varius first became attracted to the sport which would fascinate him throughout his life. However, for reasons which will become apparent, it may be that young Varius did not mingle much with the young boys of the area and might have been happier with dolls.

In the old days of the Republic, the father of the house – *paterfamilias* – would hold the ultimate position in the household. He even had power over the lives and deaths of his children. But that had been in a period which would have been medieval to the citizens of the ancient world at this time. The modern trend was to spare the rod and corporal punishment had been all but phased out. The modern stress was on praise and reproof to instil morality into the child. Moreover, although Rome was still a patriarchal society, women had for the last three centuries been enjoying a certain amount of emancipation. They could instigate divorce, own tracts of land and achieve a measure of power, albeit not directly in the senate-house. Roman women were flexing their political muscle and many old-school moralists did not like it at all. It had even been claimed that such a decline in masculine omnipotence was responsible for the decline of the Roman Empire, a poor excuse for such a phenomenal catastrophe.

At some stage, when Varius was still an infant, Julia Soaemias moved back to Emesa. She left behind her pleasant Italian villa for the sun of Syria. In his 1911 book, Professor Hay shows some bewilderment at this, and it does seem that Marcellus stayed behind in Rome. But reasons for her departure are surely not so difficult to discover. Soaemias found the atmosphere of Roman politics uncongenial, and this would have been made more uncomfortable by the attitudes of her sister Mamaea and her grandmother. Besides, Severus had sired a son and the imperial family would rule the Empire successively, which left little for her to do. As well as this, her son was needed back in Emesa. The line of high priests had to be kept intact, and as he was the next in line to the rule the family may have desired the return and asked her to come home. She may have been homesick, too, and longed for the familiar terrain of her native land.

Soaemias was renowned for her beauty, but that beauty was of a decidedly Eastern stamp. In the quiet backwaters near Rome she may have felt different from the other ladies. Being known to have had a strong attachment to her native religion, and probably for her country of origin, it may not have been difficult to persuade her to return to the people she felt at home with and the Temple at which she had worshipped so devoutly. Besides, no-one really knows how successful her marriage had been and she may well have been alarmed at the prospect that her only son, a scion of high priests, may be contaminated by the customs and gods of the Roman people. It is not difficult to imagine how a conflict of interests might have estranged husband and wife, both adamant on the future prospects of their son. Prospects which were poles apart. In this regard, a clash was inevitable and in those times it was quite acceptable for Soaemias to instigate a divorce herself.

Writing in the fourth century, historian Eutropius suggests another reason for the move to Syria. In his *Brevarium Ab Urbe Condita*, ('Breviary of the Founding of the City') he states that 'after his father's death, fearing betrayal, he fled for safety, as it were, into the priesthood of the sun-god'. The insinuation is that Marcellus had enemies in the state, and that mother and son were forced to flee for their lives. However, the tale has no basis in fact; Marcellus was alive and well when mother and son left their home for Emesa.

Interestingly, Gannys soon reappeared in Emesa, and it may have been for the sake of Soaemias that he did so. It is possible that they may have had a liaison, as Soaemias was known to be of a hot-blooded temperament, and such a liaison would not be all that surprising. Marriage was not a legal state and divorce could be brought about simply by a separation. After her return to Emesa, little is heard of Marcellus, at least not in connection with Soaemias. We know that in 196 he was made Procurator Aquarum; early on he reached the grade of Prefect. At time of death in 217 he was *Legatus Legionis II Augustae, Praeses provinciae Numidiae* ('legate of the Second Augustine Legion, Governor of the Province of Numidia'), which nullifies Eutropius's claim that he had died before the journey of his wife and son.

Gannys must have been a common sight in the household of the young Varius, and at some stage would seem to have married Soaemias; at least Dio would remark later that he was 'virtually her husband', and was Varius's 'foster-father'. Varius, who was strongly attached to his mother, may well have resented this usurpation of his father's place by his grandmother's ward – someone he may have been old enough to see as his uncle. There are, however, conflicting reports about his original position in the Bassianus household – one suggestion is that he was a eunuch and a tutor, but this hardly fits in with his role as foster-father or his subsequent significant contribution to the battles on behalf of Varius. There are also murmurs of surprise that Gannys carried himself so well in fighting, and later he seems to have reached the rank of general, an incredible feat for a eunuch. On balance, it is more probable that Gannys was an experienced soldier, and perhaps an eminent one, when he was first introduced into such a regal family as that of Maesa.

Another possibility is that, having ingratiated himself with Maesa, he may have been thought suitable as a tutor for the young Varius and was sent to Syria to fulfil that function. As he became more intimate with Soaemias, she may have thought it beneath her to have a public liaison with someone of his low status, and so he may have sought a suitable career in the military, perhaps at the local camp of the Third Gallic Legion. If this was the case, and he had gone off to seek his fortune when Varius was still small, he could have gained enough experience to have all the makings of a potentially high-ranking soldier. This would explain his subsequent success in the scenario which was to follow. However, given the lack of historical data, everything is speculation. All we are told is that he had been a tutor to Varius, and there all information about his background dies away.

It must have been a time of great confusion for the little mite who was packed off with his mother to leave the outskirts of Rome which had been his small life. No doubt it was a great adventure. He left behind the greenery and the orchards of the Roman suburbs and would have seen the countryside pass him by as his great journey took him farther and farther away from the world he knew, to a land of sands and sun, of flat-roofed Middle-Eastern houses and the great Temple by the riverside. To a grown-up, the country may have seemed harsh and unyielding, but to a child it would have seemed magical and new. Soon he would be ready for a new adventure – to play the pontiff.

The boy who left Velletri was little different from other noble Roman children of his time, even in looks, as he seemed to have inherited Avitus's more western appearance. A handsome lad, he was used to the rather staid magnificence of the Roman world – his trips to see his aunt and grandmother, the wonderful buildings, may only have been a misty remembrance in his young mind. His very early education had been to initiate him in the *via Romana*, and his clothing chosen to suit his position as a rich child of Rome. Around the columns of the villa he could see stretches of orchard and fertile hills, while, apart from his mother, his young memory might have kept a special place for his father, the dignified officer who would reappear every so often in his robes of state, and Gannys who, with a steady and serious eye, had begun to teach him Roman history and the early basics of Roman customs.

For a child to be bundled off to an alien land and to be given boundless power is hardly the way to promote normal healthy psychological development. Varius was strongly attached to his mother – obsessively so, perhaps – and the secret tales of a faraway land in which marvellous ceremonies accompanied the worship of El-Gabal, the real god, must have sent his imagination reeling. He must have been a very confused little boy. On the one hand, his father and tutor were preparing him as a normal child of Rome with opportunities to rise in the social structure of the Empire, while on the other hand others were seducing him with stories of the great god of the mountain who was waiting for his return. That day had now arrived; the boy was leaving Rome and its paganism and returning to the bosom of his god, but not as an ordinary boy going home. Varius was arriving in a blaze of glory as a High Priest, and the child, who throughout his life would nurse a wild and vivid imagination, must have felt his heart race as he thought of the magnificent temple he would inherit and the status he would enjoy as the mightiest boy in Syria. It was a fairy-tale which would have delighted and entranced him, but most importantly it was a fairy-tale which was real.

No amount of talk or teaching by his mother could have prepared him for the role he was expected to take on in the town of his ancestors. Yet Varius Avitus was the high priest of Emesa, and before long he found himself being taught subjects about which he was utterly ignorant; dancing steps, the playing of the cymbals, the cries of supplication to his new god. The whole world would seem different to the boy, now that sand replaced grass, flat-roofed humble houses the proud valley villas, tumbling merchants' stalls the plush supermarket of the Circus Maximus. Knowing no-one but his mother it would be natural that the bond between them would grow even stronger, whereas, for her part, Soaemias had finally come home.

Varius was shown the great Temple for the first time. Passing through the great phallic-shaped columns, he cannot fail to have been awestruck by the magnificent black meteorite of magical properties which linked him to El-Gabal himself. Having seen the somewhat reserved words of prayer uttered by the Romans he had known, the fury of the sun-god rites must have seemed exciting and thrilling. This, he was repeatedly told, was his inheritance, the fortune which had been prepared for him and which was now his to take. All of this – the town, the temple – were his to lead.

As the months went by, Varius was quickly taught the ceremonies by the priests of El-Gabal, and particularly the role set out for him as High Priest. Although Varius gained the power of an autocrat, he began as a student. Varius was a receptive bright child who quickly absorbed the information and put it into practice. It must have been a wonderful and moving time for the future Emperor, to lead the massive processions to the Temple, to address the newly-arrived bands of pilgrims, and to conduct the ceremony. This was not Rome, and the Middle-Eastern character was not bound by the stifling *sang-froid* of Roman etiquette – the Syrians were used to a spontaneous expression of emotions and little was better designed to move them than the orgiastic fervour of the El-Gabal rituals. Starting with prayers and dancing, the ceremony would gradually rise in tempo until the congregation reached frenzied levels; it was a furious, and in many cases therapeutic, outlet for pent-up energies and emotions.

It is arguable that the situation may not have been psychologically beneficial for the young boy. In his earliest – and some would argue, formative – years, Varius had experienced a family background in which the women were the dominant members, especially his formidable grandmother, Maesa, and his ambitious great aunt, Domna. His mother, Soaemias, would seem to have been an affectionate, loving woman who may have smothered him. Now he was exposed to, and led, a religion whose core was fertility rites and a celebration of growth and procreation. Phallic symbols surrounded him everywhere. Sex – even if he didn't fully understand it – stood in stark relief against the pulsating rhythm of the dancing and the pounding of the drums and cymbals. This absorption with sexuality, together with his status as demi-god, was not a happy psychological background for a boy already confused by the contrasts between the two lifestyles he had been exposed to.

Although it may well be argued that Varius was a boy robbed of his childhood, it may also be suggested that he was a child who never really experienced manhood. The youthful experiences he had had during these years would stay with him throughout his short life, and his opinions and predilections would never alter significantly. He retained a passion for pomp and extravagance and the love for his religion, which had been dinned into him almost from infancy, continued to burn like a beacon inside him. Paradoxically, his love of play would also cling to him and would be expanded in later years almost as an attempt to reclaim the lost years of childhood. Throughout his short life he would be committed to re-enacting the life he had lived in Emesa, claiming the love of his people through his own magnificence, and much of his actions and behaviour could be best explained by viewing them through the eyes of a child.

Dressed in a luxurious robe crusted with jewels he led a procession of countless chariots to the *sanctum sanctorum* – the black phallic-shaped meteorite which symbolized fertility and piety. All around him grown men and women gave him deference, bowing and scraping to him as if he were an avatar of El-Gabal Himself. From that moment on splendour and luxury became natural to him. He would remain enamoured to them for the rest of his existence.

It isn't too difficult to imagine how such adulation and deference would have gone to the boy's head. For the people themselves, the sight of young Varius was enough to send them into raptures, as here before them was a true descendent of the great priests of old, like a scion of old Sampsiceramus himself. Without a figurehead they were like sheep without a shepherd, and like most sheep they felt ill at ease wandering on their own. It is all but impossible that the child did not feel this love stretching out to him, and it was a feeling he would cherish and remember; his abiding needs were to be a figure of devotion and to be loved by his people.

He may have been born near Rome, but Varius was a Syrian by descent. He was very young when he returned to his Emesan roots, young enough for his child's mind to be flexible and to adapt quickly to his new environment. The Roman civilization had grown up quickly and, influenced by the Greeks, had developed a complicated and nationalistic set of ethics and values based around Jingoism and social etiquette. The Syrians were relatively unaffected by the stiff-lipped pragmatism of ancient Rome, and it was natural for them to express basic emotions freely. Besides, the moral persona of the ancient Roman was an unattainable ideal which was at best threadbare and at worst double-sided; one had merely to scratch the surface to reveal the cauldron of repressed desires beneath. The result was a neurotic hypocrisy which would erupt behind closed doors in sexual promiscuity, corruption in politics and crime in general. The history of ancient Rome, and particularly the lives of the Emperors, is littered with examples of the lust for sex and power.

To a large degree, the history of Emesa was free from such intrigue. Apart from being a trading centre for the Northern villages, its main claim to fame was that of a pilgrimage site for worshippers of the sun-god, and its only brushes with power struggles was its absorption into the great Empires of its time, first by the Seleucids and now by the Romans. There were few plots or conspiracies because the city was a theocracy run by the familial line of clerical monarchs, each successive king being a lama for his people. When Varius took over as a child priest, there was no war cabinet or senate as such, because there was no-one to oppose him. During these years, Varius's experiences of leadership were to be that of an adored figurehead whose role was heaven-sent and whose word was inviolate, and this was the model entrenched in his mind when he later transferred his office from the Syrian backwater to the full glare of the Roman Empire.

Although Soaemias had brought her son back to Syria to follow his hereditary destiny, the family were still strongly tied to the helm of the Empire. The Bassianus family had risen in the imperial ranks. Great uncle Severus had cut a wide swathe for the rest to follow, yet no-one knew to what heights his great-nephew might climb. Virgil's tales of battle and bloodshed were mixed with those of the power game in the hub of the Empire, the intrigues and in-house fighting. The Year of the Five Emperors had taken place only ten years before Varius's birth, and he was eight when Severus lay dying in York.

Severus was a good role model for the growing Varius. He had been the first Roman Emperor to have been born in Africa and his Arabic origins set a happy precedent. Moreover, he had gained his title through a lifetime of hard work and good soldiery, opening the door of heredity to the rest of his clan. For the first time in Syrian history, the corridors of power were opened up to their elite. It was an opportunity Julia Domna could not fail to appreciate. Virtually overnight, the royal line of high priests had been further elevated to the head of the great Roman Empire, and the possibilities added fuel to Julia's already glowing fires of ambition.

If Soaemias lacked such ambition, that certainly wasn't the case with Julia Maesa, who had a thirst for power which seemed unquenchable. In Emesa, she was used to being at the helm of royalty, being a high-ranking lady of the religious order there, and it is obvious that she relished her exalted position in a community whose very existence revolved around the worship of El-Gabal. Frustrated at being unable to wield power directly, she lived her life vicariously through the rule of her progeny, the line of religious priests to which Varius was heir; and although Varius would experience an omnipotence which went with his position, the influence of his great aunt and grandmother was never far away. It was not a big step to transfer her lust for power from the relatively small settlement of Emesa to the Roman Empire itself.

When Varius was eight years of age that same Empire saw something of an upheaval. The reign of Severus shuddered to an abrupt end. It had not been a popular reign; he had grasped the Empire with the might of arms and had made several purges to rid himself of those hostile to him. When his right-arm man, Plautianus (who was a Sejanus to his Tiberius) was accused of treason, and had been killed, Severus had become paranoid and many senators feared for their lives. They became so afraid that when it was revealed in the senate that (following a dream) a bald-headed senator was suspected of plotting against the Emperor, the terrified historian Cassius Dio felt the top of his head to make sure he had a fine covering of hair.

If the old fox Severus had bad points, he was nothing compared to his weasel-like son, Antoninus. During a visit to England, Antoninus plotted to kill his father, who in fact died in York, the suspicion being that his own son had poisoned him. Immediately Antoninus was declared Emperor, jointly with his brother Geta; but Antoninus did not care for this arrangement, so he quickly had his brother murdered. After this patricide and fratricide Antoninus excused his actions and sadistically refused to allow his mother Domna to mourn for her loss. Soon he began a killing spree which included all his own enemies, not even sparing the elderly or infants, while giving the Praetorian Guard *carte blanche* to revenge their own private grievances. He killed Commodus's sister, Cornificia, Plautiana, his own wife (as he'd threatened previously, she was the daughter of Plautianus, whom Antoninus detested), as well as all governors who had been loyal to Geta. He was certainly his father's son.

While these reckless murders were being committed, Antoninus was spending more and more of the treasury in his leisure pursuits, as well as enriching his armies. As the Empire's coffers became depleted, he turned to the age-old and detested expedient of increasing taxation, as well as manufacturing new taxes to drain the wealthy of their resources. Tax levels were increased – in some cases doubled – and tax exemptions (such as those dealing with bequests and succession) abolished. Personally, he continued with rash expenditure and indulgence. He spent much on public buildings, especially the amphitheatres in which he spent much of his time, but he would not permit any public funds to be wasted thereby. So the phenomenal cost of these projects had to be financed directly by the government – in other words, from the pockets of the senators. While he drained them dry, he would organize lavish shows which included a number of bloody gladiatorial contests and the killing of hundreds of rare exotic beasts. The only possible way to avoid destitution was to become the Emperor's flatterer, in which case he had no qualms about handing over largesse and gifts. According to Dio, Antoninus soon gained a reputation for debauchery and made a name for himself as an adulterer; later in life he was almost impotent and resorted to 'lewd practices' to gain sexual satisfaction.

It must have been a frustrating time for Julia Maesa, who at this stage would have been one of the most influential and politically aware people in Rome. It must also have been galling for someone of her expertise to be able to do nothing except watch events unfold. Although she advised her nephew on matters of state, her influence was limited. Antoninus had inherited much from his father, not least a stubbornness and selfishness which would brook no interference with his conception of how to run the Empire.

The two branches of the Bassianus house had sprung from the two sisters, Maesa and Domna. Julia Domna produced the Severan branch, and this consisted of the two sons Geta and Antoninus. The Avetan branch was sired by Avitus and mothered by Maesa, and she produced the two sisters Soaemias and Mamaea. Whereas the

Severan side of the family had produced fruit poisoned by cruelty, paranoia and brutality, the Avitan side had yet to be tested. The male heirs were both small children – Soaemias's son Varius and Mamaea's Alexianus – and their mettle had not been tried. The time for that would come sooner than anyone had anticipated.

There certainly seemed something rotten about the genes on Severus's side of the family. The menfolk appeared to be tainted with mental instability. There are signs that Antoninus was also suffering from paranoia, brought about by the guilt of his patricide and fratricide. Mental disturbances being relatively unknown at that time, it was natural to put it all down to witchcraft, and Antoninus became convinced that his enemies were casting black magic spells against him. He began to hallucinate, and saw his father and brother running after him, swords in hand; even the ghost of Commodus appeared to him, calling: 'Come nearer, Judgment! The gods demand it from you for the sake of Severus!'

While Antoninus was doing battle with his demons – and the rebellious Parthians – Varius Avitus was passing through a painful puberty and entering his teen years. During this time matters of the Roman state meant little to him, except perhaps a natural interest in the fortunes of his Uncle Antoninus, and the increased respect the attachment to the imperial family gave the Bassiani. This attachment enhanced the grandeur of his royal position, and his regal bearing was almost on a par with the old Caesars in the extravagance of his train and the size of his followers. He became a celebrity, not only to his own people, but to the multitudes who flocked to Emesa to join in the festivities at the Temple by the river.

In comparing his future life as Emperor of Rome, it is clear that Varius was well aware that the populace loved a spectacle, and much of his pomp and ceremony while driving through the streets of Emesa was an entertainment for the people. It was almost an extravaganza. Even to non-believers, Varius became something of a living legend.

The soldiers stationed in Syria would often come to town to see the procession and to watch this nephew of the Emperor perform his dancing and the local rites to the chimes and the beat of local music. Far from being disgusted with his actions, the soldiers became enamoured of this handsome young man dressed in sumptuous robes who was attracting the love and admiration of the crowds. In fact, he was soon well known and recognized by the military visitors, and he even managed to secure converts to his religion.

Looking back with the benefit of hindsight, the puberty of Varius must have been a difficult, even traumatic, one. He began to develop a love of clothing which was almost fetishistic, and adored the feel of rich silks against his body to such an extent that he hated wearing woollens or any inferior material. Part of the religious office meant that, as high priest and king, he needed to have his face painted and wear jewelry, and this gave his appearance an effeminacy which was remarked upon by the soldiers and which did not go unnoticed by Varius himself. It would not be long before this would lead to much condemnation, but at the time he hid a feminine nature behind his priestly garb. There is absolutely no doubt that he was already in the midst of a gender crisis.

The complicated nature of Varius's sexuality will need to be considered in much more detail later, but his powerful attachment to his mother as well as the love of all men were both contributory factors to his sexual confusion. In the short life ahead of him, Varius would show strong homosexual leanings, inwardly as well as outwardly, which must have had been exacerbated in his transition from boyhood to the estate of man. These would have been urges which needed to be suppressed, and in denying them he became frustrated and disorientated. At least part of these strong urges were sublimated in his religious duties, which promised some outlet in the orgiastic climax of its rites.

The possibility of becoming Emperor of Rome would not have even entered his young mind, nor that of his mother Soaemias. That honour was held by the other branch of the family and would be passed on from generation to generation. The Avitan branch was concentrated on the role of Syrian pontiff, even after the Severan branch had been effectively weeded by the murders of Severus and Geta. The imperial family of Rome were honorable cousins and Varius, as nephew to the Emperor, had no lineal right to the diadem. His task was to oversee the temple rites and to act as a guiding light to his people.

All of this changed abruptly in 217 AD, when the madcap Emperor finally met his end. His downfall did not come as a result of drawn-out conspiracies but, as often happens, on a sudden impulse. Antoninus was in Parthia, warring against their king Artebanus. Like his father Severus, Antoninus was popular among his men as, when on campaign, he roughed it with the lads and lived the life of a common soldier. He had a special cloak designed for himself – a *caracallus* – so after that he was nicknamed Caracalla. He even resorted to baking his own bread. But not everyone in the army liked their Emperor – his habit of ridiculing his senior officers and threatening them in public led to a number of outraged commanders who even feared for their lives. One such man was the commander Macrinus, a man whose fate would be closely intertwined with that of the future Emperor Heliogabalus.

Behind the scenes Maesa and Domna were still manoeuvring and manipulating events to promote their own interests and, of course, those of their family. Domna had got over her period of mourning for her lost husband and son and had taken on the role of personal secretary to Antoninus; while she had no real decisions of importance to make, she dealt with day-to-day correspondence and acted on those whose import was trivial. All went smoothly enough until, one day, she opened a communication from the commander of Rome's city forces, Flavius Maternianus, which filled her with terror. Although she tried to act accordingly, it was too late. That letter was a presage of doom for the house of Bassianus.

As often happened in those days, because the state religion supposed the gods had power to send messages to chosen people, professional fortune-tellers often found high favour around the Empire, and their reputation grew in accordance with the outcomes of their prophecies. A well-known soothsayer from Africa declared that the Roman Prefect Macrinus, as well as his son Diadumenianus, would eventually become Emperors, and the prophecy was soon spread about and reached the ears of both the commander of Rome's city forces, Flavius Maternianus, and the senator in charge of the census, Ulpius Julianus. Straightway Flavius sent a warning letter to Antoninus, while Ulpius did the same for Macrinus, knowing how dangerous life could be once Antoninus discovered the news of the oracle. Unfortunately for Flavius, Antoninus had decreed that all seemingly unimportant letters should be sifted first by his mother Julia Augusta in Antioch, and there the warning went; whereas Ulpius's letter reached Macrinus directly.

Macrinus had good reason to fear. Of the two generals, Adventus and Macrinus, Antoninus had shown much favour to the former, while he became increasingly scornful of Macrinus. Knowing Macrinus's love of food, he taunted him with it and called him cowardly and effeminate. On occasion he even threatened to have him murdered. When an oracle seemed to indicate that Macrinus was conspiring against him, his mind was made up. He sealed up the oracle, put it with other letters, and later gave them all to Macrinus as he was about to drive off for a chariot race; as Praetorian Prefect, it was his job to sift incoming mail. Antoninus ordered him to come immediately if there was anything of urgency, and deal with the others himself. When Macrinus opened the letter containing the oracle he realized that it also contained his death sentence.

Macrinus had also received the oracle from Africa and the two letters seemed to be messengers of fate. Buoyed up by the expectations of power, and afraid that Antoninus would have him executed, he conspired a plot with three men; one was a man called Martialis, and the other two tribunes by the names of Nemesianus and Appollinaris. Between them, they resolved to assassinate the Emperor. The attempt took place on the 8th of April, 217. Antoninus, still unaware of the African prophecy, was moving out from Edessa as he had decided to visit the Temple of Selene, the Moon-goddess, at Harran. It was a fair ride out to the temple, so Antoninus decided upon a small escort which included the above-mentioned centurion named Martialis, whose brother had recently been executed on the Emperor's orders and who had also been personally insulted by him. He had been in those closed-door talks with Macrinus and agreed to assassinate Antoninus if the chance arose. Such an opportunity came when the Emperor stopped, needing to urinate; as he dismounted and relieved himself, the soldiers stood far apart. Martialis came over to him, telling him he had something important to tell him. Antoninus had no reason to fear treachery, but as he turned towards Martialis the latter pulled out his knife and stabbed him, wounding but not killing the Emperor. At once Martialis turned on his heels and fled, but was brought down by a javelin and died instantly. There was a great outcry and panic, and in the middle of the chaos the two tribunes rushed up to help the fallen Antoninus, but when they reached him they completed Martialis's job and murdered him.

When the news of Antoninus's assassination came to the ears of the army there was widespread consternation, but the first priority was to appoint a new Emperor. At first the men inclined to Adventus, but he argued against his appointment as he was old and he thought the burden of the Empire should rest on younger shoulders. The tribunes suggested Macrinus as the obvious alternative, so the men all agreed. The decision was made not a second too soon; news soon arrived to tell them that Artebanus had rallied a huge army and were even now marching towards them.

After some vicious fighting, Artebanus discovered that his old enemy Antoninus was dead, so the two sides agreed on a peace, and Macrinus sent a letter to the senate, espousing his own cause while criticizing the past Emperors who had gained the diadem through inheritance, citing Commodus and Antoninus as examples:

> …**Virtue and kindness not only command admiration, but anyone who succeeds by dint of his own efforts also wins the fullest praise. What good, if I may ask, did the noble birth of Commodus do you? Or what good, the fact that Caracalla inherited the throne from his father? In fact, the two young brothers [Caracalla and Geta] abused their high positions and acted insolently, as if the Empire had been their personal possession handed down to them by heredity. On the other hand, those Emperors who are given the Empire by you are always in your debt, and work to repay those who have done them good…**

His appointment was duly ratified by the senate, who had no-one else to turn to, and once again the reeling Roman state saw a change in power. The first repercussion for the Bassiani was the expulsion of Julia Domna and Maesa. It was a terrible time for Domna, but even more miserable for Maesa, who had now lost both husband and son as well as her cherished position in Rome. Her whole life had been destroyed – and by an upstart soldier who had never even sat in the *curia*! She was left with nothing, at least in the way of power, and set out for the only place she could call home – Emesa, and the small remnant of family that awaited her.

It was then, in 217, that the thirteen-year old Varius saw his grandmother and great aunt again. As the ladies had spent a great deal of their lives in Rome – and become accustomed to their way of life – the appearance of the two aristocratic women dressed as matriarchs of Rome must have seemed odd to him. For their part, they knew that there was no-one else in the Bassianus family who had the ability to raise an avenging sword against their enemies; of the males, Alexianus was just a little boy, and the rather effeminate Varius more suited to his priestly duties than to march off to war. Julia Domna was overwrought; and quite apart from the misfortunes to her immediate family she had other worries, having contracted cancer of the breast. Even so, she thirsted for vengeance and spent the time left to her stirring up trouble among the military and trying to oppose Macrinus in every way she could. At last, seeing that she could find no redress through the might of arms, she gave up and committed suicide by starving herself to death.

Despite the failure of Domna to drum up support for the family cause, Maesa had not given up on her determination to avenge herself on Macrinus. Domna had acted in a state of rage and desperation, but that was not Maesa's way - she excelled in stealth and cunning. Varius was the only tool at their disposal – and at least he had reached manhood. The germ of a plot may well have come to Maesa in those first weeks back in their Syrian backwater. As the conspiracy gained momentum it would be necessary to watch the world stage and seek out weaknesses in the new ruler. The army were unwilling to give their support to a woman wronged, but they might do so for an Emperor. People would surely support an illegitimate heir of Antoninus – if one existed - sooner than a man with no other claims but his military prowess? An illegitimate heir was not impossible, knowing the legendary lasciviousness of Antoninus's personality. Yet, for the moment, discretion was the better part of conspiracy. Macrinus was strong and powerful and had the might of the armies on his side. The Bassiani planned a waiting game.

Chapter 3. The Rise of the False Antoninus

In many ways, Macrinus was an unusual ruler. He had mixed blood and was part Berber, originally being from Mauretanius, but he was also the first Emperor never to have been admitted to the senatorial ranks. True, he had proven himself a gifted lawyer and a proven solder, but in times gone by it was expected that one qualified to rule the Empire had risen through the senate to the major political levels, and Macrinus had by-passed such requirements. Before becoming Prefect he had served the nation as the superintendent of traffic on the Flaminian Way, but that was the limit of his political experience. As the new Emperor, he made an attempt to consolidate his claims by conferring the name

'Antoninus' onto his son Diadumenianus, whom he also styled 'caesar', or successor. Besides, he had the Roman armies under his command.

The senators were unanimous in their support for Macrinus. Not so much because they appreciated his talents, but because they felt that a great threat had been lifted from their shoulders by the death of Antoninus. They were also pleased at the new Emperor's first ruling – that all slaves who had betrayed their masters and all informers should be crucified. A mass confused exodus of those at risk followed, and, according to Herodian, men at last lived in a sense of security and freedom.

For the moment, Macrinus was strong. He followed the usual formulae of gaining popularity among soldiers, the people, and the senators alike. To his military he, of course, proffered gifts of money. He offered them the rates of pay as set down by Severus, but went further promising them an end to wars and days of peace ahead. The soldiers voted him emperor on the spot. To the senate, he vowed that he would follow the precept that it would be impious to kill anyone of senatorial rank. Finally, he revoked the heavy taxation which Antoninus had placed on inheritance and slave emancipation; this was a well-received bill against a detested act. So far, so good. Macrinus managed to please everyone at once, and his path to power was unobstructed.

For Maesa and her family – and Varius – it was a time to stay silent. Macrinus was at his height and it was not the time to court publicity. Especially after Domna's anguished attempts to thwart the new Emperor. All they could hope for was a time when Macrinus made a mistake and lost his powerful backing. That time was not long in coming. Macrinus did not have the political sense to keep the status quo and in no time at all he began to alienate many of his friends in the senate, who looked forward to a calmer time of it after Antoninus. Macrinus's major mistake was the distribution of important posts to undeservers. To curb the power of Antoninus's old adherents, he recalled the governors of Pannonia and Dacia, Sabinus and Castinus respectively; ostensibly to have them by his side as advisors . To Pannonia he sent Decius Triccianus, for the sole reason that he was well-disposed to him, even though he had no previous experience and had been a private soldier in the Pannonian army. In fact, the only background he had which in any way suited him for the position was the fact that he had once been the governor's door-keeper. Even worse was the Dacian appointment – not only was Marcius Agrippa an ex-slave, he had once been banished to an island for some indiscretion and afterwards was found guilty of pressing youngsters into the army. Not exactly the qualifications for the running of an important province.

Macrinus made two other blunders to exasperate the senate. First, he took upon himself various titles without following the correct protocol; that is, without waiting for the same honours to be allowed him by the senators. Thus in letters to them he not only styled himself Emperor and Caesar – Severus, even – but also Macrinus the Holy, Macrinus the Fortunate, Macrinus Augustus as well as proconsul. At this time he gave his son the appellation 'caesar' as well as the adoptive name 'Antoninus', which, he hoped, would consolidate his position. At the same time he made an appointment which was seen by the senate as a joke in very bad taste; he made his friend and co-commander, the elderly Adventus, both City Prefect and consul. This was unprecedented, as he had never attained the rank even of senator, but perhaps Macrinus was underlining the precedent he himself had set as an Emperor with no senatorial experience. The appointment was a failure, as Adventus was incompetent at speechmaking. He even pretended to be sick to avoid being present at his election. It took no time at all for Macrinus to realise his error and Adventus was replaced by one Marius Maximus.

Recent Emperors had climbed and fallen by means of the soldiery, and as Macrinus slowly lost backing in the senate the family of Varius must have been watching events on the field carefully. Sadly for him, Macrinus did little to endear himself with his soldiers. Naturally fond of extravagance, he diverted himself with shows and pantomimes, wearing luxuriant clothing and jewellery which his men associated with women. Soon his dissolute way of life led to many grumbles among the legions and unwittingly the new Emperor was gradually making himself more and more unpopular. His lifestyle clashed harshly with the conditions his army was living in, posted in a foreign land and living under tents while sometimes enduring great hardships. They were on half-rations, had been given pay cuts, and to make things even worse Macrinus had revived long-forgotten laws to restrict the soldiers' behaviour. He resurrected a defunct law which forbade the taking of a mistress from the enemy's civilians. Anyone who did so could now be burned alive, or the pair could be bricked up and left to starve.

Soon there was a universal air of resentment – even the gods proved themselves disgruntled, sending down fires, storms, earthquakes, as well as a Siamese pig with eight feet, four ears and two tongues. The people, sick of living under the mismanagement of several emperors, showed their dissatisfaction at the horse races, where the chanted that they only needed one leader – Jupiter himself. It was soon apparent that there would have to be changes, or this dissatisfaction would grow into something more dangerous.

This was exactly was the Bassiani family were waiting for, and before long Macrinus played into their hands and gave them the leeway they needed to enter the fray. Artabanus, the King of Parthia, had been slowly fuming after the barbarous treatment of his country by Antoninus, and behind the scenes he had been gathering together a mighty force of arms to exact reprisals against the Romans. Seeing a weak Emperor in charge, he saw his chance and sent envoys to Macrinus whose message reflected Artabanus's angry mood. There were three main demands – to rebuild all the forts and cities Antoninus had so recklessly destroyed; to get out of and stay out of Mesopotamia; and to make significant reparations for the sacrilegious treatment of the royal tombs, which Antoninus had ransacked. It was made apparent that if Macrinus refused to accept these terms there would be war.

For a good leader and commander of men, war could have been just the answer Macrinus was looking for. A chance to gain renown, to plunder cities, to make profit, and to regain much *dignitas* in the eyes of the senate. It was also a chance for him to recapture much of his lost popularity. But Macrinus was not a courageous man, so he sent a message back to Artabanus blaming the past on Antoninus and offering to free all captives. The offer was scornfully rejected, so Macrinus had no choice but to confront the Parthian King. Macrinus was badly defeated at Nisibis and by now he had had enough and chose not to continue the war. Instead, he acceded to all of Artabanus' requests, as well as gifts costing 200,000,000 sesterces. Then, to save face, he sent words to the senate that he had concluded a peace in Parthia, for which the overjoyed senate voted him sacrifices of thanksgiving, sacrifices which the red-faced Emperor felt bound to refuse.

The humiliation of Macrinus did not end there. Cowed and beaten, he seemed to lose any feelings of pride and did not lift a finger when, encouraged by the success of Parthia, both the Armenian King Tridates and the Dacians sent ambassadors to him. Instead of resistance, he surrendered to their wills, sending Tridates a crown and all the plunder Rome had confiscated from Armenia, while he gave back all hostages to Dacia. The Empire had never known such shame.

As Macrinus fell at hurdle after hurdle, Maesa had not been idle. While the Emesan menfolk might have climbed the heights of success, the Emesan women had always been there in the wings, prompting and steering the ship of state as best they could. Maesa had lost her colleague in intrigue, Domna, but there were always her daughters Soaemias and Mamaea, and Mamaea at least was made in the mould of her mother. Macrinus's star was waning and it was time to strike – but for whom? The Severan branch had died out with Antoninus, who had left no heir to claim the title after him.

The ever-restive soldiers picked this of all times to mutiny, particularly the troops in Syria. The long-anticipated time had come for Maesa to play her trump card. Her fellow conspirators began to spread the rumor of Antoninus's relationship with Julia Soaemias, and how she had subsequently given birth to a boy who even now was planning to take back his birthright. The astonished soldiers wanted to know more, and they were told that the true heir to the diadem was none less than Varius Avitus Bassianus, the youth who at present was the most dignified person living in Syria, a royal priest, a young man of dignity and responsibility. If they had any doubts on the matter, he would come himself and they could see how the image of Antoninus once again lived in his true son.

As we know, there was no truth in the rumour of Varius's birth by which he claimed a direct descent from Antoninus; it had merely a political expedient. But such a claim might, as the family realized, throw a dark shadow on the respectability of their house. Centuries later, this was to be the case. Lampridius, in his untrustworthy *Historia Augusta*, makes much mileage out of the supposition, accepting it only insofar as it exaggerated his negative view of Varius and his family. He goes much further; as an extension of this claim he suggests that Soaemias was therefore a lady of easy virtue and would remain one throughout her life, living 'like a prostitute' and practicing 'all manner of lewdness'. Taking this to extremes, he even recalls the gossip that the boy had been named 'Varius' became he seemed to be the offspring of 'various men', 'as would be the case with the son of a whore'. None of which has the slightest basis in truth.

The story which now unfolded did much to soil Soaemias's name for all eternity and all the historians – even Hay – suggest that she led an immoral life. However, the facts that come down to us contain little to support this idea. True, she seems to have inherited the Bassianan character for strong libido, but apart from a failed marriage and a possible liaison with Gannys, there is little else to confirm the idea that she was promiscuous. Under the goading of Maesa, and considerations for the future of her son, she had been persuaded to acknowledge that Antoninus had fathered him; but the deception was transparently thin. In later years, other rumours would abound – that Antoninus also fathered Alexianus, for example – and Soaemias's reputation would pay the ultimate price for her acquiescence to the will of her mother. Knowing her almost neurotic love for her son, she may have been worried about the new role which was being cut out for him – certainly, about his safety – but Varius's welfare had to be balanced against the huge rewards which he stood to gain. To ensure her son's glory, Soaemias sacrificed her own good name and this must have been obvious to her as they plotted around the table in the early months of 217.

The lie told by Soaemias was the cause of the odium heaped on her by later historians, but she was not the main target. Heliogabalus was to be one of the most hated rulers of the Roman Empire, and to emphasise the point these writers were hell-bent on blackening his name by whatever means they could, and did not swerve from telling lies and distorting the events to which they were not even privy. Varius's life would be scandalous enough, but there was a concerted effort to paint his picture as someone whose depravity existed from his birth and even before, in the form of his mother. These Syrians were a debauched lot, and it made sense that Varius had sprung from the seed of Severus and Antoninus, whose reigns had been marked with bloodshed and licentiousness. It dovetailed neatly into the sequence of events, and the readers of the works of Dio, Herodian and Lampridius would notice a natural progression from the cruelty of Severus, the madness and megalomania of Antoninus, then finally the worst of them all, the crazed and perverted Heliogabalus.

So it was that Heliogabalus's life began in scandal. It would be interesting to know how Soaemias herself felt about the plan, but none of the historians discuss the matter. It does seem that Mamaea took after her mother - she was an ambitious lady whom Maesa would later take into her confidence and plot with – whereas Soaemias was not a cruel and calculating woman. She more resembled her dutiful if somewhat nondescript father Avitus, and her life revolved around her adored son. As there was little love lost between Soaemias and her sister, Mamaea's entreaties would have carried little weight, especially as she herself had designs for her own son Alexianus and later would conspire for his advancement – Alexianus was already Varius's successor as high priest and served beneath him at the celebrations. Perhaps a mother's rivalry caused the rift between them. But few people could withstand the tough person of Maesa, and if Soaemias had reservations they would have been quickly quashed by her mother. There is no evidence that she was anything but a dutiful daughter at this time, and whatever was discussed among the family, Soaemias agreed to verify the story of Varius's birth. There were two factors which would have been important in reaching her decision – the thirst for revenge for the killing of her cousin Antoninus, and the lure of the Empire in the hands of her son.

First, they had to convince the army, but, as fortune had it, many of the soldiers had already seen Varius. In Emesa, the men were stationed to protect Phoenicia, and had become accustomed to the native ways, and of course were familiar with the aristocracy, in particular the Bassianus family. Everyone knew Maesa, who had been an important figure in recent times and had spent the reigns of Severus and Antoninus living in the royal palace, so she had become something of a dignatory and a celebrity of royal status. Moreover, she was powerful and extremely rich; Macrinus had been merciful to her and allowed her to return home in full possession of her properties as well as the fortune she had amassed during her time at Rome. She also commanded huge respect in her native Emesa, where she had mothered the line of high priests so important to the religion of the day.

As the conspirators now met and discussed tactics in the palatial house in Emesa, there were few in the group as informed and knowledgable as Maesa. A major problem was that of Varius's extreme youth; but nothing was impossible should they get the backing of the military, and in the end the Praetorians could easily be bought. A small rainfall could develop into a torrent and she knew that, just as Severus had rallied his men and collected allies once the campaign was in motion, so Varius could persuade the military to throw in their lot with him. There was no time to lose – Macrinus had reached a popularity crisis and the time was perfect to sow the seeds of rebellion. Should the Emesan legion back them, and spread the message of an Antoninus reborn, things could start to snowball.

At the head of the debating table was Julia Maesa, sombre, determined and hard as adamant; the aging, inflexible woman had learned the wisdom and the craft of two Emperors, and knew that the new regime was ready for shaking. Everything depended on the fourteen-year-old high priest who was the only sure weapon they had to smash through the trappings of the Roman state. He had to be coached, quickly and thoroughly. At his side were a pile of clothes, and a picture which had been painted of his uncle, dead over a year ago. In the boy his uncle's spirit would rise again, and with him all the fortunes of the Bassianus family.

One of the rebel leaders was a man called Eutychianus, slippery and as cunning as a serpent. He had already had many meetings with Maesa, and also certainly with the boy's mother, Julia Soaemias. The stakes were set, and were high. There was one major problem – the personality of Varius. By now it must have been obvious to the family that Varius was not going to be a man's man. His penchant for clothes of the most expensive materials, his habit of overdoing his make-up, and his passive gentle nature was already giving him a strongly effeminate character. His obvious femininity, married with questions concerning his uncertain sexuality, must have been a cause of much anxiety for a family who were trying to pass him off as an heir to the Empire.

Antoninus had been a soldier's Emperor and had won their approbation by his prowess in the field. As things stood, Varius little resembled his alleged father and Eutychianus must have realized that the army would never accept a candidate who was more girl than boy, one who had never even seen a battlefield. But if the army wanted a soldier and a scion from the loins of the Severans, then that's what they'd get. Time was running short.

Varius had reached his teens as a youthful dreamer and visionary. The sexual maelstrom of adolescence merely brought a sharp increase in his urge to become more and more female. The life he had been brought up in fuelled his narcissism and day after day huge crowds turned up to follow his impressive figure to the temple. A boy who was adored, his main attachment was to his mother, in whom he relied for encouragement and advice. She was the one who made dreams come true. He had been heir to a kingdom; but now he was told he was the rightful heir of the Roman Emperor and that too would be his. It must have seemed as if he were born for blessings to fall upon him, and there was no reason not to believe that the second prediction would come true. Throughout his life Varius always called himself the son of Antoninus, and while this may have been expedient it does suggest that he might have believed it. How his ever immature mind might have reacted to the revelation that the man he had called father in the Roman villa was not his father is open to conjecture.

If there could have been any doubts in Varius's mind about the truth of what his mother – and the rest of his family – was telling him, proof was not far away. On the outskirts of town, an army was there just ready for him to command. Now, from the part of high priest he was being called to play the part of all-conquering Caesar.

For someone whose dreams always became reality, Varius had no reason to doubt; he was always an immature boy and lived in his own little world. There was only one thing he felt a strong passion for, and that was his religion. He believed in the Father El Gabal with all his heart and it was a belief that would never be shaken away from him, and which would lead him to serious trouble in the years to come.

It was time to get young Varius into training. The Bassianus faction might not be able to turn him into a soldier, but he could look like one; all he needed was a uniform and a weapon. The problem was, of course, that the army would not just want to see their new Emperor, they'd want to hear him too and it was important that Varius knew the right things to say at the right time. As for Varius himself, a new role would not have daunted him too much. Up to the present time his whole life had been an act which had been a substitute for play. Throughout his time on earth he would be drawn to the stage and to playacting, probably because it was at the heart of his very existence. All of his life had been a fairy story in which he had been cast in the starring role. As such, he was flexible and easily manipulated.

It cannot have been easy – it was probably impossible – to mould the soft-featured, sensitive boy into a warrior the soldiers would follow. But with hard work he could look and sound the part. It was not necessary for Varius to hobnob with the common soldier or to rough it with the troops as his supposed father had done – the deception would soon be discovered if he did – he simply had to appear like the rising sun and rally his subjects around him. To that end, the conspirators wrote speeches for him to learn and dressed him up to suit the character.

It must have been difficult for the boy who had grown to love the feel of silk next to him and who loved ornate make-up to dress in the coarse uniform of a man of war, complete with a *caracalla* or cloak, especially when one bears in mind his sensitivity to rough materials. But this was, after all, a temporary measure, and above all things he trusted his mother and she must have persuaded him that it was the only way to win his destiny.

So after an unspecified time, Varius was as ready as he would ever be to act his part. He had good teachers in Eutychianus, who had experience as an actor himself, and Gannys, who had military experience and, as a former servant of Maesa, would have been in a position to have seen Antoninus and witness his bearing in the field. As well as this, there was the indefatigable Maesa herself, who had lived in the royal palace and knew her brother-in-law's bearing and idiosyncrasies. As far as Varius was concerned, as with everything else in his life, it is likely that he saw the whole affair as another adventure.

Varius had completed his training not a moment too soon. Macrinus had made yet another mistake by allowing the army to winter *en masse* instead of ordering them back to their individual fortresses. Here they went stale and soft, and seeing the weaknesses of their leader began to conspire together, wanting as much as they could while doing as little as possible. They also were annoyed by a new edict from the Emperor that stated that, while all soldiers presently in the army would continue to enjoy the privileges given them by Antoninus, future recruits would join up under the old guidelines of Severus. Whether the men misunderstood the new edict, and concluded that they would lose out in the new deal, or disliked the new course *per se*, it added more fuel to their discontent.

The timing could not have been better to exploit the new rumour – the supposed existence of Antoninus's son in the form of Varius. Gannys, it seems, played a major part in the forthcoming mutiny. The soldiers, angry at Macrinus and enraged by the defeat at Nisibis, were ripe for revolt. As well as the goading of Gannys, the men were further influenced by the efforts of Euthychianus, who besides being a soldier had also been a gymnast and an entertainer and knew how to play to an audience. Besides extolling the virtues of Varius, he remarked upon his incredible likeness to the dead Emperor and even produced oracles which categorically stated the Varius was to become the new ruler at Rome.

The Roman soldiers, the Third Gallic Legion, were based near Emesa at their encampment at Raphaneae, in a valley of the coastal mountains some 22 miles north-west of town. *Legio III Gallica* had a long and proud tradition, having been formed by Julius Caesar during the Gallic Wars in about 49 BC; it had therefore been in existence for over two and a half centuries. Their symbol was a bull and can be seen on coins minted during the reign of Heliogabalus. After a prominent role in Gaul, they were absorbed into Mark Antony's forces and fought in the world-changing Battle of Actium, after which Augustus was proclaimed Emperor. They first moved into Syria during the reign of Vitellius, and after they had defeated him they paved the way for the Flavian Dynasty. Impressed by the religion of the area – that of El Gabal – they began the custom of saluting the rising sun, so it is obvious that even as far back as the middle of the first century, *Legio III Gallica* felt strong ties with the natives. This, coupled with the fact that they fought alongside Severus against the Parthians, would have made a favourable impression when they heard that a new Antoninus had risen among them. They would have been so much the easier to persuade to fight for such a man's rights to the diadem, and the men must have been excited at the prospect of meeting and hearing the imperial candidate at first hand.

The important moment at last arrived. The cavalcade which accompanied Varius was heard rumbling towards Raphaneae under the cover of darkness. When they arrived the sun was rising on the 16th of May 218 and the timing was surely not accidental. Varius played his part to perfection, stepping off the chariot with the cloak of Caracalla and looking for all the world like a youthful ghost of the last Bassianian Emperor. The army all cheered, and Varius accompanied Eutychianus to hold a parley with the soldiers' superiors, including its commander Verus. Ushered into the presence of men in whose hands his future lay, Varius was ready to play the first part of his role – that of a regal leader of men. It was the easiest part of Varius's ordeal – he already had a royal bearing and now, dressed in the costume of a Roman commander, he certainly looked the part. There is no record of what transpired during the meeting, but certainly the commanders would have wanted to know more about Varius's claim, and Varius would have needed to convince them with all the eloquence he could muster.

For Maesa, this was the crunch. It was no longer a matter of overweening ambition – or even of revenge, although she thirsted for it. It was, she knew, now a matter of survival. It was true that Macrinus had allowed her to leave Rome with all of her possessions, but then, it was normal for new Emperors to display signs of mercy on their inauguration; she knew that as well as anyone alive. She also knew that deep-harboured resentment and malice could lie dormant for some time before the purges began, and before Macrinus started to look further afield for his enemies. The decimated Bassianus family had no teeth at present – the menfolk had been killed off and there only remained two boys - but Varius was close to reaching an age when he might prove to be a further annoyance, and it was more than possible that Macrinus could decide to sweep any danger from his sight rather than leave it to fester. That may come sooner rather than later; Macrinus was surely aware of the treacherous troublemaking of Julia Domna before her death. The older Varius got, the more precarious would be his position. All Maesa could hope now was that Varius played the part well, and that Eutychianus would convince the senior officers – something which he was using all of his craft to do.

Maesa left nothing to chance. She know that soldiers had one Achilles' heel – their love of money. Maesa was a powerful lady in Syria, and over the years had hoarded great wealth as well as real estate. To win their goodwill she had given a large donation to the camp, large enough to turn their heads. Thus softened, it was left to Eutychianus to ply them with all the oratory he could muster, and he did it with all the eloquence he was possessed of.

Charmed as Varius seemed to be, the officers were persuaded that Antoninus did live on in the figure of a son, and this son now stood before them. Whether they were fully convinced of Varius's claim is not certain, but they were on the brink of mutiny anyhow and Varius was as good a figurehead as any. After all, he did look the part, and his appearance did match that of the picture of Antoninus the conspirators had brought with them. The important thing was to bring down Macrinus; and if the soldiers were eager to fight for this new pretender, all well and good. It would seem that the commanders gave some sort of consent, but now it was up to the soldiers to decide on whether or not to ally themselves with Varius or not. It was time to face the army and for Varius to act the second role of the day – the warrior.

Having massed together all the people, the experienced actor Eutychianus began to harangue them with a stirring speech. This Macrinus, whom they hated, had no right to the throne. He had taken it by force and had no prior claims. Moreover, he had proven himself unworthy as Emperor and a blight on that name. Here, on the other hand, was a true branch of Antoninus, one who had been deprived of his true right and to whom all true Romans should give allegiance. Eutychianus turned to Varius – it was time for him to speak.

Varius himself backed up the story, using his well-rehearsed speech. He claimed the allegiance of the men, referred to Antoninus as 'my father', and, using all the rhetoric the Bassiani could muster, exhorted the army to fight for his cause. His speech does not survive, but it would appear that Varius played his part well, stressing the false claims of the usurper Macrinus and wooing the soldiers to rise up in his name. When the soldiers saw the old images – which may or may not have been those of Antoninus – and saw Varius clothed as the old Emperor, they were convinced. They all believed the story, denounced Macrinus, and resolved to fight for the rights of Antoninus's son.

So it was that Varius Avitus Bassianus, the fourteen-year-old son of Soaemias, later to be called Heliogabalus, was declared Emperor by the Syrian soldiers. They put him in the protection of their camp, along with women and children, and brought in supplies from the town and the neighbouring villages. They realised that there would be reprisals and were prepared for a siege, no matter how long or bitter. So far, Maesa's plans were working like clockwork.

Varius was no more than a puppet in the hands of his family and now the army. He was accepted as the son of Antoninus, even though he was really his nephew, and his name was accordingly changed to Marcus Aurelius Antoninus. It must have been a thrilling time for the boy, but then again he must have known also – or have been made aware – that this revolt was one of life or death for him. If the army was suppressed, there could only be one fate for him – death as a pretender and a traitor. It was therefore in his interest to convince the soldiers of his right to the imperial title, and to continue to do so. There was no turning back; in front of him was the promise of riches and power beyond all dreams – behind, ruin, death and disaster for himself and his family. The prize was great, but the risks appalling.

Varius may well have felt that his cause was just. After all, both Severus and Antoninus had been Emperors, and were both members of his own family. Who was left but himself to lay claim to the succession? Besides, his own line was a strong one – his great-grandfather, Julius Bassianus, claimed his descent from the house of Julius, which in reality could trace its lineage from Aeneas and his mother, the goddess Venus. Moreover, he sprang from the royal line of the high priests of Emesa. Such high birth cannot have failed to impress Varius, and if he had to tell a small lie to achieve his rightful dues, then he was prepared to do it.

Opposition was not long in coming. After the downfall of Macrinus, the Prefect Julianus was mopping things up things when word came to him of the Syrian uprising, and the sudden appearance of a supposed son of Antoninus. As Raphaneae was not far away, Julianus gathered together all the troops he could muster and marched to face the rebels. He decided first to scare them with a show of strength and to demonstrate how seriously he took this revolt, so he stormed the fortress as if he were fighting Medes or Parthians. The prolonged assault was nearly the end of Varius, as Julianus managed to smash down the gates and was threatening to rush inside. If he had done so, the result would almost certainly have been a rout, but he decided to retreat and rest his men, hoping that the rebels would by now see sense and voluntarily surrender. He was wrong. Overnight Varius's followers speedily reinforced and rebuilt the gates, and were ready for Julianus when he returned the next day. Furious, Julianus renewed the assault, but this time it came to nothing.

The rebels knew that Macrinus was unpopular among the troops and that if they could persuade Julianus's soldiers to their side they would win a victory without bloodshed. From the walls, the leaders began to shout down to their attackers, reminding them of Macrinus' perfidy, and how much better off they were under Antoninus; then they presented Varius himself, along with old pictures of Antoninus, as proof that he was really his son and heir.

'Why are you doing this, brothers-in-arms? Why are you fighting against the son of your patron?'

To push home their advantage, they pointed out Varius to the men, and, under their instructions, he made a speech to them. Once again Varius had to act like Antoninus to win the new soldiers over to him. He praised Antoninus and all his deeds, again calling him 'my father'. By this, the men began naturally to compare the largesse they had received from Antoninus with the actions of Macrinus, and as memories are short they recalled the latest edicts passed by him as well as his humiliating defeat at the hands of the Parthians. Next, Varius followed the well-worn rules of how to soften an army. He made the usual promises, being careful to ensure that all the promises were akin to those made previously by Antoninus; by these means he convinced them that he was really his son and heir. Among other things he promised that those who had deserted under Macrinus would be restored to their homes and properties, and that there would be an amnesty for exiles. He also promised that he would ensure good remuneration for all the soldiers. The tide began to turn and many men turned to the side of Varius.

As Julianus made an attempt to restrain the men by issuing orders to his centurions, Eutychianus sent out his freedman Festus to spread the word around the soldiers that a bounty would be offered to anyone who killed them – they would not only be given their title, but their possessions and property as well. By this expedient all of the remaining opposition to Varius disappeared, and Julianus had to run as fast as he could to escape the carnage. He did not run far enough – soon after he was found in hiding and killed.

When Macrinus heard news of the Syrian revolt he raced off to the Alban troops in Apamea for fear the rebellion would be successful. If it was he would need trustworthy men to fight and support his cause. So he mustered them together and spoke to them all. It was a difficult task, as he was well aware how he had been criticized for his latest edicts, and also keenly aware of his rapidly falling popularity as Emperor among the soldiers. His actions were those of a man in a panic; he resigned the empery in favour of his son Diadumenianus, and went on to restore any privations he had previously caused the soldiers, made extravagant promises and even went so far as to promise them 20,000 sesterces a man. To prove that he was in earnest (and because he was desperate) he handed out 4000 to each of them there and then. To further soften the astonished troops, he offered them a magnificent banquet to celebrate his pledge.

At this point, the soldiers knew nothing of the revolt in Syria, and Macrinus had no intentions of telling them just yet; he himself was ignorant of the outcome. As he had promised, he organized a sumptuous meal, with many rare delicacies, and invited his men to sit and join him in the feasting. Macrinus announced that the banquet was in honour of his son Diadumenianus, so they cheered and drank to his health. While they were celebrating, a soldier came with news that caused Macrinus to heave a sigh of relief; Varius, the 'False Antoninus', had been defeated and captured. The army must have wondered where this False Antoninus had come from. Then the news became widespread – Julianus had moved against a rebellion in which a certain Varius had claimed to be Antoninus' son; but the revolt had ended in disaster, and the pretender had been executed. As a gift, the soldier laid a parcel on the table – Varius's head, covered and bound up in cloths.

Elated, Macrinus began to unravel this most welcome gift; but no-one noticed that the unknown soldier had crept away. When the wrappings were removed, Macrinus saw that he had been tricked – instead of the head of that traitor Varius, he found the head of his Prefect Julianus. There was an ominous silence as Macrinus understood that he had been hoodwinked.

The soldiers knew it too, and now everything was clear to them. Once again they had been duped. This Emperor had not given out of love for his army or for the sake of fair-dealing, but out of fear. He had known well enough about the Syrian revolt and had kept it from them to buy time to bribe them. By now they had had enough of this false Emperor, this trickster, this double-dealer. They also knew that Macrinus's forces had been defeated by someone claiming to be the true heir of Antoninus, whereas Macrinus had no claims at all. Vast numbers of soldiers left in disgust and Macrinus was aware that his situation was precarious. There was one option left open to him, and one only. To flee as fast as he could. He made his way to Antioch.

As always, when a regime falls, there was widespread fear and universal reprisals. No-one who had supported Macrinus was safe. Throughout the Empire, confused news spread about the outcome of the civil wars, and many that thought they were safe as representatives of Emperor and state were cut down. Dio mentions the uprisings in Egypt, where Macrinus had appointed Basilianus as governor in place of Julianus. When news of Macrinus's defeat reached the province there was widespread bloodshed and Basilianus only just escaped with his life, fleeing towards Brundisium. From here he wrote to a friend in Rome for supplies, but was betrayed and caught, being taken to Nicodemia where he was executed.

As for Macrinus, there was only one thing on his side; he had been appointed Emperor by the senate and only the senate had the right to depose him. He felt (rightly) they would not be willing to do this in favour of some unknown upstart in Syria styling himself son of Antoninus and heir to the throne. In despair, he wrote a letter to the Prefect Maximus which was read out to the senate. In it he bemoaned the fact that the soldiers had been insisting on the pay allotted to them by Antoninus, and were stirring trouble among the new recruits by telling them of what they had been deprived. It was impossible to satisfy these soldiers, he stated, because the total expenditure would run to 280,000,000 sesterces per annum; but it was also impossible not to pay it, if they were not to revolt. Part of the letter ran:

I know that there are many people who would prefer to see an Emperor killed than to live themselves. By this I don't mean myself, that anyone would either desire or pray for *me* to die.

An ex-consul, Flavius Diogenianus, muttered: 'We've *all* prayed for it.'

But if the slow and somewhat dim-witted Diogenianus was against Macrinus, he was in the minority, because the parliament of Rome could not happily to sit by and see their appointed emperor deposed by Syrian rebels. Besides, for once the people were on his side, having heard that a province had dared to stand up to the Roman Empire and set up this false Antoninus, not only a Syrian but a figure who had not even attained manhood. The senate therefore spoke, condemned this usurpation, and had no option but to declare war upon the rebels.

Varius's army were quickly marching upon Antioch, so Macrinus gathered together his troops and set out to meet them at Immae, less than twenty miles away. Here, facing the general Gannys, they prepared for the attack. The short battle took place on 8th June 218. Although having won little renown as a commander, Gannys realised that the pass between the mountains leading to the village by which they were encamped was of great tactical importance, so he went off to hold it against the Praetorian Guard. As the enemy approached, the Guard stood ready for battle, and Gannys did well, attacking the imperial army and making great progress. It was a desperate time for the rebels and they chose this time to reveal their secret weapon.

They handed a sword to young Varius and told him what to do; then Soaemias, and even Maesa, who realized that this was a decisive struggle, donned armour for the final thrust, for the first and last time dropping their masks of femininity and unleashing their warlike alter-egos. So far, Varius had done well. He had convinced the commanders of his royalty, and convinced the soldiers that he was a scion of Severus and worthy to rule in Antoninus's place, but he had not yet shown himself to be of the selfsame mettle as his warlike father. Now the time had come for him to act this final role. His devoted mother, in armour, was by his side, encouraging him. One final thrust would bring victory and the whole world would be his; he merely had to ride and raise up his sword. Given Varius's fortunes up until that day, the matter was a simple one; all he had to do was step into a warrior's shoes and he would become a warrior. For a boy whose life was a catalogue of dreams come true, this was not too hard to swallow.

As a contingent of Varius's force charged, even Soaemias and Maesa, and the young Varius himself ran into combat, his sword brandished over his head. This was the first time his army had seen the son of Antoninus as a conquering warrior, and it lifted their spirits; any doubts as to the validity of his claim was extinguished and the soldiers, encouraged, charged with renewed vigour. Despite the quality of the fighting men doing battle for the Emperor, the sight of the False Antoninus and the rest bearing down upon them seemed to cow their enemies and the Guard made a hasty retreat. When Macrinus saw this, he knew all was lost and he himself fled and left the field to Varius and his men. Once again, Varius had merely to make a wish for it to come true. He was the darling and the hero of the hour.

That Varius made an impressive account of himself that day is reflected in the fact that his actions were noted and would find their way into the annals which would later condemn virtually every aspect of his life. It is doubtful whether Varius actually participated in any hand-to-hand fighting – he was hardly equipped for that – but as an encouraging presence his appearance won the day. Certainly he was acting a part, but he acted it with confidence and majesty. No doubt the youth found the fighting and the cut and thrust of war thrilling; but it was the first and last battle Varius would ever be embroiled in. For the rest of his life the peace-loving boy hung up his sword and showed no inclination for military exercise or warfare. It had been his one and decisive foray into war, and while it did much to temporarily raise his *dignitas* – and at just the right moment – it was poles apart from his true inclinations and tastes. Most importantly, the final barrier to his advancement had been removed.

This had been one defeat too many and Macrinus knew that his only chance was to somehow make it back to Rome and gain help from the senate. For the safety of his son, Diadumenianus, he ordered Epagathus, a profligate politician who had been a favourite of Antoninus, to accompany him to the safekeeping of Artabanus in Parthia. Then he made for Antioch and, to gain a short respite, pretended that the victory had been his. In no time at all his deception was uncovered, and revealed not only his pitiful plight but also his deceit. There was nothing left but to flee again. He shaved off all of his hair and beard, put on a cloak and in this disguise stole away from the city.

It did not take long for Varius's camp to become aware of the flight of Macrinus. They also realized that the only safe course of action was to kill him. If he succeeded in returning to Rome he could persuade some of his followers to aid him, which could result in a drawn-out conflict. The Varians turned to the Praetorian Guard and persuaded them that Macrinus had run off like a coward in the face of battle; is this the sort of unworthy man they wished to protect? Moreover, should they put in their lot with Varius, there was a promise of reward and amnesty. In no time at all the Praetorian Guard was convinced and they turned against their old Emperor.

From this time on Macrinus stayed alive by stealth and cunning. With a small number of trusted companions, he rode off, keeping as much out of sight as possible, and, in the guise of an ordinary citizen, he finally made it as far as Aegae in Cicilia. There he rested for a short time and gave out a story that he was a courier for the army; by this he managed to commandeer a carriage. Almost as soon as he had arrived he sneaked away like a ghost, traveling through the land in secrecy and fear. He drove through Cappadocia and Galatia, and finally through Bithynia to the harbour of Eribolon. It was his intention to strike for Rome, and to do that he hired a boat in the town.

So Macrinus sailed off; one story suggests that he was close to Byzantium when the wind blew him back to Asia. He got as far as Chalcedon, where again he rested for a while. It had been a difficult journey and now he faced another problem – he had nothing, no money on which to subsist. The solution was to send to someone he could rely upon, and he chose one of the procurators; it was not a good choice. Secretly, the procurator betrayed Macrinus and sent word to Varius's men, who came in force to capture him. Macrinus knew nothing of this as he lay in hiding, waiting to hear from his friend; he hardly expected the arrival of soldiers under the centurion Aurelius Celsus. He was promptly arrested, tied up like the commonest criminal, and put on a carriage to be taken back to Cappadocia. On the way, he was told that his son had also been captured by another centurion, Claudius Pollio. Macrinus grew desperate and tried to escape by leaping from the carriage, but all this achieved was a broken shoulder. Although he was put back in the cart and the journey continued, Macrinus was not destined to reach his destination. He was sentenced to die before they reached Antioch and so was stabbed to death by the centurion Marcianus Taurus. His head then sliced off.

It is an unlikely addendum that he was not allowed to be buried until the young Varius, who had ridden over from Syria, had arrived at the camp and seen it. According to Dio, he gloated over the body, which was then hastily buried. This would seem very much out of character, although it would have been politic to ensure that his enemy was truthfully out of the way.

So the Emperor Macrinus died at the age of fifty-four. Dio himself was generous in his praise for this incapable ruler, describing him as a man who had been 'distinguished for his practical experience of affairs, 'a man who displayed signs of excellence and commanded so many legions, [who] was overthrown by a mere boy of whose very name he had previously been ignorant'. It is noticeable that although Dio mentions the command of many legions, nothing is said about military prowess. This silence is probably the most charitable statement that could be made.

Chapter 4: Promises From The Sun-God

It would be an understatement to suggest that the senate were in a quandary as to what to do next. Having recently declared war on the False Antoninus, and having been unable to lend help to Macrinus, they were left with the fact that their Emperor had been defeated, and that their enemy had been chosen by the massed armies of Rome. To contradict their wishes would have been suicidal, but there must have been a number of senators – virtually all of them – who trembled to think of the possible repercussions. The only one who may have felt partly secure was that idiot Diogenianus. Perhaps he had not been so half-witted, after all.

The advent of the young Varius clashed strongly with the ethos of the government of Rome, with past precedent and form. In effect, the conflict between the Emperor and the senate was to create an unbridgeable rift which was to alienate Heliogabalus from the Conscript Fathers for the rest of his reign. In the unwritten tablets of etiquette, the acceptance of Varius demeaned the high profile of that which the Conscript Fathers had come to represent. A senatorial life was not always an easy one. Much depended on ambition, and the desires motivating an individual to rise into the government. Many were driven by the most praiseworthy motives; to actively promote the basic morals and noble tenets which had formed the backbone of Roman jurisprudence since the forming of the Republic. The Elder Cato, for example, during the time of Julius Caesar, was unswerving in his battle to maintain a strict moral code. Cassius Dio in many ways resembled Cato, but he lacked the fire of the famous orator; however, he did have a sense of proprieties which reached such fanatical levels that he comes across as something of a fusspot.

If the senate had grumbled because Macrinus had no senatorial experience, it isn't difficult to imagine their feelings on being told that the Empire was to be run by a boy who not only had no valid qualifications in Roman government, but had not even lived in Rome since he was little more than an infant. It was unprecedented. Although the great days of the Caesars were over, it was desirable that an Emperor Elect should have some virtues to justify his claims, but this young Heliogabalus had none, other than having held the office of High Priest in some Syrian backwater. It had been traditional for an honourable man to climb through the senatorial ranks and at least have served as Consul before dreaming of anything higher, but now, to Dio's disgust, the old standards were slipping away. In these days, when a man could grasp the Empire by feats of arms, at least the new ruler should have a proven track record of might and ability; but this supposed son of Antoninus had none of these either. His claim was through a supposed indiscretion of the part of his mother, which must have seemed paper-thin to the assembled senators.

The resentment of Cassius Dio and many others against Varius is understandable, as his appointment would undermine the nobility of the senate even further. The dignity of this time-honoured establishment was grounded in the Roman Constitution itself. After the last of the legendary kings, the hated Tarquin Superbus, the Republic was based on a strict democracy. To avoid submitting to the will of one man, the state was run by the senate, an oligarchy headed by two consuls, or head magistrates. The plan had been to foil individual ambition, but since the adoption of the Emperors the original ideals, which had served Rome well for four centuries, had been corrupted. The people now were accustomed to, and needed, a regal figurehead; in fact, they were lost without one. At the time of Heliogabalus, few people would have advocated a return to the republic, no matter how dear the theme of democracy was to both people and senate. Besides, the people were used to the advantages of having an Emperor who gave them gifts and lavish games as well as horse-racing.

The election of Varius as Emperor went against everything the constitution held sacred, that, fundamentally, it was the people who ruled Rome. As Cicero once said, *'Cum potestas in populo auctoritas in senatu sit'* ('While power lies with the people, authority lies with the senate'). But *auctoritas* was more than just 'authority'; it meant the esteem in which a senator was held, and would grow with individual feats and acts of great moment. The more triumphs one was awarded, for example, the greater his *auctoritas*. And this was not merely an empty honour; men with the greatest *auctoritas* were asked to speak first on senatorial matters. The kudos accrued from deeds of great acclaim therefore had an important practical significance, and could lead to promotion through the ranks; praetor, for instance, was the consul's second-in-command and took upon himself one of a variety of duties – for example, an army commander. Other magistrates included the quaestors, mainly responsible for criminal law and the treasury, and aediles, responsible for public festivals and the maintenance of public buildings. Appointment to any of these titles would be an important stepping-stone in Roman politics.

Now that an unknown boy was set to take over the Empire, it was obvious that the senate had again been sidelined, and senators like Dio were left to wonder whether the acquisition of *dignitas* and *auctoritas* had any real meaning any more. But for every Dio there was another less scrupulous. Too many were fired by greed; the wish to carve a position of eminence through pride and avarice led them to play on the proverbial pride of the Emperor through ingratiation by flattery or straightforward bribery, and the most unscrupulous by intrigue and deception. Not everybody was appalled at the coming of Varius. For every proud and therefore, to some extent, weak Emperor there would always be a Plautianus or someone plotting to feather their nest at the best opportunity. Human nature was not so different two millennia ago. It may seem peculiar that in these violent and chaotic times anyone would be so foolish as to take such immense risks to seek power and status, but there would always be people ready to fill in the vacuum left by those fallen by the wayside. No-one had a crystal ball to tell them whether the newest imperial model would be swept away or become another Augustus and reign till extreme old age. Of course it was a desperate gamble, but the golden prize at the end of the political rainbow was often too alluring to ignore.

Precedents were never far from hand; they were widely read in the old histories of Suetonius and Tacitus, as well as Livy. But you didn't have to go so far back. The Year of the Five Emperors was warning enough to demonstrate the extreme dangers of partisanship. Many had perished for the simple reason that they had backed the wrong horse during the terrors of 193, and those bleak lessons were repeated throughout the family strife between the house of Bassianus – those followers of Severus and Antoninus – as well as the factions warring between Macrinus and Antoninus. Repercussions had been swift and brutal and it had been a hard task to choose the most favourable winds blowing and swirling through the government of the Empire. Who, a year before, could have guessed that the fourteen year old lad from Emesa would have been proclaimed Emperor by the most powerful generals of Rome?

The most wise of the senate held a strictly middle course. Perhaps it was not the quickest way to eminence, but it was the safest way to stay alive, and when the regime was corrupt, life was cheap. One such senator was Dio, who always prided himself on doing the right thing at the right time. But no-one was really safe, especially in the case of an untrusting and paranoid Emperor; we have already seen how Dio was put in an agony of fear when, for the sake of a dream, a bald-headed senator was put in danger of an accusation of treason. Again, certain other circumstances spelled fear for the most unbiased of them. During times of revolt the senate could not afford to remain impartial, but was forced to make decisions for the common good of Rome. Such a situation they now faced – when there had been a revolt against the appointed Emperor Macrinus, they had no choice but to condemn the rebels. Now their head of state had been murdered, and they were faced with the inevitability that this 'False Antoninus' had seized the empery.

It seemed that there would be troublesome times ahead, and the senate could expect a turbulent time if the political climate was correspondingly turbulent, more so in times of warring factions and schisms within the imperial family. But if the senate feared the new Emperor, Varius's advisors also feared the senate, especially if his title stood on uncertain ground. There was the constant danger that it hid enemies among its ranks who could endanger his security, and if these dangers became apparent a purge would be necessary – a worrisome time among senators, who may well have feared that in some way they may be implicated in some devised plot. Even if they were innocent, they may find themselves a victim of an old adversary who may wish to play on the Emperor's insecurity – and therefore credulity – to condemn anyone on the flimsiest pretext of subversive behaviour. The worst possible scenario was to be in dread of a madman such as Caligula or Nero, who thought nothing of snuffing out a life on a whim; and 'madman' is precisely how Macrinus had described Varius.

Macrinus's assessment of the character of Varius was nonsense; he had never even seen the young pretender, and he was probably hardly aware of his existence. It had been a comment of propaganda designed to discredit his rival and rally his men to his own cause.. Macrinus had been failing fast, and his only chance was to persuade his followers of the worthlessness of his opponent, a worthlessness demonstrated by his extreme youth and a doubt placed upon his sanity. Macrinus's desperate attempts failed in the end, but his comments proved too alluring to be missed by the historians, and the reader could not fail to draw the inferences.

By now, the damage was done and the lightning *putsch* had been a total success. There was nothing that Rome could do but await developments in the knowledge that the succession had been a *fait accompli* and she was powerless to resist the oncoming storm. The Romans would be aware that Varius was a descendent of the line of Bassianus, and therefore of the imperial family, but little else. The only clear thing was that Varius was a scion of the house of Severus and his son, and such credentials would have done little to ease the tension felt by the Roman governors, who could do little but hope to weather the tempest.

After Immae, Varius had made the leisurely journey towards Antioch. Word of his sudden advancement had swept through the countryside and the natives rejoiced that one of their own had again taken over the Roman Empire. The histories remain stubbornly silent about his reception, but there is no reason to suspect it was anything but rapturous. Maesa, however, knew that he must make the journey to Rome as quickly as possible, to consolidate his position before rival factions could have the opportunity to strengthen and wrest the diadem by brute force. After any coup, the state was at its weakest, and it was vital that any opposition should be crushed speedily and mercilessly. Maesa had not watched through the reigns of two Emperors for nothing.

Word of the earth-shattering change in imperial power spread quickly and, as the royal cortège approached Mount Taurus, a deputation from the local temple of Faustina approached and asked Varius if he would re-dedicate it to the honour of El Gabal. Varius, who would remain deeply attached to his religion throughout his life, readily accepted, and the local priests must have felt the great honour of being visited not only by their Emperor, but also by a boy whose reputation as El Gabal's pontiff went before him. Sadly, no description of the ceremony survives, but it must have been a joyous and a festive occasion. His advisors did not prevent Varius from climbing the mountain and performing the requisite rituals; after all, this was a great piece of propaganda showing the new Emperor in the light of a people's man. It was publicity that money couldn't buy. For his part, Varius always loved ceremony and being in the public eye as an admired celebrity. It was also a welcome chance to cast off his soldier's costume and again revel in the feel of silk and make up his face.

There is another reason why the worshippers of the sun should have a double celebration in the coming of Varius. It seems that, from the first moment he knew he was to rule the world, Varius had given great thought to the worship of El-Gabal and there is strong evidence to suggest that he arranged for the great black stone of Emesa to accompany him to Rome. Such an upheaval must have produced cries of despair from the Emesan inhabitants, but the worship of Elagabalus was too important a subject to bow down to provincial desires. Coins minted at Antioch depicted the transport of the holy black meteorite on a cart pulled by horses. So here the natives had not only the presence of a great High Priest of El-Gabal, but a token of the god sent down from heaven as his holy sign.

After the ceremony, Varius and his troop continued on their way, and finally stopped at Antioch. By now there was no doubt in anybody's mind that he was now the new Emperor, and everyone looked forward to see how the heir of Antoninus would conduct himself. With him were the powerful figures of his mother, Julia Soaemias, his aunt Mamaea, and his grandmother Julia Maesa, who was the Livia to Varius's Tiberius. Through these women Varius had been led to dreams of greatness and power, the leader of the greatest Empire the world had seen. It is easy to visualize the grasping, manipulating women using the boy as a pawn in their grand plan. As he was so young, the three became his chief advisors, although others, of their kind, were employed to steer Varius on the right direction to his imperial destiny. All of them, with the exception perhaps of Soaemias, saw Varius as a stepping-stone to power and prestige; whereas Soaemias, while eager for his advancement, was also solicitous for his welfare, something all too rare over the next few years.

Varius himself had virtually no knowledge of government or politics. In Emesa there had been virtually no opposition to his rule and so he needed to know little of the crooked by-ways and the cut and thrust of Roman intrigue. Although he would learn some of this later – to his cost – at the beginning of his reign he was an innocent, coached and taught by his family and their powerful allies. Varius's dependence suited Maesa very well, and now she had what she had always wanted –a puppet she could manipulate while using her own influence to steer the Empire whichever way she wished.

What happened next is an old story Rome had witnessed a number of times. It was not enough to grasp power, Varius must wield it. The wreath of empery was of little use if it sat on an unsteady head, so Varius' position had to be solidified. Winning the one battle was not the end of the war, and Varius' advisors knew too well that there would be many in Rome watching closely, ready to spring if Varius miscarried. While he had the Roman legions behind him, no-one could make a move. Fear was a strong weapon, so while he held the affection and loyalty of the troops he could feel secure enough; meanwhile the soldiers, who were old hands at this game, awaited their bribes.

At least money was soon in coming. Over the years it had been quite a lucrative business, being a soldier; besides the huge bonuses they had been awarded by sundry emperors in the recent past, there was always the promise of booty while on campaign, unless they were prevented from doing so for political reasons or reasons of diplomacy. Looting and pillaging was a profitable and well-established pastime; the wealthier the city, the more booty to be had.

Apart from lining pockets, there was also the promise of lusty maidens on which to slake their sexual appetites, which had been sharpened by the months of warfare. Rape may have been a dirty word among the citizens in Rome, but it was not only expected but occasionally actively encouraged in times of invasion and punitive raids. There was much to be said for a successful attack or siege, when the mercy of the town was left under their control.

Antioch promised much. At that time, it was the capital of Syria, had been the administrative centre of the Seleucid Dynasty, and subsequent beautification programmes had earned it the title 'the Golden'. It had been fashioned along typical Roman lines, with a Forum and a temple to Jupiter which probably dated from the time of Augustus. There was a theatre and a fine Circus, and as a city of eminence it produced artists and writers such as Apollophanes and Phoebus. The city was a bustling melting-pot of nationalities and religions, and although earthquakes periodically did great damage to its structures, it remained a splendid fortified gem on the river Orestes. It was a town of some antiquity, having been founded by a general of Alexander the Great – Seleucus - and had grown much in prestige over the centuries. Not only did it boast numerous temples and theatres, but it was a trading centre for the region, a regular stopping-place for caravans from the East; it was a buzzing, prosperous, cosmopolitan settlement and an important base for the Roman Empire. Varius's advisors saw this, but the soldiers only saw profits. Besides, hadn't Antioch given Macrinus shelter after the final battle – albeit they were unaware of the true outcome?

Even so, they were prepared to act as a friend to their enemies, and wasn't that in itself worth a bit of pillaging?

Maesa knew that the only way to save the city was to compensate the soldiers in some way – that way being, of course, money. She and Domna had seen this under the reigns of Severus and Antoninus, and Maesa had made good use of the ploy when she bought off the legion at Emesa. 2000 sesterces apiece was enough to bribe them, but Varius did not have ready cash with him, so he raised it from the citizens of Antioch themselves. After all, which would they prefer – to be violently raided, or to pay a ransom? The money was collected and distributed to the army, the soldiers appeased, and the city left in peace.

Having sorted out outstanding business, Maesa in particular was chafing to leave for Rome; she missed the political intrigues at the nerve-centre of the Empire. It must have been difficult for a woman of her temperament, not only in Rome but also in Emesa, where the royal line was again a masculine affair. Arabian women were thought of as chattels. Women fared little better in Rome, but at least were treated with dignity as far as their roles in society went, chiefly as keeper of the home and educator to young children. It must have been daunting for the young Varius. His mother still smothered him, and he could hope for no aid from his real father, Sextius Varius Marcellus; but at that time his foster-father, Gannys, was still an important soldier and would at least have been able to advise his party on everything military.

Entering his teens, the picture of Varius is one of a young man in a state of confusion, caught between his own beliefs and that of Rome, whose religious experiences wavered between orgiastic excess and fertility rites. As for the question of sexuality, he was in a peculiar situation in that the strong stabilizing influence was distinctly female. Whereas other boys saw their female relations as dignified servants, and the men as the strong masculine role model, Varius had instead forceful and powerful women which he could emulate in the forms of his aunt and grandmother. The assimilation of power and intrigue with the female, and his own hopes and aspirations, could well have been a factor in his obvious struggle with sexuality. His leaning towards the ideal of femininity would very soon become more dominant and almost fetishistic.

The influence of his mother is hardly to be denied, but of course we don't know anything about his constitution, or his genetic make-up. In retrospect, it is certain that he was a latent homosexual; but more of that later.

Maesa and Mamaea chafing at the bit, their aim now was to ensure their safety and to cultivate friends in the Roman administration. It was impractical to govern the state machine with force of arms and so diplomacy was the only choice. A letter was carefully drafted to the senate, its intention being to mollify them with regard to their own safety and to stress the good intentions of the new Emperor. As well as this, the letter had to persuade them that the emperor elect merited the title and had qualities which were fitted to one aspiring to such heights. In this, they rather overdid things, and the missive could have backfired; for Varius styled himself with several epithets he was not privileged to use. He began by referring to himself as 'Emperor and Caesar, the son of Antoninus, the grandson of

Severus, Pius, Felix, Augustus, proconsul, and holder of the tribunician power.' These titles were all very grand, but, perhaps due to the inexperience of the advisors, they had not followed the proper protocol. It was not for Varius, even if all of these appellations were true or deserved, to take them upon himself; custom dictated that they should be accepted after being formally offered by the government. This may have been a formality; but formality was important to the ancient Romans, and the letter had begun with a slight which may or may not have been intended. Dio was furious. However, protocol had been broken in this way on so many recent occasions that the Bassiani might well have felt that a precedent had been set and that it had become the norm for Emperors to style themselves in this manner.

The substance of the letter was encouraging enough – Varius promised to take up Augustus as his role model. It was encouraging, but not exactly original. Every emperor who wanted to prove his worthy intentions was used to taking the great Emperor Augustus as a yardstick. Nonetheless, for form's sake it was a good idea. And Varius went on to say that he could see parallels between the youth of the two men, himself and Augustus. As well as emulating him, he also promised to use the last of the 'good emperors', Marcus Aurelius, as a model too. Such an avowal could not fail to have been appreciated, even if the senate had seen no signs of that yet, and Augustus would certainly never have styled himself in the same way that Varius had.

Knowing that the senate had backed Macrinus against him, Varius next went on to explain why he had rebelled against Marcinus' authority. His argument was based on the late Emperor's lowliness of birth, his low rank at the time he was elected, and his professed part in the death of Antoninus:

> **This man, who was not allowed to even enter the senate-house, after the proclamation barring everyone except senators, dared treacherously to murder the emperor whom he had been trusted to guard - dared to appropriate his office and to become emperor before he had been a senator.**

He also attacked Macrinus for having mocked his age, and in a back-handed defence of that he said:

> **He decided to disparage my age, when he himself had appointed his five-year-old son emperor!**

This was not true, of course, but it was important that Varius should blacken Macrinus's name as much as possible, both to promote his own claim and to drum up as much support for his case as he could. Apart from this, Maesa knew that future trouble from Macrinus's supporters should be nipped in the bud at the earliest opportunity. To this end Varius also sent messages to legions throughout the Empire, and his secret police hunted out letters and incriminating notebooks written by Macrinus, which they then distributed to the soldiers to blacken his name even further. At this time the followers of Macrinus comprised Varius's biggest threat; as yet no-one else had appeared to question his claim to the imperial title. The first priority was to maintain the loyalty of the army by whatever means he could.

He, and his advisors, knew that they needed the goodwill of the senate, and Varius's letter had done everything it could to convince them of his sincerity. Still, if they would not submit voluntarily then they could be forced to do so. He made sure that the senate were aware of that, and he 'commanded that if anyone resisted him, he should call on the soldiers for assistance.' This, he knew, would not fail to show the senate his intentions and his strength, and suggests Maesa's influence. The senate could hardly refuse.

Of course, the result was general fear. When the letters of Varius had been sent and read, Dio expressed the feelings in the curia:

> ...Because of the great need hanging over them, they couldn't do any of the things that were proper or expedient . . but were panic-stricken by fear . . . and Macrinus, whom they had often commended, they now reviled, together with his son, regarding him as a public enemy; while as for Tarautas [Antoninus], whom they had often wished to declare a public enemy, they now exalted him and prayed that his alleged son should be like him.

Praying was the best they could do. It was all very well for Varius to maintain that he would emulate Augustus, but the senate had heard such things before. It is hardly surprising that they were 'panic-stricken by fear'. Even if it were hard to cobble together a case against individuals, they all shared the responsibility of the declamation against Varius at the outset of his rebellion. Persecutions were still a recent memory to the frightened senators and now it was not only the bald-headed who feared for their lives.

Varius himself was in no great hurry to get to Rome. His future certain, he remained for some time in Antioch, and while he was there he strengthened his hold on this key city. His advisors began to put their mind to administrative matters. They appointed Pollio as Governor of Germany, as he had successfully subdued Bithynia and it would take a general of some experience to deal with the warlike, aggressive, barbaric tribes. Germany had been a spear in the Empire's side since the days of Julius Caesar, and even he had been unwilling to cross the Rhine and invade their territories. Pollio undertook the task with his usual dedication and often called in Gannys to help him.

It had made good political sense to spend a little time in Antioch, and it was only natural that Varius wished to give honour to the city that had ousted Macrinus and had proven its faith in him. It was a time of great celebration for the citizens, to have the new Emperor among them, one who had shown them mercy and kindness. Varius performed his own rites at the temple, but there may have been another reason why he decided to linger here. From the relative backwater of Emesa, Antioch would have seemed very cosmopolitan and modern to him; besides, the passing of time had given the city a slightly dubious reputation, and extravagance had become the trend of the day. As Gibbon explained:

> **Fashion was the only law, pleasure the only pursuit, and the splendour of dress and furniture was the only distinction of the citizens of Antioch. The arts of luxury were honoured, the serious and manly virtues were the subject of ridicule, and the contempt for female modesty and reverent age announced the universal corruption of the capital of the East.**

It is easy to imagine the attraction for a young boy at visiting the fun city of the East. Among the flesh-pots of the bright, fashionable capital, the young ruler would have felt quite at home among the trendy youth of the time, resplendent in the lavish clothes to which he was accustomed.

Having spent a number of months in Antioch, and having garrisoned the city to his (or his grandmother's) satisfaction, Varius at last decided to travel through Bithynia and spend the winter months of 218-219 in its capital, Nicodemia, where he again consolidated his position with the people there. Nicodemia was one of the most important towns of North-West Asia Minor and lay at the head of the Gulf of Astacus which flowed into the Propontis River, some two hundred kilometres North of Antioch. Once again there was much local excitement, and the pious new Emperor again agreed to participate in the celebrations to his deity. He visited the Temple of the Sun-God, and, dressed in the robes befitting his position of high-priest, performed the necessary rites, rites which seemed a little strange and outré to the Romans there.

The decision to linger in Nicodemia was a strange one, and marks his first clash with his grandmother, who had ordered him to move on to Rome as quickly as he could. There were many reasons to do so; having been proclaimed Emperor it was important to make an early appearance, to appease the senate and to crush any possible dissension from amongst the ranks. Moreover, the people themselves were anxious to see their new figurehead. To Maesa's amazement, Varius dug in his heels, and openly defied his omnipotent grandmother. Such a response was hardly expected and little welcomed; no-one would have thought the young boy to have so much courage and independence. It became obvious that the new status had gone to his head and would soon have to be addressed if Maesa was to attain the control she had schemed for. For the moment, she did nothing apart from grit her teeth; she was a cunning lady and never did anything precipitously; but she did mark the offence down in her personal grudge bank, to be remembered at a later stage.

This act of defiance by Varius demonstrates another important aspect to his character, and one which would become more important as his reign progressed. Admittedly, he was green as far as government went, but he was a determined young man with a strong sense of independence, something Maesa and Mamaea had not bargained on. During his time in Emesa, he had acted the part of high priest with style and panache, and if he knew anything at all it was how to act a regal part. Now he had reached the ultimate height, he had agendas of his own, and not even the intimidating figure of Maesa would stand in his way. It was a recipe for disaster.

It would have been interesting to assess the personality of Varius at this point in his life, but again the records are silent. Perhaps it is not so amazing that he found the courage to disregard the orders of the matriarchal Maesa and tarry in Nicodemia. Immature as he undoubtedly was, he had entered man's estate and was beginning to act on his own initiative. This was, after all, not about his grandmother or his aunt, it was about himself. His god had decreed that he was the anointed one, and as such it was incumbent upon him to act and think for himself, as far as he could. In his brain he was entering adulthood, but his mind was forever trapped in that twilight world of childish fantasy and dream. Given a perverse psychological make-up, the recipe could have been one of universal disaster. As it happened, Varius was a kind-hearted, emotional young man who had not inherited the cruel streak of the other branch of the family.

Although no-one is really sure why Varius lingered in Nicodemia, there may be a possibility which has been overlooked. As some point Varius decided to have his portrait painted, and in a specific pose. It was to be a large canvas depicting him sacrificing to El-Gabal in his sacerdotal livery and was to be sent to the senate-house in Rome before his arrival there. Unfortunately, the picture was not intended merely as a gift but was to have a very practical use, one which would stir the embers of revulsion and dissatisfaction among the Conscript Elders.

Other reasons have been put forward to explain his delay in setting off for Rome. Coins minted during this period have the inscription SALUS ANTONINI AUGUSTI ('the health of Antoninus Augustus'), and Hay has suggested that the new Emperor was recovering from some illness, of mental or physical origin. The idea does not hold much water. Salus was a goddess based on the Greek Hygeia, and she was not only the goddess of health but also of security and social welfare. She was commonly printed on coins between the first and the fourth century, and is depicted as feeding a snake which is either coiled around her or shown on an altar, the snake representing that of Aescipilus and so the personification of health. Salus was usually chosen to signify welfare of the emperor (*Salus Augusti*), of the soldiers (*Salus Militum*) and of the state (*Salus Republicae*). In this case, the coins suggested a prayer for the well-being of the Antonine house to which Varius had claimed kinship and which Macrinus has opposed; as such it most probably reflected a pointed political comment.

There was another reason why such a delay in Nicodemia, of all places, should worry Maesa. Varius's latent homosexual leanings – or at least his femininity - were likely to have been noticed by his immediate family, and in that age it was crucial that such a sexual orientation should be kept from the general public, and especially the senate. Nicodemia was a city with a reputation. Julius Caesar had also lingered there for longer than was good for him, at the court of King Nicodemes; at the time he was also a young man who had only just begun on his journey towards glory. The Hellenistic King seemed to take to Caesar, and rumours circulated that they were lovers, Caesar taking the passive role. It was a rumour he tried unsuccessfully to live down for the rest of his life, but the gossip was too good to miss. Even as his soldiers marched home after the triumphant Gallic campaign, they would sing:

> *Gaul was shamed by Caesar,*
> *By Nicodemes, he!*
> *Here's Caesar, wreathed in triumph*
> *For his Gallic victory!*
> *Nicodemes wears no laurels*
> *Though the greatest of the three!!*

Although this happened over two centuries before, it had not been forgotten; the annalists of the time ensured that, especially the scandal-mongerer Suetonius. These histories were still extant and were popular books; there was nothing the Romans liked better than the whiff of scandal. The stories were common knowledge to the senators, and as they waited with impatience for the arrival of their new ruler, the news that he was hanging around in Nicodemia – for no apparent reason – would have started off dark whispers and speculations. Parallels with Julius Caesar would be unavoidable; but then, if Varius was destined to follow the same star as Caesar, then there came the promise of greatness and a glorious reign.

By May 219 Varius felt ready to face the journey, and his relatives may have sighed their relief as they set out for the Roman capital, travelling through Thrace and Moesia, and eventually passing down into Italy. Here, Varius made preparations for his entrance into Rome. The arrival of a new Emperor was not an event to pass by unnoticed, and both precedent and tradition demanded a spectacle of some grandeur. To act the part of a powerful ruler would have come as second nature to Varius, but this was Rome and form had to be observed on all points. Varius had to look the part of an impressive Caesar, deserving of high office and a young man capable of filling the Roman people with pride and admiration. Although he had a determination to take on the purple as his own man, he had an intelligence above average and was no fool. He knew that his complete naivety concerning matters of state required good counsel and trustworthy advisors – and on political matters he was quite prepared to listen to them.

As Varius entered the seat of his newly-gained Empire, it would take a brave man not to raise a cheer or two. There were, in fact, many reasons for the people to rejoice. The unpopular Macrinus had been disposed of, the Empire was at peace, and here came a new Emperor with the promise of celebratory games, gifts and a new era of the Antonine Dynasty.

Herodian describes the entry of Heliogabalus into Rome that June as one might expect someone who was antipathetic to his subject to do so, stating that he arrived dressed in his native garb just as he appeared while performing his religious duties. The suggestion is one of the Emperor dressed in luxuriant robes, face painted, adorned with trinkets, and dancing while surrounded by eunuchs and chanting women. It is another example of the historian twisting the truth to stress Varius's depravity from the very start of his reign.

The picture is a silly one, because no-one, even someone as empty-headed as Herodian tries to describe, would be foolish enough to flout Roman sensibilities in such a way on their triumphant arrival to Rome. Even Lampridius draws the mark at such a portrait, which in any case is refuted by the more reliable Dio, who states that he arrived dressed in military costume as would be fitting for a new Emperor. It also must be remembered that Dio himself harboured no little resentment for the Syrian interloper, and if Varius had arrived as Herodian described he would not have hidden such a spectacle from his readers. The scandal would have been too good to ignore.

Almost certainly, the Emperor's arrival into Rome was a grand occasion, a time for great celebration and joy. As Varius had been triumphant in battle against Macrinus and the Praetorian Guard, he would have appeared as a conquering hero, dressed in the uniform he wore while charging down on the enemy hordes. The Roman citizens, who adored a party, would have thronged the streets in anticipation and curiosity, and roared their approbation to the slight figure who had put an end to the man who had brought so much shame on his country. Young, handsome and proud, this new Nero had the potential of resurrecting Rome's good name and heralding a new Golden Age of prosperity. Such a huge demonstration of loyalty could not help but affect Varius, who always cherished the love of the people. In his turn, his natural grace had the power of seducing men to his favour, and he is said to have had a natural magnetism which was very winning.

The cart with the ominous black stone, however, was never even mentioned. No-one even knew what it was.

As the new Emperor, Varius took pride in conferring upon himself the name of the sun-god to which he was bound by virtue of his rank in the religion of El-Gabal. In fact, Varius was to have a bewildering array of names; first of all he was called Varius Avetus Bassianus, which he changed to Marcus Aurelius Antoninus on assuming the role of Antoninus's son. As Emperor, he became known as Sardanapolis and Elagabalus, after the sun-god himself. However, the name he would be more usually known as in future history would be the Hellenised version of the same name, Heliogabalus. This is the name he will be referred to from this time forward.

It is important to recognise that in taking upon himself the cognomen of Heliogabalus, he was in no way comparing himself with the god himself. That would have been a blasphemy for someone as devoted and religious as Varius. He took the name as an act of reverence. Far from seeing himself as a deity, he saw himself as his god's ambassador. Heliogabalus was to be an evangelist, not an avatar.

And what of the appearance of the new Emperor? Of course he was young, and Dio describes him as 'handsome'. Professor Bury describes him thus:

In form he was attractive and exceedingly graceful; his hair, which was very fair, glistened like gold in the sun; he was slender and possessed of glorious blue eyes, which in turn were endowed with the power of attracting all beholders to his worship; and he knew his power over men; he had first realised it when the legionaries flocked to the temple at Emesa attracted by the reports of this Prince Charming.

One bust of him exists, kept at the Capitoline Museums; it was carved in his lifetime (221), and shows a rather rounded face, with a prominent Cupid's bow and an attractive dimple on is chin. His hair was brushed forward in a short fringe, and hair was short although some ringlets fall in front of his ears. He was clean-shaven, and had somewhat soft features. It is tempting to say that he looked almost feminine.

Varius had donned the uniform of a soldier as a costume, just as he had done in the Battle of Immae, to impress the Romans. In battle he had played the part of an avenging warrior; on his entrance to Rome as the dignified and worthy warrior-emperor. Now that the theatricals were over, Varius discarded the costume forever. He resorted to the fashions he was used to, which shone with magnificence and grandeur. The times of war and battle were at an end, and now it was time for the new Emperor to shine forth with all the resplendent majesty he could muster. It was a role he felt very much at home with: the centre of attention as a spectacular and princely sovereign – and to Varius there was no good reason why his old life in Emesa should not continue in Rome.

So it was that, at the very start of his reign, there was great hope for a successful and peaceful rule. For the time being, the senate were mollified by his vows of setting a good imperial example, and they must have looked forward to a time of harmony, should all of his promises not prove hollow. The soldiery had another Antoninus at their head, and had been paid their bribes to protect him. And finally the people had their Nero resurrected from the tomb; although Nero's reign had been a malicious one he was still the darling of the people and the new boy seemed like a forgotten scion from the line of the old Caesars. The board was set for success, and the scheming women in the background must have been thanking their god for their new twist of good fortune.

Little did they know that in less than four short years Heliogabalus would become the most hated Emperor in the history of ancient Rome.

Chapter 5: The Boy In The Candy Shop

> **The life of Elagabalus Antoninus, also called Varius, I should never have put in writing — hoping that it might not be known that he was emperor of the Romans — were it not that before him this same imperial office had had a Caligula, a Nero, and a Vitellius. But, just as the same earth produces not only poisons but also corn and other useful things, not only snakes but sheep as well, so the thoughtful reader may find himself some consolation for these monstrous tyrants by reading of Augustus, Trajan, Vespasian, Hadrian, Pius, Titus, and Marcus. At the same time he will learn of the Romans' discernment, in that these last ruled long and died by natural deaths, whereas the former were murdered, dragged through the streets, officially called tyrants, and no man wishes to mention even their names.**

This is an extract from the *Historia Augusta* – 'The Illustrious History', and is a fair summary of the general feeling at the time following his reign, and during it. Unfortunately, the *Historia Augusta* is a most unreliable work, packed with important facts juxtaposed with forgeries and fictions. In the case of this particular quote, however, the complaint of Lampridius is supported by the histories of both Herodian and Cassius Dio, both of whom were contemporaries of Heliogabalus and so were not written from the hindsight of the fourth century. Despite the prejudices of Dio and the brevity of Herodian, their testimony casts a dark shadow on the memory of the young Emperor, and as in the case of the *Historia* there is a hardly-repressed shame even at mentioning his very name. To each of them, Heliogabalus was a man to be scorned and detested, a pariah whose acts filled the writer with disgust and revulsion. To determine the validity of such censorship is the goal towards which this account is aimed.

Heliogabalus was little more than a child when he took over the running of the Empire, physically and mentally. As such, he was dominated by his aunt and grandmother, each ambitious and thirsty for power. The most conniving was Maesa, certainly the most experienced in the affairs of the Roman state, but it would be wrong to consider her as an ogress. She was also wise and cautious, an able advisor; apart from having many negative aspects, not least an overweening superiority, she was also a steadying hand on the life of her young protégé. Always there at hand, always working behind the scenes, was the figure of Maesa, industrious, razor-keen, intelligent.

Although hers was the voice of reason, Heliogabalus's character and the strange driving force within him made it impossible to obey his grandmother at every turn, and once he had been given imperial power he gradually followed his own inclinations. But it was a slow process, and at least at the start of his rule he followed her advice to the best of his ability. Maesa was in fact aware that Heliogabalus was his own worst enemy and tried on numerous occasions to curb his excesses. In the end, when the final catastrophe came, Maesa had already made other arrangements, and made sure she had other cards in her hand when all hope seemed to be lost.

The interference of women in the running of the nation was an obvious goad to Lampridius, who in his fabulous *Historia* lampooned the womenfolk in a passage wherein he imagines that Heliogabalus has set up a women's senate on the Quirinile Hill. This, he claims, was instigated by Soaemias, and in a paragraph in which his sense of outrage is heightened, states that several decrees were issued concerning Roman women, 'namely, what kind of clothing each might wear in public, who was to yield precedence and to whom, who was to advance to kiss another, who might ride in a chariot, on a horse, on a pack-animal, or on an ass, who might drive in a carriage drawn by mules or in one drawn by oxen, who might be carried in a litter, and whether the litter might be made of leather, or of bone, or covered with ivory or with silver, and lastly, who might wear gold or jewels on her shoes.' His ridicule is poorly aimed; as he well knew, etiquette was an important consideration to the Romans, and many of these decrees were necessary ones; besides, there were other more important issues which were indeed debated by a body of women. This was not a new organisation, and although Soaemias may have been involved in such activities, the President was more likely to have been Mamaea or Maesa.

The idea for this lampoon was obviously inspired by the long-respected *conventus matronarum*, an organization dating from the early republican period. Its function was to deal with matters of court etiquette, and it had some kind of approbation due to its ancient establishment. Judging by the words of Lampridius, it had not been held in universal favour among some of the menfolk – for obvious reasons - but the *conventus* was a traditional and well-respected establishment held in great esteem by the citizens of Rome; and Lampridius's carping has probably more to do with chauvinism than disgust at the Bassiani family. It says something of his temperament that he was prepared to take cheap swipes at them through such an eminent institution.

Lampridius takes female influence to ludicrous proportions. Unreliable as he is, Lampridius states that Heliogabalus demanded the right to allow his mother to attend the senate meetings, and take part in the drawing up of senatorial decrees. This would have been an unprecedented violation of protocol; only once had a woman attended such a meeting – Agrippina, Nero's mother - but even then she was hidden behind a curtain. Should Lampridius have been serious in such a declaration, it can only be assumed that he was writing a satire on the influence of women over the Emperor. He was, after all, writing to Constantine, and the new state religion had at last put the woman back in an inferior position – as a being grown from Adam's rib and doomed to be man's maidservant.

Apart from this, Heliogabalus was young, and the Romans had already had bad experiences of what can happen when a boy takes the imperial chair. Nero had only been seventeen after his mother had engineered his own rise to power, and his reign had been tainted with bloodshed and perversity, even though his family name had survived his outrages and was still held in respect. Again, Commodus had hardly shone through as Emperor, proving to be the rot which began the Empire's decline. In this regard, the senators had little hope for Heliogabalus, who was younger than both – a boy, merely, and the youngest Emperor ever to be been appointed.

Even worse, he was of Arab blood. Before he had even begun his reign, local prejudice was strong against him.

Although the senate had little hope, it still did have a lot of fear. Cassius Dio himself was unnerved; as he said, 'many individuals and communities alike, including the Romans themselves, both knights and senators, had privately and publicly, by word and by deed, heaped insults upon both Caracallus and himself, as a result of the letters of Macrinus.' Fortunately for them, the senatorial baby was not thrown out with the bath water. It may well have been that Heliogabalus's family and advisors were sensible enough to realise that it was hardly diplomatic to decimate the ruling body of Rome, and indeed to some extent the tactic was successful. The apparent magnanimity of the ruler and his people was not lost on the governors, and they must have breathed a sigh of relief when they finally realised that they were safe. As Dio was to remark, it was the one 'action of his worthy of a thoroughly good emperor'. Hardly a surprising comment; after the debates during the wars, Dio himself had chimed in with the opinions of the *curia*, and was certainly in the firing-line should the imperial family choose to wreak revenge. They never did. Though this was more due to politics than to compassion.

But this is not to say that Maesa was the soul of leniency. On the contrary, she realised that the senate were a mob with herd instincts, and they ebbed and waxed with each phase of the political moon – no harm to be seen in that; on the other hand, the safety of the regal seat was of first priority, and it would not do to allow it be at the mercy of anyone whose interests were in direct conflict with it.

Certainly, there were little fears in the yes-men who raised their hands to the nod of whoever assumed power - for that reason it was politic to give a show of clemency and fair-dealing - but those who had proven themselves the true enemies of the Bassiani, they were the ones to fear, and against whom stern measures had to be taken.

These enemies were to be found among those of Macrinus' supporters who had actively opposed them, and who could be expected to harbour open grudges against the new regime. So began the reprisals, and the start of the negative propaganda against Heliogabalus, of which Dio wrote that he: 'drifted into all the most shameful, lawless, and cruel practices, with the result that some of them, never before known in Rome, came to have the authority of tradition.' Whether or not these epithets apply to Heliogabalus will be a question to be looked at throughout the remainder of this book, but the first taste of bloodshed occurred very early in his reign, while he tarried in Nicodemia.

His foster father Gannys had won great renown in the revolt against Macrinus, and was now reaping the rewards of his labours. His imperial ward had much to thank him for – not only had he been instrumental in the rebellion, he had cared for him as his own son and guided him to the path of regality. But Gannys was a wily and ambitious man, and although even Dio had to concede that 'he did no-one any harm and bestowed many benefits upon many people', he also saw through his ambition and noted him for impiety and for a love of taking bribes. The giving of benefits to many people could be construed as buying friends, and his accumulation of wealth made him a powerful man. Like Caesar, Heliogabalus's party may have thought him 'as a serpent's egg, which, hatched, would, as his kind, grow mischievous'.

There was another reason why Heliogabalus may have resented Gannys, and that it his attachment to his mother. It is not difficult to see how jealousy may have led him to hate the man who had robbed him of some part of his mother's love and affection, and this neurotic tie to his mother-image may well have led to an unconscious aversion to the man he called both 'uncle' and 'father'. Always Soaemias remained as the main guiding star of his life, and the dominantly irrepressible figures of Aunt Mamaea and his Grandmother were an abiding and powerful force inside him. His advancement was the fruit of their limitless ambition, and nothing was to stand in their way.

Perhaps not even Gannys.

In this Agatha Christie whodunnit we have many suspects but no real evidence. It is transparent that nothing, not even family honour could restrain the Bassiani women from fulfilling their dream of power, and it could be that Gannys himself had been nurtured as a tool to pave the way for their success, as he did so effectively in the revolution. Had they suspected that he was feathering a nest for his future, gathering wealth and an unassailable position in Roman politics, he himself could have been an enemy to be reckoned with – and the women knew well enough his ability to stir up animosity and begin a revolt. They also knew how ambitious he himself was; and should he have joined with the Macrinus faction he could have been a great danger to them. Of course, now that the dust of almost two millennia has settled, we are left with little but guesswork.

But if we are to believe Cassius Dio, Gannys over-reached himself when he demanded a powerful marriage alliance from Heliogabalus, and that he himself should be made 'caesar'. This at last revealed the full extent of his ambition and would not have been welcomed by either Heliogabalus nor his scheming relations. Should they have suspected Gannys's loyalty or motives for one moment, this would have been sufficient to convince them; by such a request Gannys was looking beyond petty ambition, to the throne of Rome itself! This was something which was hardly to be borne. His whole attitude was reflected in his continuous interference with Heliogabalus's life-style, curbing his activities and ordering him in how to run his life. According to Dio, 'he was forced by Gannys to live temperately and prudently.' Perhaps so; but this was written after the death of the Emperor, and when his character had been assessed as a psychopathological one; it is statement made to fit in with what were seen as the facts. As he was considered as being lacking in moral fobre, so Gannys was seen as a guiding influence on him. Whatever checks Gannys may have made on the plans or intentions of Heliogabalus – and it will be shown that there may have been many – would not have been congenial to a boy who considered himself as omnipotent, perhaps god-like. A boy in a candy shop who was denied the right to taste the wares.

Gannys had other enemies, in the form of the supporters of Macrinus, who saw him as the author of their own downfall, and as the engineer of Heliogabalus's rise to fame. The young new Emperor was at this time carefully working to gain support, as his mild treatment of the senate had proven. If there was to be a counter-rebellion, the greatest of the opponents would be the slippery Gannys. So there were many snakes hissing into Heliogabalus's ear at the time, and Gannys' rapid rise to popularity may well have worked against him. For whatever reason, Gannys' presence was thought too much of an irritant and he was murdered.

Dio puts the blame for the murder squarely at the door of Heliogabalus…

He himself was the first to give Gannys a mortal blow with his own hand, since no one of the soldiers had the hardihood to take the lead in murdering him.

The quote itself betrays the fact that it was suspected that more than one hand was responsible: 'the first' to give a mortal blow suggests there were more. It is difficult to believe that a mere boy, with little battle experience, should oppose himself a military man of Gannys's reputation, unless it be by a stab from behind; and if that had happened – even if in rumour – Dio would have been the first to expose such cowardice. In any case, throughout his life Heliogabalus showed signs of a delicate and sensitive nature. In the final analysis, it would appear that Gannys died as a result of a conspiracy, no-one knows by whom.

The assassination of Gannys exposed the intentions of the new rulers of Rome, in that they were determined to remove any threats or dangers from their fold. Macrinus's followers had been dealt with summarily, and swept from sight. Rome itself was safe enough, although the eagle eyes of Mamaea and Maesa were always on the lookout for potential trouble. Now it was abroad where the danger loomed – discontented governors of far-off provinces, with armies and military might at their back, ready to give defiance to the new order.

The first to feel the cut of the new scythe was the governor of Arabia, Pica Caerianus. Word had come to him of a revolt in Syria, and that a young pretender was claiming the empery; a boy claiming to be the son of Antoninus. Thinking nothing of the latest disturbance – one of a great many which had taken place over the last few years – Caerianus did little about it, and in so doing neglected to send vows of allegiance to the boy Emperor. So it became obvious that his loyalty was in doubt, and moves were made against him lest he should decide to deploy the armies resident in his land. Caerinus was killed and replaced with an official more suited to the Bassiani allies.

There was further bloodshed in Syria in the aftermath of the rebellion against Macrinus; the massed soldiers of Heliogabalus swept away all prominent supporters of the last Emperor, and among the assassinated were Nestor and the Syrian governor, Fabius Agrippinus. After that, the whole of Syria was made safe against any possibility of effective revolt. The lessons afforded by Severus's early career had been well learned.

Among Heliogabalus' allies there was one Comazon, who was given the privileged position of head of the Praetorian Guard, despite the fact that he had little senior military or experience. He was despised by the senate, who called him Comazon, a name, they said, he took from mimes and buffoons. The scorn of the senate was certainly well-placed, as Comazon had already something of a disreputable reputation before the campaign to advance Varius; in the past, he had committed a crime in Cyprus for which the governor, Claudius Attalus, had sent him to the galleys.

The identity of this Comazon is difficult to unravel. Most writers, including Dio, assume that he was Publius Valerius Comazon Eutychianus, the same Eutychianus who had played such an important part in the original rebellion against Macrinus and who was one of the first to fool the armies into accepting Varius as the son of Antoninus. For him, it is reasonable to accept that he was nicknamed 'Comazon', the Greek for 'Reveller', as he was originally an acrobat and an actor. But it is not certain that this was the same man. It could well have been M Valerius Comazon, who was prominent at this time, and whose surname was a real name and not an epithet of scorn. On the other hand, Eutychianus had proven himself an able soldier and a wily tactician, who might well have received rewards for his labours.

Attalus had had a stormy career, which was now coming to an abrupt end. He had been appointed governor of Thrace under Severus, but during the war against Pescennius the Black he was dismissed from service. However, when Antoninus took over the empire Attalus found himself back in favour, and was sent off to govern Cyprus. There, he survived the takeover of Macrinus, but when Heliogabalus succeeded him Attalus's luck finally ran out. The wheel of fortune had now turned in Comazon's favour, and with the aid of his powerful allies he revenged himself upon Attalus by having him executed. Comazon continued to stay in favour with the new ruling family, and in their first year he was made both consul and city prefect, to the disdain of the senate; as Dio wrote of his advancement to the prefecture, 'and that not once only, but even a second and a third time — a thing that had never before happened in the case of anybody else; hence this will be counted as one of the greatest violations of precedent.' Precedent, of course, was food and drink to the fastidious Dio.

The puppeteers pulling Heliogabalus's strings knew well from experience how easy it had been to forge a rebellion, and had themselves set a precedent for mutineers. There was little about rousing a multitude that they did not know, nor how to use such an influence for violent ends. The widespread use of terror was a tool to snuff out the embers of revolt before even a modest flame could be ignited. Self-taught, they kept a watchful eye on the reaches of the empire, and acted quickly when suspicious actions excited their doubts, and doubtless many innocents found themselves in the firing-line. Armies of provinces were kept in tow by tame governors, and anyone in communication with hostile forces was a threat.

There was no time to plan a *coup d'état* than in a time of great weakness, and many saw that time as still being now. Dio's complaint about Heliogabalus's cruelty and oppression, written after his name had been blackened, does not bear scrutiny when one considers the scramble of would-be rebels gathering forces under the shadow of secrecy. Dio himself gives the truth away in his Histories, with the following passage:

> ...there were many others elsewhere, since it was the simplest thing in the world for anyone who wished to rule to stir up a rebellion, being encouraged in the act by the fact that many men had seized the Empire against all expectation and lacking all merit. And let no one doubt my statements; for what I have written about the other attempts of private citizens I learned from trustworthy men, and the information about the fleet I personally learned by accurate investigation in Pergamum, close at hand, when I was in charge of that city, as well as of Smyrna, having been appointed by Macrinus; and in view of this attempt none of the others seemed incredible to me.

Dio cannot have it both ways. Either Heliogabalus was a little monster, delighting in cruelty and massacring citizens in a bloody Reign of Terror, or he was defending himself against possible uprisings, which Dio himself admits to be a matter of fact. The incident of the fleet refers to a nameless individual who attempted to stir up mutiny among the ships of war moored at the port of Cyzicus, while Heliogabalus was in Nicodemia. And many other attempts are known of, most of which at least indicate definite designs against the new Emperor. Two soldiers mentioned by name were Verus, commander of the Third Gallic legion, and Gellius Maximus, who was lieutenant of the Fourth Scythian legion. Both of these men aimed at the empery, and both were summarily executed as a reward for their temerity. They were made an example to others, although these were by no means isolated cases.

It seems surprising that Verus, who had been commander of the fort at Raphaneae and who had been instrumental in forwarding the cause of Heliogabalus, should so quickly have risen up against him. The historians suggest that he was already disillusioned by the young

Emperor's lifestyle, but although many people had cause to fear for their lives, he was not one of them, and at that moment Heliogabalus had not betrayed those traits for which he would later be condemned. There are many possibilities: he may have feared that Heliogabalus and his retinue may resent being in debt to him; as someone who had succeeded in dethroning an Emperor he may have been seen as a future danger; he may have exploited the claim of Heliogabalus to aid in the mutiny against Macrinus; or he may have even then have nurtured dreams of taking over the Empire himself. He had demonstrated how possible that was and he may have seen himself in the mould of the soldier-emperors who, like Severus before him, had snatched the diadem through force of arms. Whatever the true reason, his rebellion was a rash act. If he had thought that the best time to strike was when the Emperor was weak, at the start of his reign, he was proven wrong – Maesa had ensured that, and with a speedy and hard resolve she had quickly bolted up all the doors against revolt. His ill-advised attempt to snatch power was easily and ruthlessly quashed.

At one point Heliogabalus summoned the governor of Cappadocia, Sulla, back to Rome, as he (or his advisors) had heard that Sulla had been interfering with matters outside his remit. Either fearing that he had incurred the wrath of the new Emperor, or as part of a preconceived plan, Sulla instead visited German troops on their way home from Bithynia. This may have been an innocent encounter, but it only served to deepen suspicions against him. Whether or not his fate had already been sealed, he was executed on suspicion of treason.

The rumbling uncertainty over the future of Rome sent its tremors to all corners of the Empire. For instance, there was discontent in the Alban Legion, where a commander by the name of Triccianus had ruled his soldiers with a rod of iron and so made himself unpopular with his troops. It was not difficult to engineer accusations in such perilous times, and after his reliability was called into question, he too was eliminated. As well as Triccianus, the grandson of a former city prefect, Seius Carus, was also held in suspicion, and his case is interesting as it is the only one in which we know that Heliogabalus took part in the proceedings. Carus was summoned to the palace, where the Emperor himself arraigned him on charges of treason. It is interesting, because it is the only accusation in which Heliogabalus was named as the accuser, and the conclusion is that it was uncommon, perhaps even unique. The inference is that the Emperor was rarely involved in these reprisals, and perhaps it was thought that the experience would be valuable to him. The boy had already sufficient experience as a regal leader, being a scion of high priests and having been trained as the great high priest and participated in many holy ceremonies and rite, but he had to get used to Roman administration. Heliogabalus simply repeated the accusations, and as a result Carius was sentenced to die, the execution taking place in the precincts of the Palace itself. It is probable that the idea to show Heliogabalus in the mould of frowning judge might have come from Maesa.

In those topsy-turvy days, some eminent citizens caused their own downfall. It was wise to keep a very low profile and play a patient hand, but some individuals made themselves conspicuous and foolishly put themselves in the full glare of Maesa's roaming searchlight. Valerianus Paetus was just such a person; rather inadvisedly he had images of himself plated with gold, and when he announced his intentions of returning to the unsettled area of Cappadocia, near to his allies and his place of birth, suspicions were soon aroused. He was swiftly arrested and questioned; the conclusion having been drawn that he was planning to use the gold pieces as part of a conspiracy to attack the regime. That was quite possibly true, and the excuse that he had the pieces made up as pretty ornaments for his mistress did not wash. Taking no chances, the imperial family had him condemned and killed.

Other death sentences were less convincing and reflected badly on the Emperor himself, particularly in hindsight. When he succeeded to the imperial throne, Heliogabalus had shown clemency to the senate and others, two such being Julius Asper and Castinus, writing of his decision to the senate and claiming that he had restored to liberty these men whom Macrinus had banished. However, in the wake of the reprisals, the same two men had become dangerous through their past association with Antoninus and the command they had procured over the armies. Now regarded as enemies to the state, they were condemned to die, the Emperor himself, as in all such cases, directing the sentences. It is, again, doubtful whether he was acting in his own initiative; more than likely, he was more or less a cipher acting on behalf of his aunt and grandmother, who might have reversed Heliogabalus's original decisions. These actions, which served to undermine Heliogabalus's authority, must have been galling to the new Emperor; but bowing to Maesa's experience in all things political he did not think it prudent to stand in her way. Asper and Castinus were accordingly recaptured, arraigned and subsequently executed.

It is easy to overstate the reprisals which took place in the early reign of Heliogabalus, and the historians go to some length to distort the truth and to exaggerate the extent of the killings, suggesting a brutal and ruthless extermination of all those who fell out of his favour. That there was bloodshed is undeniable, but counting the victims, relatively few names have passed into history – hardly the bloodbath depicted by Dio and the others. It might well have been the case that Heliogabalus might have been a steadying influence, although in these matters again he would have been influenced by the greater experience of Maesa and her confederates.

Dio once again in his work displayed his prejudice by his curious account of the deaths of Silius Messala and Pomponius Bassus. Their attempt at ousting the Emperor has already been dealt with, and their execution, after a bid to stir up the senate into revolt. After their deaths, Heliogabalus wrote to the senate, refusing to send proof of their plots because it was too late – they were dead already.

Dio's account does not ring true and although in the main he was an honest and conscientious historian, he had obviously written this much later and coloured the facts. To begin with, he states quite clearly that the men were 'condemned to death *by the senate*'. Dio does not even infer that they had been ordered to follow this course of action, but bluntly writes that the decision was the senate's alone; any pressure from above would certainly have been emphasised by him. Dio had, especially when writing his account, a great antipathy to his subject and would have not missed an opportunity to expose such corruption. Again, Messala had 'lain many facts bare before the senate', but he does not expand on what they may have been, only hinting that they may have been instrumental in turning the senate-house against the Emperor. If that had been the case, then clearly the subterfuge had failed; the senate did not take his side – on the contrary, they found him guilty and punished him accordingly. Furthermore, the politicians must have had good reason to condemn Messala, the flimsy complaints of Heliogabalus hardly amounting to a water-tight accusation. No, the senate had acted because they had been aware of the plots that had been hatched against the imperial throne.

There is also a hint of world-weariness about Heliogabalus' response to the senate, and a sense that things are going over his head. The senate, or perhaps the invisible forces manipulating him, had gone ahead with the execution, and now were asking Heliogabalus for proofs, as if they wished to cover their own backs. What was the point? What had it to do with him?

This discrepancy belies a fact that Dio did not wish to express, but which was inescapable – at this point, Heliogabalus had done little politically to arouse the enmity of his people. True, his reign would prove to be the most scandalous of any in the history of the Roman Empire, his name would top the list of such despicable rulers as Caligula, Nero and Tiberius – and there were already scandalous tales whispered about his private life, and of course there had been dark rumours about his birth and his claims to be Antoninus's son – but so far his reign hadn't been particularly extraordinary. The bypaths and plots by which he reached the imperial chair were still a question of dispute, but the young Emperor had shown mercy to his administration and had also shown a strong hand when dealing with opposition; and it was a firm arm that was needed to guide the beleaguered Empire into peace and stability.

The purges which had followed Heliogabalus' rise to power had been ruthless and, more important, successful, but not excessive. Enemies, real or potential, had been ferreted out and dealt with quickly, ruthlessly and effectively, by removal or, in extreme cases, death. Any root of civil strife had been dug out and eradicated with a thoroughness and aggression which admitted no argument, and for the rest of the boy's reign – a mere three years or so – there was, in the main, peace throughout the Empire. This achievement is too often missed or glossed over by historians determined to heap odium on the reign of one of Rome's most reviled rulers.

What part did Heliogabalus personally play in these purges? It is a case of heads he wins, tails he loses. If his part had been prominent, then the accusations of his terrible ruthlessness and cruelty would appear to be proven, and the argument that this would have been the action of a strong emperor discarded, as his reign proved the opposite. If, however, he was not instrumental in the executions, he would appear as weak and ineffective. One can easily understand a boy only in his mid-teens, having had a taste of regal power, wielding that power sadistically with all the relish of our proverbial boy in the candy shop. Give a child unlimited power and what he does with it would surely be attended by a childish relish; besides, the child was a high priest of a religion which had once actively supported human killing. But the sheer scale of the reprisals, and the careful planning of them, suggests a hand more subtle and cunning, a hand with political insight. The systematic elimination of all opposing influences was a carefully considered plan worked out with a ruthless logic which was surely beyond the boy who had been trained in religion and used as a puppet in the political machinations of his day, despite the fact that he had given up his *bulla* for his *toga virilis*. And more convincing than all of this is the examination of the executions which have been described above, none of which can be ascribed to the will of the Emperor alone. There can be little doubt that, just as he was hoisted up during the first rebellion to play the part of Antoninus' son, so he was set up as a puppet emperor in name only.

So far, the Bassiani had played their cards to perfection. All opposition broken down, there was every possibility of a peaceful and productive reign. The shadows of real scandal had not appeared as yet – though the clouds were gathering. For his own part, the intrigues of life at the nerve-centre of Rome meant little to Heliogabalus and his real interests lay elsewhere. While his family were mopping up after the insurrection, he concentrated on his role as the most powerful person in the world. The senate may have had some misgivings to begin with, but when the purges stopped they felt relatively safe; in fact, in the next four years their lives would be spent in quiet and peace. The bulk of the people, initially, looked to their new Emperor with hope and warmth.

So it was that, despite some misgivings, the entrance of the new incarnation of Nero was applauded by the country. The universal hope was that his inauguration would usher in a new phase of peace and prosperity. In his turn, Heliogabalus found his new capital much to his liking, having been brought up in the lap of luxury and extravagance. Everywhere he looked, he was met with splendour on such a scale as to have impressed every passing dignitary with wonder; ultra-modern palaces burnished with gold, vast temples without number, the Domus Aureus of Nero glistening in the sun, gold-inlayed and so sumptuous that even the cellars were decorated. The skyscraping Coliseum rose higher and higher within sight of the Forum, built on a lake which had been drained for the purpose. Beautiful baths of porphyry, ivory-inlaid ceilings, no expense spared to create a fantasy-world of rich delights. Gorgeous statues rose high in all directions, with painted faces and eyes which stared at the passer-by with a disturbingly life-like countenance. It is hardly any wonder that the new boy-emperor was enchanted by what he saw, and in his childish fancies, dreamed of building a Rome even more fabulous than had yet been created.

Heliogabalus went to work with all the enthusiasm and joyful eagerness of the child he was. He cannot fail to have been moved by the cheers of welcome he had received on his entry to Rome, nor the affection in their salutations. He wove fantastic plans to return their love with gifts of inordinate cost, and how to remain a great star in the eyes of the people. Genuinely affectionate, he had a love of people which was seemingly boundless, and a generosity which, had his reign been a successful one, would have made him one of the most admired of all the Roman Emperors. Sadly, that was not to be, but here at the beginning of his rule his main aim was to impress and to be admired by all.

Heliogabalus's visions of grandeur prompted him to exceed even Nero in greatness. He was stirred by the grandeur he saw about him and his imagination ran away with him as he considered how he could make his own mark on the city – a mark more grandiose than ever before. Almost immediately he made himself known by his reckless expenditure. Great shows had been given before, some of them legendary; now Heliogabalus planned to outdo them all. As with everything he did, he planned things on a phenomenal scale, and never before nor after would the world see such incredible splendour. It was a well-known tactic, to please the people – the Romans delighted in show and spectacle – but Heliogabalus had an ever-generous nature which was almost obsessive in its need to give and give in abundance. His shows are the stuff of myth.

The anticipation must have been tremendous when the posters advertised a spectacle of unsurpassable magnitude. After the long years of war, now that peace had been visited on Rome, the people were more than ready to be entertained. The Romans loved nothing better than a great spectacle, but this one promised to be the most spectacular of all. The new Emperor had proven that he was a crowd-pleaser, and on the day of the show the Forum must have been buzzing as crowds shuffled along the Via Sacra towards the Coliseum.

The audience arrived in droves and bustled to get their seats, some haggling with the ticket-touts or *locarii* stationed at the entrance. Eighty thousand or more, piled up on terraces climbing to a huge height. Saffron was given them to dust on their clothes, and they were protected from the strong sunlight by giant canopies – not of cloth, but of real silk. The crowds chattered in expectation, and the voices reached a climax as the performers readied themselves for the show. A blare of many trumpets sounded – and the new Emperor himself climbed up to greet his people, who responded with deafening cheers. Flowers, countless in number, fell from the skies, the waft of incense rose among the people. Flutes and other instruments played around the amphitheatre as the events of the show were about to begin.

And what events they were! No simple gladiator contests for him; the show was meticulously planned and co-ordinated to astound and amaze all who watched. There were exciting chariot races, yes, but not only drawn by horses, but by wild beasts – lions, stags, tigers, and even women, to add a touch of the exotic to a traditional delight. There were gladiator contests as well, but here the hunters were pitted against strange beasts. In one show alone, no less than fifty-one tigers were killed, a terrible waste of life to the modern eye but a roller-coaster of excitement to the spectators who cheered and yelled as the battle went on, sometimes pushing back a fleeing competitor into the fray if he tried to escape. Up to one hundred lions would prowl into the arena, and the deafening thud of a horde of rampaging elephants vied with rapturous cheering.

On a lake of pure wine, ships floated and famous battle scenes were re-enacted, each side cheered on or booed by the enthusiastic crowds. With the rest, Heliogabalus would roar and shout out as ships were attacked, sunk or stoutly defended. Excitement was intense.

An interlude. Music again filled the air as the acrobats danced and performed feats of wonder, flying high into the air, somersaulting and forming human pyramids. Tame lions wandered around the arena, neatly groomed and decorated; horsemen rode around on zebras chasing ostriches. The historians sometimes over-exaggerate in their descriptions, and one can hardly credit a tightrope-walking lion or another playing the cymbals or writing Greek obscenities; but such accounts merely prove the sheer scale of the spectacle.

The players left the arena, and the animals were led down to the subterranean quarters. More trumpets. The star attraction – as with every Roman spectacle – was the entrance of the gladiators. Nothing aroused the excitement of the ancient Romans more than a gladiatorial contest, and they had lost none of their appeal after almost half a millennium. No-one is really certain where the contests originated; Nicolaus of Damascus suggests an Etruscan origin, others suggest they came from Campania and Lucania, where they started life as funeral games. In the late second century BCE, the games had passed on from a funerary ritual to public performances.

Outside the amphitheatre, a notice was fixed by the entrance, listing the names of the gladiators who were to perform for the show. The Romans were very knowledgeable at the sport, and would soon see the names of their champions and the household names who were facing death or glory. Bookmakers would size up the odds and take bets from the punters who were all too ready to place their money on their favourites. The attitude of the public to the fighters was mixed; in one way they were looked down upon, as many had begun life from lowly origins, often as slaves; but some had won great renown and were seen as sporting heroes. Girls especially loved the sport, and would look admiringly at the pin-up physiques displayed to them with adoration and lust – the Thracian gladiator Celadus had quite a fan-base at Pompeii, where he was described as 'the sigh and glory of the girls'. Souvenir bowls depicting gladiators were often snapped up by fans.

When the fighters entered the arena they did not face the Emperor and, while saluting, cry out: 'We who are about to die salute you.' At least, not as a custom; this was only ever noted once, in the time of Claudius, and those crying '*morituri te salutant*' ('those about to die salute you') were ready to participate in a mock sea-fight. Gladiators would usually fight in pairs unless requested otherwise, and the object of the exercise was to defeat and not to kill. In fact, life expectancy was around thirty years, which sounds poor until compared with the average life expectancy of a Roman citizen, which was twenty-five. Sometimes, the crowds would will a gladiator's death; in that case, the victor would cut his throat or plunge his sword through his neck. In the case of a mortal injury, the fighter would be carried out and humanely killed – by means of a mallet blow to the head.

The fighting would be under certain rules, now lost, and watched over by a qualified referee. As the fight became more violent, the crowds would become more vociferous. It was well for the gladiator to put on a great show; if he impressed the audience enough, he could even earn his freedom, and it was usual to gain this anyway after five wins. The crowd would cheer a particularly deft tactic and shout on a courageous rival. As a fighter wavered, there would be cries of '*Habet! Hoc habet!*' ('He's done for! This one's done for!') until a result was forthcoming; a competitor could surrender at any time by holding up a finger, but that could be dangerous as it might incite the spectators to call for his death. The winner was always paid, by coin or by a valuable present; and often there would be a whip-round in the crowds, any offerings being placed on a silver tray.

After the contest, the result would often be marked on the playbill outside the entrance; v for *vicit* (won), p for *periit* (died) and m for *missus* (lost).

Even the most elaborate of games have to come to an end, and so it was with those of Heliogabalus. But he had one more treat in store for them. Flutes and a myriad instruments played to delight and enthral the crowds, and then the Emperor himself, with his Syrian contingent, took to the arena and dance a native round for their amusement. Heliogabalus always needed to appear centre stage, to be admired and adored, to entertain – and he had no intention of missing out on an opportunity to appear at such lavish spectacles, despite the fact that dancers and theatricals were seen as of dubious sexuality. Still, bemused as they might be by such an unfamiliar sight – and at being entertained by their ruler – the audience erupted into ecstatic applause which eventually died away to mark the end of the proceedings.

Heliogabalus loved the games. He was no rugged gladiator, although some Emperors before him – notably Commodus – had stepped into the arena to take their chances (not that any gladiator would dare kill their emperor). However, he loved chariot-racing, and would often spend leisure time following this pursuit in the vicinity of and inside the Palace, or the Garden of Hope, being pulled by a variety of animals from dogs, lions, even naked women (although this last item was probably a piece of lurid titillation, coming as it does from the pen of Lampridius). While riding the chariot he showed great nerve, and careered recklessly round the makeshift arena with an abandon that scared his spectators. Then, like a naughty child, he would insist that his guests would do the same, and as none dare refuse they were forced to put themselves at some risk, especially if they were unfit or aged.

Careering around the gardens at full speed while controlling wild animals is no game for the faint-hearted. It calls for a certain amount of fearlessness, and at various stages in his life Heliogabalus proved that he did have a certain amount of courage in him, which exhibited itself when dealing with his grandmother and, at times, even the soldiery. There were also times when he would assert his individuality even at times of great personal risk. This side of his personality is rarely appreciated by his few biographers.

The Emperor was not a vindictive or malicious person, but he did have a fondness for practical jokes, and often the victims of these jokes would be hard pressed to see the funny side. He was little more than a child, and childish pranks amused him, although many caught up in his youthful play did not appreciate them. It was analogues to a child setting up a tripwire and giggling as his victim falls over it – no more malicious than that. But the sweating nervous senator careering around the Palace in a chariot drawn by wild animals, while being the butt of universal laughter, probably wished himself elsewhere.

Many important guests were invited to the palace, but sometimes they would wish they had not come. If a guest felt sleepy after drinking too much wine, he would be taken up to a guest room in which to spend the night. When he awoke, he would stare goggle-eyed at the sight before him – a tiger wandering around by his side! The poor terrified victim would not be aware that the creature was tame, and his terror would be unbounded, to the glee of the young prankster. It is said that he had another favourite pastime – of giving his guest a gift of a most beautiful maiden for the night, but when he found himself locked in his room he would be confronted with an aging crone. It was even said that he would enjoy having his guest tied to a waterwheel for his pleasure, but this does not seem in character and was most likely a fabrication made by those who later hated him.

But no matter what indignities his guests suffered for their host's sense of humour, none were ever harmed, and all came away well rewarded. Heliogabalus was the epitome of generosity, and they would all leave laden with expensive gifts, even the golden bowls from which they had eaten. He also had a habit of having them draw lots, and the prizes would range, we are told, from enormous riches to the body of a dead dog, another example of the boy's sense of the comical. What's more, this was no Caligula or Tiberius, and no-one feared for their lives when in his company; more probably, they had an extremely entertaining evening, so long as they had not fallen foul of his jokes or at least had the good sense to take it all in fun.

These activities, which seemed so odd to the Romans of the day, may be seen as a regressive attempt to play. During his hectic childhood, he had very little time to indulge in play with other kids; he had had much to learn and do and his sacerdotal duties kept him busy. From a modern perspective, this lack of a normal childhood is potentially very damaging to the development of the personality, especially in the form of group communication skills. Such interactions were not allowed to grow and mature, so Heliogabalus did not properly understand the concepts of sharing and deference – in fact, his position in society would have strengthened a feeling of egotism. According to the American Academy of Paediatrics, 'as they master their world, play helps children develop new competencies that lead to enhanced confidence and the resiliency they will need to face future challenges.' Lack of play can lead to emotional distress and depression. In his leisure time, Heliogabalus would often look for play in the world around him, and sometimes he displayed a characteristically infantile insensibility to the discomfiture of others; but his play never displayed evidence of sadism. What's more, he seemed to need play. Something he cherished but had been deprived of.

The habit of having his guests draw lots soon expanded to cover all of Rome. He became the founder of a lottery, following the example of Nero before him; tickets were free, and again the prizes varied from a lump of meat to a hundred pieces of gold, from ships to estates, from food to a small fortune; all provided by the Emperor himself. It is hardly any wonder that, at least to begin with, the people were enamoured of their new ruler. He was also enamoured with them, although especially so with the young beautiful people of the day, to whom he was in the habit of showering gifts. He gave the pimps and whores of a district a year's supply of corn for pleasing him; and he once gave circus actors and theatrical performers three pieces of gold, whispering: 'Don't tell anyone Antoninus gave you this…'

Heliogabalus's proverbial extravagance may have bought him a certain number of friends, and, for the time being, the love of the people, but it also made his some enemies. The gigantic sums he frittered away wantonly must have had the senate reeling, yet their seemed no way to curb this spendthrift boy, whose pleasure consisted of literally throwing away gold at an alarming rate. Having no head for economics, he simply lived life on a whim, and his whims were outrageously expensive ones. A detailed summary of Heliogabalus's spending would have given his treasurer cardiac failure, and soon the money would dry up unless something could be done. For the moment, there seemed to be no easy solution – so Heliogabalus simply went about his everyday life as he had already done before.

There is no doubt at all that power had gone straight to his head. Who could be surprised? Give a young boy unlimited greatness and who would not pander to his own will, the boy in the candy shop, wide-eyed and with every good thing within his grasp. Nero had outdone all the emperors before him in extravagance, demanding a retinue of 500 carriages – so what was Heliogabalus to do? Out-Nero Nero, of course – and that meant a convoy of no less than 600, attending on him, his followers and his favourite flatterers and the beautiful people. An astrologer predicted a violent death for him – so he built a huge tower overlooking a bed of gold on which he could fling himself if the time so called for it. Everything had to be on a grand scale, grander than anything that had come before. Part of the gift to his people was to see the lavish spectacle of their Emperor travelling as none had done before, a breathtaking sight of rich chariots and finely-plumed horses. It was a banquet for the eye.

But the gods sent messages through their favoured ones, and even if Heliogabalus never fully accepted the Roman pantheon he still took their omens seriously. To be forewarned of a bloody death was no trivial thing, and the Emperor took certain precautions to ensure that he could avert any likely threat; he took to carrying poison with him, and a cord so that he could strangle himself as a final expedient. Even in this did he show his extravagance; the poison was kept in a precious bottle kept in a jewel-encrusted purse, and the cord was of the finest silk. He was determined that he himself should be the only one to terminate his life, and in a way becoming his station.

The boy had riches in plenty, and like a child found a great deal of satisfaction in flaunting the fact to the world. Not only did he do so in the – perhaps understandable – way in which he furnished his table of his Palace, but also in ways less reputable, if the old stories can be believed at face value and not simply as an exaggeration to caricature them. It is said he had a huge mound - a mountain – of snow built in his gardens, to cool the warm air. While that lies within the realms of possibility, it is harder to imagine that he would collect cobwebs by the ton, just to prove he had the power to do so, or that he had fully-laden ships sunk in the harbours, just so that he could compensate the owners and demonstrate his enormous wealth. These acts may or may not be factual, but even if they are fabrications, it is certain that the Emperor had gained a reputation for wastage which crossed the boundaries of the abuse of power.

Heliogabalus has been, and is, widely regarded as a megalomaniac, a word coming from the Greek meaning an obsession with greatness. It is not an easy matter to come to any true conclusion, as it can with justification be said that all the Emperors of ancient Rome were, to some extent, megalomaniacs. Most of them, at any rate, revelled in their power and had a great appetite for self-glorification. Julius Caesar conquered wherever he went, and surely his *'veni vidi vici'* smacks of self-aggrandisement. Caligula was so pleased with his own prowess that he had himself deified while a young Emperor, and Augustus wrote a list of his great achievements to be a lasting monument to his glory. But surely the difference between, say Julius and Caligula, lies in their true inherent worth? In other words, are they truly great or do they merely think they are great? The term 'megalomania' suggests either an abuse of power by someone who is granted it, or a delusion of power in those who are undeserving. It remains to be seen whether Heliogabalus fits into either of these categories.

To begin with, there is every suggestion that as a child Heliogabalus had all the conditions for its development. Virtually from the moment he could speak he was made aware that he was not like other children and beyond his normal education he was different from they – that he had been chosen as a great leader of men, someone who could communicate with his god and would inherit the ultimate position as high priest among his contemporaries. What made matters worse was the fact that when in his homeland, as a boy of regal status, he had become used to a life of extravagance. Although it may be something of an exaggeration, we are told that whenever he walked abroad he was followed by an impressive entourage of no less than sixty chariots, and that even Maesa herself shuddered at the scale of such ostentation. He was born to this way of life and accepted it as being his inheritance, right and proper. He had no delusions of grandeur; he was in every way grand, and as regal as his status reflected. There would be no-one to explain the benefits of the simple things of life, of charity or austerity, because such sentiments were both unnecessary and useless. The people adored him as their representative of god, and loved him in much the same way that the Tibetans loved their Dalai Lama in his gorgeous palace in Lhasa.

It is hardly to be expected that a boy in such a situation would not get a taste for luxury, although no-one seems to have realised that much of his way of life was set down in his religious office, that shows of might and prowess were expected. The child Varius was performing his duties as set down by tradition. But he would have been an extraordinary child indeed if he had not become accustomed to his aristocratic way of life. He knew nothing else. The new life in Rome was simply an extension of the life he had lead in Emesa, but now on an even more lavish and grandiose scale; he had slipped into it so easily that it was hard to see the joins. Just as the good people of Emesa had expected the glare and glitter of spectacle on a huge scale, so the circus of this spectacle was carried straight to Rome, with the blare of trumpets going before. And although Heliogabalus excelled himself in everything he did, there was one area of life in which he became most celebrated – that of food.

Food was of course important to the Romans, and they were fortunate in that they lived in a fertile country surrounded by the sea. Wheat was the staple cereal, and it was used to make porridge and to bake bread. These, with the addition of meat and vegetables when available, were the usual diet of the poorer citizens. Even the more wealthy usually only ate one main meal a day, which had shifted from midday to suppertime. This was most often split into three courses, a starter, a main course and a dessert. The starter was usually a fish dish, the main course meat and vegetables, and the dessert would be fruit or pastries sweetened with honey, of which the more well-to-do were inordinately fond. But the food prepared for Heliogabalus belonged to another world.

We can rely upon Lampridius to besmirch the Emperor even in his description of his feasts. 'At his banquets he preferred to have perverts placed next to him and took special delight in touching or fondling them, and whenever he drank one of them was usually selected to hand him the cup.' While safely ignoring such fantasies, it must be said that the banquets given by the Emperor were lavish affairs; even the furniture glistened with silver and gold and was supplied with ornate cushions for his guests (his own were stuffed with hare fur or partridge down). No hint of the plebeian classes here; the dishes and cutlery were of solid silver – even the saucepans. There were vases of great beauty, etched with various indecent scenes, weighing, according to Hay, over 45 kilograms each. Such pomp and luxury seems absurd and indecent, but the Emperor was the Emperor and had to put on a show; besides, it would be alien to Heliogabalus's sense of decorum and generosity to stint at meal-times.

Fitting with Heliogabalus's love of extravagance and ceremony, the courses of food surpassed the superfluity of even the most gluttonous of Emperors before him. Lampridius may have been exaggerating, as was his wont, but his suggestion that they entailed up to twenty-odd courses and cost between 100,000 and 300,000 sesterces is not impossible. The wealthy Romans, of course, loved their food to an almost abnormal extent, and vomiting between courses was said to be the social norm; such a tendency was not lost on the Emperor. Courtesans and entertainment were provided as a matter of course; Heliogabalus would have been a poor host had he neglected those. To make meals a more sociable affair, Heliogabalus instigated a tradition that each course would be enjoyed at the houses of each guest, which meant much travelling between districts. This would be unthinkable without customary shows of excess, so after every plateful the carriages and gold-laden chariots would be seen in formation wandering about the streets of Rome.

The food served at these feasts was not merely a matter of taste, it was an art form. Hay describes some of the dainties which may be expected at these gastronomic festivals: 'sows' breasts with Lybian truffles; dormice baked in poppies and honey; peacocks' tongues flavoured with cinnamon; oysters stewed in *garum* - a sort of anchovy sauce made of the intestines of fish - flamingos' and ostriches' brains, followed by the brains of thrushes, parroquets, pheasants, and peacocks, also a yellow pig cooked after the Trojan fashion, from which, when carved, hot sausages fell and live thrushes flew; sea-wolves from the Baltic, sturgeons from Rhodes, fig-peckers from Samos, African snails and the rest. He would also serve 'grains of gold with his peas, rubies with lentils, beans and amber, for the mere pleasure of sight; though his salads of mullets' fins with cress, balm mint, and fenugreek'. Food fit for the gods, and washed down with the finest wines available, the delicate Greek vintages being fashionable at the time; although following youthful fashion Heliogabalus often adulterated them by the addition of crushed pine or fir cones. Trust the *Historia Augusta* to stain this pleasant scene; we are asked to believe that the Emperor mixed wine with the water of the baths and invited guests to drink it. In another off passage he insists that during the summer Heliogabalus would hold 'theme parties', in which the food was all of one colour, of from the same beast. He even mentions pork, an obvious lie as the boy never ate it on religious grounds.

He did, however, have a penchant for fish and for fishing which probably went back to his early years in Velletri; he was also something of a conservationist, building gigantic salt-water tanks in the countryside and filling them with sea fish. It became a hobby for him. He even developed a method of mass fishing, using oxen for haulage. He loved eating the fish, of course, and even invented sausages made from varying types of seafood, and his sauce became the toast of the city. He formed the conceit that the sauce should resemble the sea water in which the fish lay, with the appearance not of being cooked, but swimming calmly in the water; it was of a transparent turquoise colour. So interested was the Emperor in the culinary arts that his dishes became proverbial in their excellence, and cooks of the city would try to emulate his inventions in their own confections, food made fit for the Emperor – a good slogan for sales.

Nothing was forgotten which might add a touch of added splendour to these banquets. Even the menus were astonishing, embroidered as they were on the tablecloth and accompanied by pictures representing the dishes on offer. Heliogabalus was always eager and happy to please, and his magnificent feasts were not only reserved for the aristocracy as he would also treat politicians and, in fact, any guests with fine dining. With a lack of finesse which suggests his childishness, he would often play a game with his guests and ask them to guess at the cost of the dishes, amusing himself by seeing their looks of astonishment when they were told of the staggering sums he had lavished on them. This may well have impressed the visiting dignitaries, but hardly the most die-hard senators, who would have seen such reckless expenditure as frittering away the national treasury – which of course it was. Not for him the coldness and simplicity of the meals customarily held in the past; dining was an art to Heliogabalus and he perfected that art with the touch of a connoisseur, as well as that of a wastrel.

It would hardly do to throw such exquisite feasts and pay no heed to ambience. Everywhere, flowers were strewn – a particular fondness of the Emperor – and the cushions of the especially important guests would be sprinkled with saffron and gold dust. The banquets were the stuff of fairy-tales, as rich and elaborate as legend or fantasy could make them. They were the talk of the town.

Even in matters of urination - piss-pots were provided made from precious metals.

The boy Emperor was not mean-minded and loved giving as well as receiving. His generosity was not limited to his guests, but he is reported to have opened his windows and distributed these gourmet delights to the man in the street as well. Such a charitable disposition does not fit well with the malicious portrait of him which has passed down to posterity. Although hardly a matter for praise, he was even generous with his animals, feeding them on expensive titbits which although well-meant, hardly comprised a suitable diet for these beasts. Like the Shakespearean character who, in kindness to his horse, buttered his hay. His dogs were fed on foie-gras, his horses on grapes, his lions on rare fowls. He simply did not see why someone poorer than himself should be relegated to eating mean food when he had plenty of his own to share; there was nothing niggardly in his nature, although even his open-handedness would lead to complaint and censure.

Another of Heliogabalus's great loves was music and he himself was an accomplished player, often delighting guests with his repertoire on the *hydraulis*, an organ worked by hydraulic pressure, or the *pandore*, a stringed instrument originally attributed to Pan and was in effect a three-stringed lute. Doubtlessly Heliogabalus loved music *per se*, but he may have been copying the musical inclinations of Nero as a role model. He also copied Nero in his concept of 'divine right'.

The idea of 'divine right' was in stark contrast to the ways and traditions of the Romans. True, they worshipped their Emperors, but usually after their deification; there was widespread fury when the Emperor Domitian insisted on being addressed as a god. Although they fawned and flattered the most feared of rulers, the Roman people held fast to the old ideas of morality and austerity. Of especial merit were those Emperors who had been modest and even austere in their habits, the most beloved being Augustus Caesar and Marcus Aurelius. Julius Caesar gained the respect and adoration of his troops by fighting alongside them and often living like a common soldier; the 'common touch' was greatly admired and thought to be a great quality among men of power. They may have accepted their new Emperor, and the people always loved great spectacle, but the arrogance and conceit of Heliogabalus would not have sat well with his governing senate. From his point of view, Heliogabalus would not have understood; he simply transported his position in Emesa to Rome.

The major mistake he made throughout his short life was not to acknowledge the good advice of his family, particularly Maesa, who knew well how to retain the respect of the senate and the people of Rome. Tired of being led by their apron-strings, Heliogabalus felt that, in his mid teens, he was old enough to act on his own initiative, an opinion shared by most pubescent children. He wanted to become a model emperor but used his own judgement as a yardstick, a youthful judgement which often failed in the cold reality of the political arena he lived in. Like Caligula, he felt that his own position of power was unassailable.

The logical, almost adult side of Heliogabalus was probably right. Despite the historians' insults, he was an intelligent and eager to learn. He knew quite well that he needed Maesa'a advisors, and to a large extent Maesa herself, to keep him afloat on the alien sea of politics which surrounded him on all shores. But he was aware that while he needed able people to act on his behalf, to surrender complete power would mean that he would become little more than a puppet in the hands of his family and subservience was something he was not prepared to stomach. He might have known little about the power game, but he did know how to act like a sovereign and needed little encouragement to do so. In his personal life and in the centre stage which was the Empire he intended he would shine and dazzle just as he had done in Emesa.

The little boy inside Heliogabalus exulted in his new position as the leader of the entire civilised world. A new chapter in his fairy-tale existence had unfolded and the throne of the earth was his to enjoy. The prince was now the king. Apart from acting the part, which was play to the little boy, he needed playmates with whom to act out his games in the schoolyard of Rome. These new acquaintances were fitting to a youngster who was looking for fun in his new milieu, and were chosen for his own amusement.

Heliogabalus was too young to have learned of the ways of the world; he knew nothing of people, let alone high politics. Naturally friendly, he accepted all friendships at face value, making him easy prey for flatterers and fortune hunters. As a child, he loved to be amused, and took a great liking to all those who could entertain him; and so a good part of his entourage consisted of actors and theatricals, what the senate would have thought of as ne'er-do-wells. The status of a man never bothered Heliogabalus at all, and he found more enjoyment in the company of comedians and acrobats than he did with the grave greybeards of the senate house. Completely innocent, the Emperor made his Palace a haunt of sycophants from all over town, many of whom were only too ready and willing to take advantage of their imperial friend's renowned generosity. Fortunes were wasted on scroungers, but Heliogabalus thought little about the money he was squandering and continued to shower his favour on those who were quick to take advantage of him. Haplessly, the boy renounced his well-meaning advisors and put in his lot with apes of idleness. All remonstrance and pleading from his family went to no avail.

    He had not learned that it was imperative to surround himself with those well-versed in public office and government, nor that to associate with vagabonds and plebeians would undermine his position as father of his nation. How could he? He was only fourteen, and in his position of seeming omnipotence, he felt that he was a free agent. It would never have occurred to him that the Emperor is never his own man, and that he was at the top of a slope down which he would eventually slide to his own destruction.

    The honeymoon was over. While the people may still have toasted the health of their open-handed and regal emperor, those in power were starting to grumble. The rumblings from the *curia* reverberated down to Maesa, whose spies kept her well informed. Preferments were being given to worthless creatures whose only virtue was that of flattery. The treasury was being emptied by a mad whirlwind of spending which beggared belief. While the soldiers received their pay – and bonuses – Heliogabalus was safe, but what would happen if the treasury ran out? While no-one dared to take him to task directly, even when his friends asked him whether he realised where his way of life would end up, finally, in necessity, he simply replied: 'What could be better for me than to be my own heir?'

Dissatisfaction started to be whispered around the senate, as well as among those who had reckoned themselves worthy of promotion only to find the eminent posts given to sycophants in the emperor's train. It was a breeding-ground for unrest and, worse of all, conspiracy. There was only so much his aunt and grandmother could do to stem the rising tide.

Clouds began to hover over Heliogabalus.

Chapter 6: Blood Mingled With Wine

To put the disastrous rule of Heliogabalus into a true perspective it is worthwhile to examine how he was viewed by the people and senate of his adopted country. Even during his honeymoon in Rome he was eyed with much suspicion by the ruling bodies. So far, his actions had caused a few raised eyebrows but little else; the bloodletting at his inauguration would hardly have been unexpected, and although he had broken protocol on a number of occasions, this could easily be overlooked in the case of a just and admired ruler. It was the fate of Heliogabalus that he would be remembered as neither of these. The matter of religion was the first of many which would cause him to be an Emperor beleaguered by scandal and tainted with moral decrepitude.

This matter was only one star in a constellation of events which were changing the face and values of ancient Rome. The argument that the search for individual enlightenment – or salvation – in the Eastern religions caused the rot which led to the Empire's decline is surely an overstatement. It may be true in part; but in that case it proves necessary to determine where the disillusionment came from, and of the many possibilities the strongest must be a growing resentment of government. Whether rightly or wrongly, national pride is reflected in the monarch, and a wave of popular satisfaction rises and falls with the strength of the ruler. In times past, the Caesar dynasty – from Julius to Nero – led the way with such indisputable strength that the Romans were content to bask in their rays, looking on their leader as an infallible pedagogue. Sheep need a careful shepherd, and it is no surprise that, from the time of Julius, the Emperors were regularly deified after their deaths and that the people looked to the time of old Caesars with nostalgic admiration. Modern times had become immoral and sinful; they always were, but the sanctity of the ultimate office was an anchor to which the common people could attach themselves and feel secure. Now that office was usurped, not by gods, but by insolent warrior-kings, who lacked the sheen of aristocracy and majesty. A servant craves a just and deserving master, but now the people saw men of their own rank climb to power through subterfuge and greed. Their beloved Empire was bought and sold to anyone who had the nous and cunning to grasp it.

Daily life had begun to lose its stability. Wolves roamed unmolested among the sheep, who had become easy prey. Rome had become both a market-place and a battlefield, a rudderless ship floating in whichever direction the prevailing wind blew. At present, the Syrian wind was directing her, and the Severan Dynasty was proving a poor safeguard for its people. The decline of the Empire surely began, not with Heliogabalus, but with the death of Pertinax, when the cream of the Roman world was fought over with such ferocity by Clodius, Pescennius and Severus; it was clear even then that the Romans were a people to be won by the might of arms. The dignity of the office decayed, and even the honoured concept of inheritance was beginning to fade in the knowledge that the imperial diadem could be snatched with a sword of sufficient might. It also meant that to ascend the seat of power was to invite insurrection and conspiracy. From Severus to the later Diocletian, the average term of office was three years, and very few of those Emperors escaped betrayal or assassination.

From the first moment Heliogabalus wore the imperial purple he came in direct conflict with the Roman senate. As Rome prided itself on its union between the ruling body and its people – the senate and people of Rome (SPQR) – it followed that, at least in the minds of the senators, he was also in conflict with the populace. This conflict led to an intense dislike aimed towards the new Emperor, and this would grow insidiously into a detestation which eventually led the senate to turn their backs completely on their ruler. At the start of his reign, three things joined together to form the basis of the stronger antipathy which was to follow. The first of these was the matter of race.

This particular dislike had been brewing for centuries and had its roots in what the senate saw as a gradual deterioration in the pride of being a Roman as well as the sickliness which dogged the Empire's fortunes. Back in the old days, in the time of Julius Caesar's youth, there was widespread horror when the dictator Sulla marched against Rome itself; this had now become a commonplace event. Then, too, there had been a jingoistic pride in being a citizen of Rome, and it had taken much effort for the Italians in the provinces to be accepted as such; now the unique pride of calling oneself a 'Roman' was nullified by the sense that anyone living within Roman territories could inherit that honour. People longed for the good old days when Rome was the awe of the world, when the world looked upon them and their Emperor with reverence. The reign of Heliogabalus was yet another spear-thrust in the side of a nation which was becoming embittered to the point of numbness; apathy and growing resentment were the order of the day.

It follows that Heliogabalus had more to fight against than simply the concept of his Emesan religion. There is no doubt that the outcry against his religious activities was deepened by xenophobia – that it chimed with his *foreignness*. It was important for the citizens of Rome to hold fast to their identity. This nationalism, this *amor patriae*, had grown in proportion to the expansion of the Empire. To die for one's native land was a great honour, and to serve one's country was the summit of every politician's ambition. The greatest virtue was to fight for Rome, and the greatest celebrations and triumphs were accorded to those heroes who had achieved greatness on its behalf, none more than the commanders who had led their troops to victory. The unmatchable might of the Roman soldiery was expected to succeed against any odds, and defeat was a matter of great shame and public outcry.

The pride of the Romans is not difficult to understand, and their attitudes are reflected in all of the great Empires which came before and after them. Conquest brings with it an air of superiority and a strong patriotism stirred up by a feeling of omnipotence. Rome had conquered all the civilised world and had emerged triumphant. The provinces, from Phoenicia to Morocco, all paid tribute to their overlords. As masters of the world, the politicians of the senate held the power to use or abuse it. From the mighty vantage point of superiority grew precepts of ethics and morality – as well as a strong sense of virtue. The Romans set themselves up as examples to the world.

The sheer size of the Roman Empire made Rome a wealthy city, as tributes from every province poured in. As in the case of all Empires, these riches enabled the civilisation to nurture other things apart from warfare and the upkeep of the huge armies needed to control the lands and keep order. It was a time for patronising the arts, and nowhere was this more evident than in Rome itself, which was festooned with sculptures and artworks. Architecture reached new heights of sophistication and the Romans were proud of their new modern temples, their lines of palaces, their amphitheatres as well as the gigantic Coliseum. Rome was the model of modernity, was its baths, its aqueducts, its underfloor heating and its sewage system. In the great houses, luxury was the order of the day, and rich families employed top-name architects and artists to embellish their homes to add to their prestige. It is hardly surprising that they looked upon the tribes of the provinces as peasants and savages.

Like the British in their days of colonialism, the Romans ruled their Empire with an iron fist. Reprisals and rebellions were dealt with summarily and violently. Examples were made of notable rebels to act as a deterrent against further troublemaking. The Romans, too, had a distrust of 'damn foreigners', as exemplified in the works of all their leading historians. Tacitus said of the Jews that 'all their other customs, which are both perverted and disgusting, owe their strength to their very baseness.' Julius Caesar wrote of the men of a Gallic tribe as being 'stimulated by avarice, others by revenge and credulity, which is an innate propensity in that race of men.' The list could go on and on.

Far from the elegance and sophistication of Rome, the dominions were seen as barbaric and uncouth; their habits and customs as strange, and their sense of morals as suspect. Syria was not exempt.

Although there was a great deal of nationalism evident in ancient Rome, this was not to say that anyone born outside the Italian boundaries could not make good – provided they adopted Roman ways, and learned to speak Latin and Greek (Greek was often used for orations). Neither Trajan nor Hadrian were Italian, and the Emperor Claudius made attempts to allow Gauls into Rome. It would be a mistake to play a racist card against the Romans; it would be both wrong and anachronistic - the Romans of this period would be bewildered by such accusations. The Romans were a noble race, according to their lights. Moreover, they accepted foreign nationals into their country – even their political arena, if – and it is a big 'if' – they conformed to their society.

Even Varius's adopted name – Heliogabalus – would have raised some eyebrows. It sounded peculiar and alien to Roman ears, smacking as it did of oriental mysticism. It would have sat easier with the Italians had he chosen a more traditional name; even simply the Emperor Varius. The foregoing Severan Emperors had been called Severus, Antonius and Geta, all names which could be easily accepted by Rome; but 'Heliogabalus', even when Romanised to 'Elagabalus', still sounded awkward to the Romans. Worse, it was the name of a god, and the assumption of a divine name, even a foreign one, drew uncomfortable parallels with Caligula and suggested a monarch who at least hinted at comparisons with a deity.

So the matter of Heliogabalus's race was an obvious goad to the senate, but it was a prejudice which could be suffered providing the boy emperor proved himself worthy of his position as the head of the state. But the fact that he was merely a boy led to the second prejudice, that of his modern and youthful outlook. For his part, Heliogabalus could see little congenial to him in that anachronistic gathering which met regularly in the senate to thrash out old rules and discuss the new regime. To a young man of tender years who basked in his glory, in the fashionable quarters of town among the flash blades and jet-setters of the city, the old greybeards would seem old-fashioned and of another time, men whose rationale dated back from the days of the old Caesars and beyond. The generation gap alienated him from their severe and dated prejudices against his appearance and his views. Although he would take into account their rulings and their debates, he had little in common with a group whose *raison d'être* was to keep the Empire in the bondage of the old order. Heliogabalus, the new broom, would see the senate, replete in its austere gravity, as a barrier to his reforms, and this intransigence led to the driving of a wedge between them.

The relationship between the senators and their Emperor was never likely to be anything less than rocky. For his part, Heliogabalus was a thoroughly modern young man who wanted to sweep away the cobwebs from the tired and sleepy government of the day. He had brought with him bold new ideas for change, and saw with some acumen the rottenness in the state of Rome. This was, after all, the modern third century, and times were changing. Moral censorship and Catonian moralism were outmoded and it was time for a revaluation of ideals. It was as if the *curia* were wrapped in a time-bubble which had somehow evaded the march of centuries and was still looking back wistfully at the fine precepts of Republican government. The old timers and greybeards of the senate did not want change; the *curia*, tucked away in a corner of the Forum resounded with the dreary old voices of long-forgotten days, of moulding morality and dying values. The Emperor saw the inevitable twilight of the old order and was ready and willing to push his Empire into the new age with all the impetuosity of youth. It was understandable that the elderly would hardly approve of the sycophantic men-about-town who copied Heliogabalus's fashions and saw him as a trend-setter. Part of the problem was their unwillingness to sacrifice the old edicts buried in library dust for a new and exciting agenda of reform.

Heliogabalus wanted no less than to bring the Empire into the new age; a revisionist and a modernist, he was prepared to stand face to face with the greybeards and fight his corner. This had been done before, of course; and the senate still had its annals reminding them of the crazy course of events following the reigns of other young Emperors such as Nero and Caligula, who also acted on their own whims. It might have been that these two acted in a disgraceful manner, but certainly their biographies were coloured by the prejudice of the annalists Suetonius and Tacitus, both holders of respectable positions within the senate. It was a fact that new young brooms were eyed with some suspicion by the diehards of government.

But the problems really began for Heliogabalus because of his non-conformist attitude. Varius had a penchant for garments made of the materials of his homeland, and he looked regal in his robes which were reminiscent of his high priest's garb and smacked of Phoenician fashion; but not everyone appreciated his dress. A Roman should be a Roman, and wear the time-honoured toga as a sign of pride in the fatherland and a symbol of masculinity. It would not be long before this antipathy to his sense of fashion would develop into a stronger dislike; but for now, they accepted it, and Heliogabalus himself argued that he hated Roman and Greek clothes because they were made of wool. This coarse material was an irritant to his sensitive skin, and although this reaction was not a true allergy it made the wearing of wool uncomfortable for him. Besides, the boy had gloried in splendour since his earliest days, and it was hateful for him to wear the garments of an ordinary citizen. His life had been a procession of pomp and magnificence, and he would not give that up even for the power of the Roman Empire.

That the Emperor was particular about his dress is apparent from all sources. The Romans were a somewhat austere people, conservative in their outlook, and they prized wool as their native material; but not only did Heliogabalus scorn wool, he refused to wear any clothes (or jewels) that he had worn once before. He had a passion for dress design, and determined to have his outfits made such that they would be the wonder of Rome, including a robe wrought from fine gold resplendent with jewels, sleeves flowing down to his legs, which were encased in thigh-high leather boots. On his hands and around his neck were priceless ear-rings, bracelets and necklaces, while on his head he wore the coronet designed by Caracalla, of solid gold encrusted with gems – he was famous for his ornate shoe-buckles, too. The people deserved to see their Emperor in his full splendour, he argued, and tried his best to outdo even their wildest expectations.

Heliogabalus was not making a concerted effort to alienate himself from the Romans – on the contrary, he was doing his best to impress them. Also, for fetishistic and fantasy purposes, the boy wanted and needed the luxuriance of his silken drapes; meanwhile the man argued that as a Syrian his magnificent appearance would not only astound the local Romans but would also provide a show of royalty and wonder for the populace. The affectation of the new Emperor with regard to clothing did more than raise eyebrows – this was an affront to the Roman civilisation. Some of Heliogabalus's flatterers naturally ignored his fault, and some (and not only from his home land) even copied his style, but his family were concerned. Maesa was incensed; she had carefully manoeuvred and plotted for the Empire, but now her grandson was risking all because of his foibles. Moreover, his dress was uncomfortably feminine in Roman eyes, and Maesa's fear may have been aroused by more than his insistence on wearing his native costume; she may have been worrying over the direction in which her grandson was heading. Foreseeing trouble ahead, she once again made her protestations to the Emperor, explaining the offence he was causing, and how important it was to appear like a Roman before Romans. The Godmother could not brook any danger to the firm political platform she had constructed, and now the only threat to the empery was the Emperor himself.

Heliogabalus would not listen to her. The boy was now the most powerful man in the world, and must have felt the thrill of that power. The senate were incensed and even persuaded Maesa to try again on several occasions; this must have disturbed her and, afraid that the child was hell-bent on alienating his people, she warned and cajoled him, with little result. As Dio resentfully wrote:

When she saw what Heliogabalus was up to, Maesa was extremely worried and tried again and again to persuade the youth to wear Roman dress when he entered the city to visit the Senate. She was afraid that his appearance, obviously foreign and completely barbaric, would offend those who saw him; they were not used to such clothing and considered his ornaments only suitable for women.

So as an individual, Heliogabalus seemed liked an oddball to the senate, but apart from odd whispers there was little else to grumble about at the beginning. It could be that the senate were a little perturbed by his Eastern origins, by his fashionable attitudes and especially so by clothing which hinted at femininity, but yet again this still could be suffered providing the boy emperor proved himself worthy of his position as the head of the state. But there would be more serious confrontations which would compound this alienation and drive all sympathy from the governmental collective. The first of these was over the matter of religious worship, which blew apart their uneasy relationship like a time bomb.

The memory of the Temple of Emesa shining in the Syrian sun never left the mind of Heliogabalus. As he had reached adolescence, and a painful, distorted adolescence at that, it is possible that he thought of the religion that he had left behind as a great emptiness in his soul. Back in the days when the chariots had followed him, dressed gorgeously in the trappings of the high priest, he had officiated and given sacrifices to the great Sun-God, and led the ritual dancing and frenzy of the rites of which he was so familiar. Sexuality had grown inside him, and with it the need to express it, but all that succeeded in doing was to drive his thoughts back to the same symbols of sex, the fertility rites and rituals which were so familiar to him. These pagan festivals, seen as so backward by the Romans, put man in his natural place among the workings of Nature, and seemed to the worshippers to be a correct and normal relationship to the creation. In the midst of life they were in the midst of Nature, and what could be more suitable than to bow down to creation itself, the witness to which was all around them, the giver and nurturer of life, the Sun itself, blazing every day in all its majesty.

The clash between Heliogabalus and Rome on the matter of religion produced a scandal and rocked the nation. It is not possible to exaggerate its importance. The crisis came quickly and its seed can be traced, as always, by the mutual agreement of Heliogabalus the boy and Heliogabalus the man. The boy had grown up surrounded by images of the sun-god and wrapped in his own importance. Travelling to Rome he had been invited to inaugurate temples and to lead the ceremonies to El Gabal, but once he had reached the capital his religious role had come to an abrupt full stop. Of course he was given the titular position as head of the priests, but only to oversee religion as the Romans believed in it. The maelstrom of Heliogabalus's childhood left a deep emotional scar in which a love of his religion and his role as intercessor struck at the very core of his being. This was a big gap in his new life as master of Rome and one which he intended to fill.

It had been about nine long years since the new Emperor had lived in his villa outside Rome – an aeon to a boy of fourteen. It is not known how much of Roman ways or religions he might have been taught but it is reasonable to assume that very little stayed with him, even with the receptive mind he undoubtedly had. Robbed of his everyday function, the boy found little compensation in the supplicatory worship practised in Rome.

To fully appreciate the storm which was about to strike Rome, one must be aware of the relationship the Romans had with their religion and how it had, over the centuries, become embedded in their traditions. The Romans had a vastly different view of religion to Heliogabalus. In the most ancient of times, the Roman gods grew up around local superstitions and a need for supernatural protection, in much the same way as the pagan gods did. These gods – known as *di indigetes* – were not adopted from religions outside the country, although a number were filched from outlying areas such as those of the Sabines and the Etruscans. The ancient pantheon consisted of deities who presided over every aspect of everyday life; because the essence of life and Nature was a great mystery to the people of that age, they assumed that everything seen or perceived was pervaded with a myriad of minor or major gods whose role was to dictate each aspect of existence. The invisible presences – *numina* – dictated life and perception, and embodied the divine plan by which all things are ruled and regulated. Hence a whole welter of deities reigned over all things imaginable, from creation, birth, death, and beyond. Gods such as *lares* protected the household, and others looked after trade, commerce, and farming. There were deities who controlled the weather, others who looked after all aspects of warfare, gods who personified the virtues, and those presiding over the Underworld.

There was even protection – in the form of Cloaca – for the sewage system.

As Rome expanded, the Romans borrowed outside gods, from the Etruscans for example, and three of them formed a centrepiece for worship on the Capitoline Hill – Jupiter and Juno (king and queen of the gods) as well as Minerva. In the fifth century BCE, the Romans encountered the Greeks and, impressed by their sophistication, took many other deities under their wing, notably Apollo, Venus, Diana, Mercury, Neptune and Vulcan, who were derived from Hermes, Aphrodite, Artemis, Hermes, Poseidon and Hephaestus respectively. Some of the established Roman gods were also linked with their Greek equivalents, such as Zeus and Hera (Jupiter and Juno). The glorious tales of the gods and their interaction with humans as expressed in works such as Homer's Iliad and Odyssey - not to mention great poets such as Pindar, Theocritus and Simonides - spurred on the Romans to emulate the erudition of their neighbours and rivals, so Virgil began doing just that, copying Theocritus in his *Bucolics* and Homer in his *Aeneid*. The *Aeneid* was possibly the most influential work of the time; taking his cue from the Odyssey, it wrote of the siege of Troy from the Trojan viewpoint, using the Roman borrowed gods as the war progressed as a divine chess game.

The Greeks may have had a major influence on Roman religion, but they were far from being the only ones. For example, in the beginning of the third century, the Phrygian god Cybele was adopted officially in Rome, and from Persia came the ancient god Mithras, whose worship spread throughout the Empire as far as Britain. These were representative of a number of 'saviour-gods' who were accepted within the list of Roman deities, as Roman religious ideas were far from stagnant, but ever-developing as they tended to augment rather than fragment the growing systems of worship within their own pantheon.

By the time Heliogabalus had ascended the throne of the Empire, the state religion was a vast tapestry of gods, old and new, interspersed between a varied and hybrid mythos developed over the centuries. Moreover, the methods of worship were long established and followed scrupulously. Religion was a serious matter and one which influenced every aspect of life; the gods had to be appeased or appealed to for each undertaking, whether it be to care for the house, or to protect a soldier in warfare. The approval of the gods was not earned, although auspicious persons in high position may gain their approbation; it was paid for by barter, and a boon could not be expected unless it was paid for in the form of prayer, offerings and sacrifices. For every god needed his or her own shrine or temple; and it was necessary to appeal to the individual god at the appropriate place, using rite and ritual passed down through the generations. During the festival of a certain god, feasts would be held, and invitations sent out in the name of the god, who would actually be present at the gathering and join in the celebration; a dish of food would actually be set out for him. In the home, the head of the house – *paterfamilias* – would be responsible for organising the required and necessary rituals.

Family worship was a central part of everyday life, but the ancient Romans participated in state or public worship too. Their priests were broadly spilt into two groups, one dealing with omens and the other with ritual. Those priests who interpreted the omens and signs from the gods were the were known as *augeres*, and they would translate signs shown in Nature or in the entrails of sacrificed beasts; an augury was a necessary part of preparation for war, for example, or any serious political decision. The most important of the ritual priests were the *pontifices*, who were in charge of important matters such as overseeing festivals and their dates, assisting the Emperor in religious matters, and determining valid business days. They were led by the Head Priest (*pontifex maximus*). As well as the priests, there were the king and queen of holy matters (*rex sacrorum* and *regina sacrorum*) who were responsible for state sacrifices, and minor officials (*flamines*) whose responsibility was for a particular god; although not as highly-regarded as the *pontifices*, a *flamen* was still an office of great esteem.

It can be appreciated that, in the old days, the Romans were pious in their attitudes towards religion, and usually the Emperor took the title of *pontifex maximus*- 'great bridge-builder'. This official line was the foundation of the trouble which would soon brew up between Heliogabalus and the state. Having been brought up in a widely different religious ethos, and with a sincere belief in the religion for which he had been groomed as pontiff, Heliogabalus was an evangelist who wanted to impress his theology on the Roman state, an intention which, taken too far, would be an attack not only on the state religion but on the fabric of Roman society itself. There would be no harm in annexing a god into the Roman pantheon – that had been done too often to excite even comment. From the Greeks they had adopted a sun-god (Helios), and many others, too, so the addition of El Gabal would be a little price to pay to buy the pleasure of the new Emperor. But the senate were worried; they had heard of the Emperor's activities before he came to Rome, especially a rite in Nicodemia over which he presided:

Immediately he plunged into his mad activities, dressed in his richest robes of state, purple embroidered with gold, wearing not only bracelets and necklaces but even a crown of gold and jewels.

News of this strange ritual spread far and wide, inevitably being reported to the senators, who assumed that, while Emperor in Rome, he would desist from such lewd and barbaric customs. The solemn role of Emperor, its dignity, did not fit with orgiastic dancing and prancing about in an alien and peculiar manner. That might have been all right when he was a priest in the backwaters of Syria – he could even be admired for it as an object of curiosity – but naturally this would stop when he sat in the imperial chair. His religion itself may command respect and even adherents, but Heliogabalus would surely suborn his actions as a religious votary to the demands of the state. They were proven wrong, and when it became apparent that the new Emperor was hell-bent on promoting El-Gabal, it was clear that something had to be done.

Heliogabalus's intentions had been clear enough from the very start. In the *curia* still hung the ominous present they had received before they had even set eyes on the boy – the painting of him sacrificing to El-Gabal. Maesa herself had cautioned Heliogabalus against a religious reform, but to no avail. Dio:

But Heliogabalus had nothing but contempt for the old woman's warnings, and no-one succeeded in persuading him. (He would listen only to those who were like him and flattered his faults.) Since, however, he wished the Senate and the Roman people to get used to seeing him in this costume and wanted to gauge their reactions to this exotic sight, before he returned to Rome he had a full-length portrait painted, showing him performing his priestly duties in public. His native god also appeared in the painting - the emperor was shown sacrificing to him under favourable auspices.

Heliogabalus sent this picture to Rome to be hung in the centre of the senate-house, high above the statue of Victory before which each senator burns frankincense and pours a libation of wine as they enter the chamber. He directed all Roman officials who perform public sacrifices to call upon the new god Heliogabalus before all the other gods whom they invoke in their rites. By the time the Emperor came to Rome dressed in the manner described above, the Romans saw nothing unusual in it - the painting had prepared them for what to expect.

This was serious. The senate must have at least half expected the former high priest to bring his god along to Rome, but Heliogabalus made it clear that he was intent upon giving it prominence too. He rejected the supremacy of the Roman deities and kept affiliation with the god he had worshipped and led the processions of in Emesa; and so the sense of his racial background came to the fore again. What was the senate to do with an Emperor who not only refused to don the imperial toga, but also seemed determined to undermine the fabric of Roman religion and sensibilities?

The senators were well aware who was the driving-force behind the new Antonine regime, and, as they had done before, they once again turned to Maesa to right their wrongs. After all, they all knew how much experience she had had over the decades, and no-one was foolish enough to doubt who was the real Empress. For her part, Maesa was aware that it was in her interests to demonstrate that they were right; a woman as ambitious as she needed not only to pull strings but to be seen to pull them. It is left for us to imagine her fury when – again – she approached the Emperor only to be ignored. Far from dissuading the headstrong lad, she only succeeded in strengthening his resolve. Once more, Maesa noted this unwelcome show of independence and would nurse these private grievances as time went by. As it was, she had the extra embarrassment of having to confront the senate and admit failure too. Such an admission must, she would have realized, diminish her standing in the eyes of the government, and that must have been galling for her. The senate now realized that their allies in the imperial house were ineffectual, and were powerless to resist the coming storm.

As far as Heliogabalus was concerned, the Roman gods would have seemed artificial and hollow. He would have been unimpressed by the staid rituals of the Romans, their stress on superstition and augury, their polytheism and their tales, legends and myths; far from seeming sophisticated, they bore the hallmarks of falsity. It would be wonderful to educate these infidels, and to show through example how it really felt to pray, to be wound up in an ecstatic orgiastic delight which was the gateway to true perception. To experience rather than simply supplicate. He was on the right lines. This perception which his religion offered was, to many men, exactly what they had been looking for, and his timing could not have been better.

Whether they liked it or not, he was the Emperor and could (and would) use his power to attain his ends. Many deplored the new religion as an affront to common decency, but the government had another reason for fearing the rise of an all-embracing new faith. The senate knew well enough how dangerous a monotheism could be to a state or a nation; once people began to believe in a religion for their own ends, then the former values of the republican gods would falter. As these were directed to the good of the state, then this in itself would be enough to put the Empire in danger. All was well and good if the religion was run by and for the state, but to give the keys to men's opinions to a self-enlightening god would be to open the doors to anarchy. The cult of El-Gabal was all very well, so long as it knew its proper – subordinate – station. It was acceptable for some of the trendy youngsters to be drawn towards these new barbaric cults – although they were still frowned upon – but trend-setters did not control government and the senate were not prepared to sweep aside centuries of tradition on a youngster's whim. They were, however, prepared to accept the new El-Gabalists as a marginalised faith, alongside the other circus attractions which seemed to be elbowing their way into the Roman pantheon.

Heliogabalus wanted more than that. In insisting that the sun god take first place in the pantheon, replacing Jupiter himself, Heliogabalus had assaulted the very heart of the Roman political fabric, and such a potentially hazardous situation was fraught with peril; should Rome's protective gods be toppled the Empire itself could fall. These fears were sound, and this is what would happen eventually – but not yet, and not by the machinations of

Heliogabalus. As *pontifex maximus*, Heliogabalus now planned to fuse the gods' *pontifices* into one official office which he himself would take up. To him, this was a necessary and harmless step, and not necessarily a political one. But he was naïve. The *pontifex maximus* was traditionally a state post and at is core held authority only on behalf of the Roman people. Effectively Heliogabalus's proposal was that he should take over as head of the Roman Church, a religious supremo whose power was limitless. In effect, he could become little less than a dictator, and if the senate's decrees ran counter to the new religion they could be quashed simply by his order. The result could be the age-old battle between the church and sovereign rule. Religion was well and good so long as it did not interfere with politics, and ideas foreign to the state could lead to dissension and rebellion.

Heliogabalus was in the throes of maturation and his mind wavered between the delights of a child and the serious matter of deciding, in an adult way, what was best for his people. In so many ways he was thinking along the right lines. Like many of the citizens of Rome he saw the twilight of the gods and the inevitable shaking of old beliefs and creeds. The almost grown-up Heliogabalus very probably knew that the Roman people were ripe for change, and what better than to give them his own sun god? Given happier conditions, Heliogabalus may well have succeeded. If he had proven a popular ruler in the coming few years, the people may have been carried forward on his wave of enthusiasm. Then again, even if the *hoi polloi* were searching for a new religious experience, among the aristocratic opponents were those still swayed by the philosophers of the day, and some poets such as Horace were openly atheistic. Given a few more years, and the conditions would be perfect, as indeed they were at the advent of Christianity. Despite his unflagging devotion, Heliogabalus was not destined to prosper; even from the very start, before he officially took office, the senate was keeping a watchful eye on their Emperor.

The methods used by Heliogabalus to promote the religion of El-Gabal have been distorted and twisted by the historians. In fact, Heliogabalus must have spent a long time in considering the most effective and least offensive way of converting his people to his own beliefs. At all times he showed reverence to the Roman gods, even if he did not sympathise with them. He tried to draw up a line of action through which his god would seamlessly blend with those of his new country. As always, Heliogabalus took into account the feelings and sensibilities of those around him.

Far from converting those in power, Heliogabalus only managed to alienate them further, although there was much interest in his activities. His first task was to establish a place of worship for his deity, as El-Gabal had no home in the capital. As he planned to raise the god to the ultimate position, the temple would have to be a building of surpassing excellence, and as this was (to him) the most important priority of his reign, no expense would be spared. Straight away he gathered the architects to him and began on the plans which were of immense scale.

The Temples were to closely follow classical architectural design; the Romans were world-leaders at building work and Heliogabalus wanted his work to be the awe and gaze of the city. Besides, his dearest wish was to reconcile the Romans with his native religion and the use of classical Roman design was a good compromise. The Roman temple was quite distinctive, with a stairway leading up to the stylobate, or base; before the front doorway were a line of columns holding up the arcatrave, above which sat the pointed roof. Normally between the arcatrave and roof were decorations in the form of bas-reliefs.

First of all Heliogabalus erected a huge temple in the suburbs of the city, dedicated to the sun-god, and had an enormous statue of himself put up too. The sheer size of the project and the numerous altars built within it staggered the senate, as well as the furnishings and cost lavished on the new site of worship. It was perhaps natural that the Emperor would wish the temple of his native god to be constructed with some grandeur; but the subject of the Syrian sun-god was already disturbing to the government, and the expense was just another annoyance to sting them with. They were already incensed at having to perform their ritual libations beneath this strange deity in the senate house, and the fact that now the new god had officially risen in rank above all others. They were not prepared to express any enthusiasm at the construction of so ornate a structure in which to worship it. Angry whispers echoed along the corridors of power.

Once again the boy and the man met at the crossroads of a fine project; the boy delighted in sheer magnificence, and the pleasure of realising his dream, while the adult considered the practicalities of construction and the logistics of such a venture. In fact Heliogabalus built two temples to the god, the main building - known as the

Eliogabalum, on Palatine Hill - and another in the suburb of Ad Spem Veterem, close to the present-day Porta Maggiore. This latter temple was to serve as a kind of summer retreat, and was built on land which belonged to the imperial family, having been part of the estate of Soaemias's late husband, Varius Marcellus. The land was known as Ad Spe Veteram, and it is likely that Heliogabalus chose it to avoid any unpleasantness caused by proportioning land. The Emperor's project would set a fine example by being constructed on his private estate.

The Eliogabalum was a sumptuous structure and its design can be seen on coins of that period. It was built on the side of the Hill nearest to the Circus Maximus – and it was a prominent spectacle, towering as it did to a great height. The façade was constructed by a symmetrical arrangement of great columns, and its grand entrance flanked by phallic statues. Inside lay the great expanse of the main chamber, dotted with various altars, and to each side were beautiful wings. He even planned to construct a gigantic column, fitted with steps, to mark the arrival of the new national deity; he did not live to see its completion. But in the meantime the large black stone, the purpose of which probably having defeated the Romans, was hauled into place in the centre of the sanctum sanctorum.

Heliogabalus went further, wishing to act the part of arbitrator between the traditional old and the vibrant new orders. He was determined that he should show, once and for all, that his new god did not displace the original deities held in so much esteem by the Romans, and to prove this he decided to publically advertise his respect by transferring the emblems of the most respected of their deities into his new Temple. To the Eliogabalum he desired to transfer the emblem of the Great Mother, the fire of Vesta, the Palladium, the shields of the Salii, and all that the Romans held sacred.

Lampridius lapses into farce and buffoonery in an unsavoury attempt to darken Heliogabalus's name; in fact, the end effect is one almost comical in its silliness. We are asked to believe that Heliogabalus – the sensitive young man – smashed his way into the Temple of the Vestal Virgins and demanded the shrine, but the Senior Vestal fooled him with an earthenware copy! Opening the shrine, the empty-headed idiot threw a tantrum, and smashed it when he found nothing inside: an unlikely scenario for the *pontifex maximus*. With his customary relish for all things unsavoury, Lampridius goes on to describe, with delight, an imaginary scene in which Heliogabalus, having sown up his prepuce so that he may follow in the footsteps of the eunuchs, participated in the rites to the Great Mother before carrying off her idol to the new Temple.

Although such preposterous tales were popular with his modern audience, there is no doubt that Heliogabalus was seen by some to be plundering sacred temples to place their relics in the Eliogabalum so that no god might be worshipped at Rome save only Elagabalus. It is also important to realise that this was not done in a spirit of spiteful malice or blasphemy, but with a genuine devotion to his god. In fact, his actions point to an attempt at conciliation between his view and that of the Romans; after all, there was nothing to stop him from simply smashing the statues of what he considered to be false idols in the name of the sun-god. Instead, he allowed their worship, but only as being subservient to his own. He tried to explain his purpose by arguing that they were Elagabalus's subordinates and may well have hoped that this would satisfy the Romans. It did not.

These desecrations of Heliogabalus must be seen in perspective. Lampridius's tale of the Emperor smashing his way into the Vestal Temple is exaggeration and untruth. It may well have been expedient for him to use brute force and to prosecute all those who stood in his way, but the boy was too genteel for a course of action like that, even though it may have helped him to carry out his desires with the minimum of fuss. When the priests of Cybele refused to accede to his requests, he submitted to them, sacrificed for them and even agreed to be ordained as a priest of that faith to win their approbation. Such an act does not suggest a violent, irascible nature but a boy of sensitivity and humility. As with all aspects of his short life, his deeds were later embroidered to chime with the portrait of a detestable monster; and although he did many unseemly things, a monster he was not.

In his idealistic and premature quest to unite his Empire, Heliogabalus declared, furthermore, that the religions of the Jews and the Samaritans and the rites of the Christians must also be transferred to this place, in order that the priesthood of Elagabalus might include the mysteries of every form of worship. It is obvious that Heliogabalus wished to consign every god under his own deity's banner, and the design in some ways was praiseworthy – to do away with sectarianism and join together under one theism. It was also another ham-fisted attempt to reconcile all parties.

The Emperor made a further blunder, which helped to alienate his religion once and for all. He had himself circumcised, although no-one is really sure when the operation was performed; it was, however, common gossip around town. In his innocent zeal to include all religions under his sun-flag, he had included the Hebrews, and this piece of body mutilation was a sign that he had begun what was in essence a Jewish revival. Moreover, he submitted to Christian baptism as well, which caused people to doubt his motives. These innovations were ill-advised in the climate of the day, only a few years after the laws of Severus had banned the Jewish religion and had allowed for a mass Christian persecution. The people still remembered that the Christians were a treacherous people who were plotting the overthrow of the state; moreover, they had caused every misfortune to have occurred both now and in the past. It was still commonly believed that they were thieves and liars who killed children and ate raw meat. Yet now the new Emperor was putting their cult on an equal footing with the Roman pantheon, these people who not long ago had been sentenced to death for treason and sacrilege! And he had even submitted to their inauguration rites! They could not realise that Heliogabalus was simply working towards a two-level programme to promote national unity, and the worship of his god El-Gabal.

Heliogabalus's plan to reconcile the senate with his priestly calling met with no success; he even took to walking in the public streets wearing his priest's costume. It simply earned him the nickname of 'The Assyrian'. Despite much remonstrance from his family, he refused to back down and went ahead with the rites of worship. If he had hoped to convince the populace of the sincerity of his religion by demonstrating the rituals, he was again doomed to failure. Already biased against the intrusive god, the senate – in secret, of course – ridiculed the performance, and felt somewhat embarrassed by their Emperor behaving in such a ludicrous way. To the pious Roman, a little wine for libation, some incense, and some appropriate words were enough to satisfy them; their attitude towards their religion was solemn and minimalist.

In contrast to the Roman forms of worship, the rites of El-Gabal seemed indeed primitive, as in fact they were, originating back to the old religions of Peru and Mexico. Throughout the Middle East, cults grew up, each group recognising its own *baal*, or local god. Inevitably, this *baal* was the originator of produce, and as life depended on fruit and animals, so they in turn depended on the climate. Nature-worship was not only seen as necessary, but a matter of common sense, and clans would bow down to gods and goddesses of the forest, of rain, and of the sun. There was a further development when it became apparent that one could communicate with these gods using sympathetic magic, and when the concept of increase became naturally linked with that of fertility. So what better way to encourage growth than by the exercise of fertility rites?

The more excessive these rites, the more powerful the sympathetic magic between mortal and *baal*. The most extreme form (and therefore the most potent) of sacrifice was that of humans. Fertility rites reached the point of orgiastic and ecstatic rituals, and in some cases the extent of licentiousness and sexuality would have horrified the Romans, who already heard dark whispers about the strange eastern cults. These activities were no less energetic in the worship of the sun-god El-Gabal, and in the old days youngsters would sometimes be sacrificed, their entrails used for augury. The common form of worship was a frenzied dance, performed to the sound of instruments, the cymbals being played by the women. The most important intermediary between the people and their *baal* was the high priest, or head witch-doctor, which was Heliogabalus.

The Emesan worship of El-Gabal was not as localized as many people assert, and the common belief that Varius brought his deity to Europe is not true. By the time of Varius it had already spread to many parts of the globe, even as far as the western shores. In the City Museum of Woerden, Netherlands, there is a memorial, which states: 'For the good health of the Emperor Caesar Titus Aelius Hadrianus Antoninus Augustus Pius, to the invincible sun Elagabal and Minerva Lucius Terentius Bassus, standard bearer of the third cohort of Breuci.' The Emperor Antoninus Pius died as long ago as 161.

The Emperor must have been a very excited young man when the sumptuous Elagabalum was finally completed and worship could at last commence in the heart of his Empire. The senate could hardly avoid the great event – they were posted within the Temple to act as favoured witnesses to the spectacle. The performance must have meant a great deal for Heliogabalus – he wanted more than anything else to impress his people with the grandness of the ceremony. At the appointed time – daybreak – the Emperor and his cavalcade made their way solemnly to the new building. Herds of sacrificial bulls and droves of sheep had been driven there for the performance, and were placed on the many altars to the sun-god. Banks of expensive spices were piled up, and in front of the altars Heliogabalus placed large jars of the best wine, which was mingled with the blood of the victims. The music began and the imperial youth began his task appointed to the *'Invictus Sacerdos Dei Soli'* – 'Invincible Priest of the Sun-God' – which was to remain his favourite of all titles given him. It was etched on the numerous medals minted in his day, along with an image of himself in the act of sacrifice.

As for the rites, the historians described them for us:

Heliogabalus danced around the altars to music played on every kind of instrument; women from his native country joined him in these dances, carrying cymbals and drums as they circled around the altars. The entire senate and all the knights stood watching, like spectators at the theatre. The spices and entrails of the sacrificial animals were not carried by servants or men of low birth; instead, they were carried in gold vessels held aloft by the praetorian prefects and the most important magistrates, who wore long-sleeved robes with a broad purple stripe in the centre, robes which hung to their feet in the Phoenician style. On their feet were the linen shoes customarily worn by the Eastern prophets. It was obvious that Heliogabalus was paying the highest honour to those associated with him....

...Accompanied by flutes and drums, he went about performing, as it appeared, orgiastic service to his god....

There is a barely disguised contempt in these words; the sight of an Emperor of Rome capering about to barbaric tunes played on drums and flutes was beyond their comprehension, and only served to degrade him in their eyes. It was bad enough to see some of the citizens following an uncouth cult which devalued the *via Romana*;

but to see it being promulgated by their own ruler was too much. Instead of converting his senate, he only succeeded in enraging them, and far from exhibiting his faith as one to be emulated the net result was derision and scorn. Moreover, the activities within the Temple were distorted and mixed with revolting fabrications. One description tells of 'the secret sacrifices that he offered to him [El Gabal], slaying boys and using charms, in fact actually shutting up alive in the god's temple a lion, a monkey, and a snake, and throwing in among them human genitals, and practising other unholy rites, while he invariably wore innumerable amulets.' Lampridius could be relied upon to go a step further than anyone else, and his description of the rituals has its place more in lewd fantasy than in any element of truth, filled with disgusting accusations written to delight and amuse his audience, who loved to hear of his atrocities, however removed from the facts they may be. Human sacrifices had been banned, in all parts of the Empire, by decree well over a century before.

Heliogabalus also sacrificed human victims, and for this purpose he collected beautiful children of noble birth from the whole of Italy, whose fathers and mothers were alive - intending, I guess, that the sorrow would be intensified if suffered by both parents. Finally, he kept about him every species of magician and had them perform daily sacrifices, himself urging them on and thanking the gods because he found them to be well-disposed to these men. And all the while he would examine the children's genitals and torture the victims in the way of his own native rites.

There is also disdain in the epithet 'The Assyrian', and the nickname reflects the feelings at the time; of an Emperor as an alien;

an Emperor who seemed to have no desire to ingratiate himself with the people or the senate, and who had not only brought his lewd and orgiastic religion to Rome, but had forced the citizens to join in its worship. This offence was rank, and, as Dio states, 'consisted, not in his introducing a foreign god into Rome or in his exalting him in very strange ways, but in his placing him even before Jupiter himself and causing himself to be voted his priest.' It was an attack on the Roman state.

The methods used in religious rites different drastically between the Romans and the Syrians. Worship of the gods was a respectable affair in Rome, and the most excessive shows of zeal were demonstrated in the sacrifice of animals or vegetable produce, and the erection of statues and shrines. Human sacrifices were thought of as barbaric, and the very concept was banned by a senatorial decree of 97 BCE, almost three centuries ago. Pliny the Elder pointed to the sacrifice as distinctly un-Roman, and Horace describes such scenes as representative of barbaric witchcraft and black magic. All of this must have seemed strange to someone like Heliogabalus, who had been brought up amongst such pagan beliefs and held them closely to his heart.

Although later the rites of the worship of El-Gabal would be later condemned as bizarre and ridiculous, that would not have been the first impression of all the Romans in the street. Already half-converted by the cults of Selene and Cybele, there seems to have been a growing interest in the trendy new ideas gaining ground over the past century. In fact, far from criticising the unfamiliar dancing and singing, there seems to have been much admiration;

Heliogabalus had been a favourite figure among the soldiers in Emesa, and a new dogma aimed at salvation was a novel and perhaps seductive set of religious values for the fashionable set. The time was coming for a psychological and religious rebellion.

These fertility sects were looked on with disgust by the authorities, but they were growing in popularity, and even the orgiastic fervour of the El Gabal cult was mild compared with the excesses of the Cybele cult. In the event, although it had a growing number of adherents, the worship of Cybele was thought of by the moralists as frankly obscene, and (as in the case of Heliogabalus) dark rumours were whispered about it. The priests, it was said, were eunuchs, and castrated themselves in a frenzy of sexual excitement. Self-flagellation was a strong element, and the wish to suffer was a parallel to their model, Attis, who swore eternal love to a goddess but betrayed her after having sex with a naiad – thereafter he castrated and punished himself. Apuleius suggested that there was a strong homosexual element among the votaries, who would select muscular farm-workers with which to copulate.

Apuleius joins the ranks of writers who, appalled by new ideas, use fictions to portray them as licentious and perverse. This is the old ruse used by Lampridius, and in his abuse he spends much time sneering at the phallic content of the new cult. In this case, he was quite correct – the worship of El-Gabal was centred on fertility and so the phallus was an important symbol - but such accusations could be pointed at many areas of everyday life in ancient Rome. There was nothing extreme or even particularly new in the worship of El Gabal and its focus on phallic symbolism. In fact, the penis had been an important fetish in many of the religions which had been admitted into the ever-increasing circle of Roman faiths and superstitions; penile amulets were commonplace, and sometimes a great wooden phallus would be set up on the town gates to ward off bad luck – along with the sign HAPPINESS LIVES HERE. It was also the central figure in the worship of many important gods, such as Liber, a straightforward fertility god whose festival involved dragging a giant wooden phallus around on a cart until it was returned to its resting-place, at which point a respected matron would lay a wreath at its base.

The moralists did not like this open veneration of sex and genitalia; it is a short step from phallic worship and fertility rites to open orgy. Even the festival of the long-admired Good Goddess became degraded, and, although supposedly run by respectable ladies, soon deteriorated into a sex-party; Juvenal describes how, to the loud blasts of music, the women would become so frenzied as to desperately seek any male to satisfy their seething passions, stooping so low as to as to suborn a slave, a scavenger – even, he says, a donkey. The cult of Isis was so well-known as an excuse for sexual licence that Juvenal simply described its priestesses as 'pimps.' The old garden god Priapus was transformed into a giant penis and so degenerated into a fertility deity, too.

In his way, by accident or design, Heliogabalus grasped something which the others were blind to – that people could be moulded into a powerful force under the banner of one religion. Even to a lad of his tender years, it was apparent that Rome was a city in turmoil, and that much of the quarrelling throughout the Empire was caused by an increasing tendency to split into opposing factions. What was needed was peace in the form of an umbrella beneath which the whole nation could unite, and Heliogabalus thought he had found the solution in the form of religion. It was more than a mere possibility, it was an inevitability. His reasoning was sound enough, but needed a strength of will and character strong enough to carry it off; unfortunately, he had none of these, and the Empire had to await the adoption of Christianity before such an attempt was successfully attempted.

That Christianity came up on the rails to win the race was more a matter of chance than theology; the worship of Isis and Mithras were thoroughbreds well in the running. It took a strong character and a readiness – even a need – to seek individual salvation to clinch the race. It is also facile to argue that pagan religions failed due to their lack of virtue, an argument common among early Christians. Indeed, their own religion was not free from moral taint; the pagans of the time complained about their behaviour, and even their one-time champion, Tertullian, faltered in his defence, admitting that some but not all of their number were at fault. The pagans themselves complained about the love-feasts of the early Christians, and if they in turned criticised the Dionysia and Bacchanalia, this was simply the propaganda commonly thrown about randomly at the time. Mud-slinging was a favourite pastime, and was an effective weapon; no-one is free from scandal, and smoke will rise from the tiniest of fires.

It is true that the worship of the sun-god, to Heliogabalus, was an *idée fixe*, but in the rush to denounce the boy it has been too simple to ignore the virtuous attempt which lay behind it. As it is, he did his utmost to promote his praiseworthy intentions; in fact, it would be fair to say that he spent most of his life working towards his dream of a unified Empire. His failure does not reflect any lack of soundness in his ideals, merely a weakness which prevented them from becoming a reality.

This weakness was compounded by his idiosyncrasies, which will become apparent later. It is a mistake to blend his way of life with his good intentions. One of the tragedies of his short life was this very fact; Heliogabalus was a compassionate, good-natured boy who was destroyed by the scandals which rocked his reign, scandals which inevitably grew up around his abnormal behaviour. They were the stuff gleefully gathered together by his contemporary biographers who delighted in using them to make the virtuous blush and astonish the strait-laced. Lampridius especially, who loved to bask in infamies, takes unrestrained pleasure in embroidering and expanding such tales to produce a pornographic nonsense calculated to titillate and tease his public. These took on a greater significance after the Emperor had become a figure of universal detestation. To distance themselves from his aberrations, they became embedded in his origins – the fact that he was not Roman, and therefore Rome could wipe their hands clean of his contamination.

For the few years of his reign Heliogabalus remained constant to his native god. In the midsummer, every year, he would hold a lavish festival in its honour, and at that time he bribed the people with great spectacle; he built race tracks around the area and erected theatres which staged shows and costly recitals. To some extent his plan to woo the men of Rome worked, as they arrived in droves to watch the chariot races and entertainments provided for them, which culminated in all-night feasting and drinking. His past spectacles had earned him renown throughout the Empire; and, as at the games in the Coliseum, there must have been an atmosphere of intense anticipation. Even at a young age the Emperor knew how to seduce the populace; he himself drove chariots and danced during the festival. Although the wooing of the people was an obvious motive for the extravagances, it was not the only one, and probably not even the most important one. As has been demonstrated, Heliogabalus was a genuinely kind person, and throughout his reign bore a feeling of goodwill to everyone, poor or rich, and delighted in his own generosity.

The bringing of the sun-god was an occasion of great pomp, circumstance – and expenditure. A magnificent chariot was constructed to carry the idol, bedecked with gold inlay and jewels, and drawn by six perfectly white thoroughbred horses. The carriage brought the god from the city to the Temple, and no-one drove it; it was arranged to give the illusion that the sun-god himself controlled the horses. In fact, the chariot was led by Heliogabalus himself, who walked backwards in front of the chariot, holding the horses' reins while looking up, adoringly, at the face of the sun-god. Dio described the scene as follows:

> **Since he couldn't see where he was going, his route was paved with gold dust to keep him from stumbling and falling, and bodyguards supported him on each side to protect him from injury. The people ran parallel to him, carrying torches and tossing wreaths and flowers. The statues of all the gods,**

the costly or sacred offerings in the temples, the imperial ornaments, and valuable heirlooms were carried by the cavalry and the entire Praetorian Guard in honour of the sun god.

The statue to El Gabal was an uncommon thing as, by common consent, idols were not usually made of the sun or moon. The reason being that as the two bodies were readily seen in the sky every day, images of these gods were superfluous anyway. That said, El Gabal has links to the ancient Babylonian god Samas, who was often depicted as a terrifying man with flames or snakes bursting from his arms. Perhaps the idol was based on this or, more likely, was a representation of one of his consorts, Astarte and Artagatis, the former offering water and fertility, while the latter bore a resemblance to Cybele and was known as 'the Great Mother'.

When the idol had arrived at the Temple, Heliogabalus performed the rites of which he was the master for the edification of the multitude. That done, he climbed to the top of a huge tower and looked down over his people and addressed them while throwing down all manner of valuables, including cups of gold or silver and rich cloths. He even loosed a variety of domestic animals for the people, all except the pig, which was offensive to his Phoenician upbringing and religion – pork was a food he never touched.

It is not hard to imagine the reaction of the mob when treasures were flung down to them from the tower looming high above them. The scramble turned into a riot, and soldiers would try to quell the disturbance, with little success; instead, many persons were injured by the spears they wielded so ineffectually. Some were trampled to death in the rioting, and many lost their lives as a result of Heliogabalus's well-meant generosity. It had been a well-planned strategy but one which turned to tragedy for many of the spectators caught up in the battle for the gifts their Emperor had so freely distributed. The feelings of the senate-house were, of course, censorious.

The argument that his generosity was 'well-meant' stands good, and his well-meaning benevolence is demonstrated again and again during his life. In fact, he could even, in this regard, be described as virtuous. In his day, the concept of virtue lay in one's outward behaviour, an embodied of a sense of justice, of courage, and honesty; applying such strict criteria to Heliogabalus there can be little doubt that he possessed all of these. When applied to sexuality, the word 'virtuous' had lost much of its meaning, and this was a reflection of the changing times; it was used, slightly tongue-in-cheek, to describe a Vestal Virgin or a mother – whose virtue, in those dark days, was now seen as improbable. It was a bitter joke that it merely applied to a eunuch.

There is an aspect to Heliogabalus's personality which has been much overlooked and is an important characteristic. He had an acute awareness of the suffering of his people, and had boundless compassion. It is a wonder, when one considers his background, his regal nature, his love of extravagance and his pampered upbringing, that the poor people around the city suburbs should have even taken up a single one of his thoughts. But they did. Throughout his life Heliogabalus bemoaned the fate of the poor, and would constantly weep whenever he witnessed suffering and misery. Even more incredible, he tried to do something about it, trying to ameliorate conditions and then help those in trouble whenever he had the opportunity. He had a love for his people which led him to come among them, visiting the poorest areas and helping out in barber's shops or as a bar assistant in the inns. He would even join the market tradesmen, sharing their lives with them, selling his wares on the dirty streets.

On a more practical level, he would help the people by insisting on holding donation days – six in all during his four-year reign – where he would distribute gifts to the people, all bought with his own private income. These ranged from gold or silver to a variety of beasts to carriages, slaves and litters, and as he handed them out he expressed a wish that they would always remember that the Emperor himself had donated them.

These laudable acts sat uncomfortably with his insistence on following his whims with regard to expenditure and religion. But Heliogabalus was little more than a boy, and had not been taken to task by the senate themselves; instead, they had weakly applied for help to his maternal relations. Having taken up the mantle of state, the boy found that he could not only follow his own inclinations – to some extent – but that he was as omnipotent as he had been in Emesa. His aunt and grandmother may have pulled his puppet-strings, but by this action Heliogabalus had proven that he could grab whatever he wanted simply by stretching out his hand. It was the boy in the candy shop once again, and although his relations had some control over him, they were beginning to lose their grip. The rein had slackened, and the fear was that one day Heliogabalus would break completely free and behave just how he liked.

It is possible that his family may have feared for him – and more importantly, themselves - if he did. Heliogabalus had had the worst possible start to his reign. The family had done what they could be ensure a secure platform on which he could stand at the very start, winnowing out his potential enemies and setting the scene for a long and peaceful rule. They had tried to restrain him from doing anything to jeopardise his security, yet he had managed to do just that on his own initiative. The colossal gold statue of him looming over the people seemed to mock them, and his new temple was an abomination, reminding them of the boy who had pulled down their religion and turned his back on Roman customs. He was an alien through and through, and not compatible with the way of life Rome had enjoyed for many centuries.

There was only one saving grace – his reign had been marked by a period of peace. This was no insignificant matter, as the years of turmoil and war had taken their toll on the Roman people and they longed for a respite from the rigours and horrors of battle. Ever since the demise of Commodus and the advent of the warrior-emperors the Empire had seen blood-letting and carnage on a grand scale. As early as the reign of Severus there had been protests and public demonstrations; during a chariot race the people all chanted:

'How long are we to suffer for?'
'How long shall we be waging war?'
'*Enough*!'

But even peace was a mixed blessing; had he become embroiled in warfare, his mind may have been occupied and the people would have stood behind him during his campaigns against threats to the safety of the state. But no external conflict had arisen – his enemies had been rooted out with some precision – and in any case there was no-one else eligible for the supreme title as yet. Idleness had turned the boy's mind to projects dear to his heat and antipathetic to those of the people to whom he was now the supreme ruler. It was a situation which could not last.

Maesa knew it, and resented the temerity of the boy in opposing her great will. Nothing had turned out as she planned; instead of being the ruling force in Rome, her influence was limited to her advisors and the meetings of the *conventus matronarum*. She had tried everything in her power, from cajoling to bullying, but the headstrong boy had shown surprising resilience; in fact, it says much for him that he refused to be browbeaten or intimidated by his awe-inspiring grandmother. Slowly, the seeds of resentment gave birth to hate. As was her wont, she kept all her scheming private and free from prying eyes, but from this time forward she began a conspiracy to topple the new Emperor. She had made Emperors before and she could do it again; only this time she had all the power at her beck, whereas Heliogabalus had little but his determination and his admirable but powerless regality.

Moreover, Maesa had allies within the family, not least of which was Mamaea, who had her own agenda and had been nursing her own ambition for some time. Mamaea was another beauty of the family, taking after Maesa, although her good looks were not, by common consent, as voluptuous as the lovely Soaemias – but she was dedicated to her cause, and at that time her cause was Alexianus. Watching the Bassianus family butcher themselves was sad enough, but it meant that her son was slowly coming forward in the ranks. From this time on she plotted with Maesa to attempt to bring down her nephew.

There was one stumbling-block, in the form of Soaemias, who was and remained devoted to her son. Although her reputation had been held up to dispute for public inspection, her sister was to fare little better, as rumours had grown that Antoninus had seduced her as well as her sister, and that Alexianus and Heliogabalus was actually half-brothers. As in the case of Heliogabalus, this is not likely. Soaemias would hardly agree to a plot against her son, whom she loved with an ardent passion, and so she herself would need to be kept under strict observation. So the remains of the Bassianus family made their dubious plans to uproot each other, while Heliogabalus continued to work towards his own ruin.

For the moment, Rome stood and watched. The senate wondered what he was going to do next, and they were not long in finding out. Heliogabalus had succeeded, despite all opposition, in bringing his native god to the Empire. He had overcome all obstacles simply by the power entrusted in him, but more scandal was already darkening the Roman skies like an ominous storm cloud.

Chapter 7: God-Like Children

Heliogabalus had gender issues. It is inconceivable that his family knew nothing about them, and must have seen the signs in his childhood behaviour. Now that he was growing, and was in the throes of adolescence, there could be no mistaking the fact. The senate had already remarked upon his native dress and how it had made the Emperor look feminine. This, undoubtedly, was one of the reasons his family urged him so strongly to give it up and wear the Roman toga as befitted a man of the time. It is likely that a love for his native costume was only part of the reason for Heliogabalus' reluctance to comply with their advice.

The Romans did not like homosexuality much. While acknowledging the sophistication and art of the Greeks, they despised their seeming predilection for same-sex relationships and dubbed homosexuality 'the Greek disease'. Even a whiff of scandal could result in unsavoury rumours and attacks, and rank was no safeguard against such abuse; it could even make matters worse. The Romans were a gossip-loving people and liked nothing better than a chance to ridicule a prominent public figure. Even a towering celebrity like Julius Caesar was not exempt, as seen by the rumours of his homosexuality after his prolonged stay at Nicodemia.

Caesar did not see the funny side; indeed, he spent much of his life living down the rumours and denying them at every opportunity. When in Rome, Caesar began a spree of affairs with women married to important men; a seemingly odd thing to do as these adulteries would be certain to come to public attention. But perhaps this is what Caesar wanted; it may well have been a desperate effort to clear his name from the odium of homosexuality. But even his sexual licentiousness could not stem the singing of the men-at-arms; now they chanted:

Citizens, protect your wives -
We lead the bald adulterer home!
You fucked away the gold in Gaul
Which you borrowed when in Rome!

When Heliogabalus began on his spree of adulteries and heterosexual excess, it could have been for several reasons. He could have been genuinely bisexual, although this hardly accords with his obvious femininity and the rest of his sexual life; he could, of course, having been experimenting in his first bloom of rising libido. He could have been energetically denying the homosexuality of which he was certainly aware, over-compensating for his infection with the Greek disease; although the boy-in-a-candy-shop syndrome may well have over-ridden any personal misgivings he may have had. Most probably, he was taking his cue from Julius Caesar.

His family and advisors would have been well aware of their protégé's unpopularity and must have suspected Heliogabalus' sexual orientation. An open avowal of homosexuality may well have been the final straw as far as the people of Rome were concerned and given the current rising feelings of antipathy among the authorities it was unthinkable that he should alienate himself even further. Heliogabalus had ignored all advice on restraint when it came to religious matters, but he had to tow the line as far as his sexuality went. He himself, even as Emperor and high priest, would have known well enough the social stigma attached to an outward show of homosexual love, and later events suggest that he even felt a deep-rooted shame and guilt concerning it. This may well have been at the centre of his next actions, which far from exculpating him from charges of what was seen as sexual perversion, simply led to more outrage as he became a symbol of concupiscence.

Sex was a thorny subject to the Romans of the time. As the epitome of virtue and sophistication, as reflected in the senate-house, Rome had, since the days of Augustus and before, grown a thin veneer of prudishness which belied the recognised and not-to-be-denied sexual needs pulsating beneath. It was not difficult to assuage one's sexual urges in ancient Rome. True, by the time of Heliogabalus, the Bacchanalia was long gone – and perhaps that was just as well. Copied from the healthier Dionysia orgies of Greece, the Bacchanalia had turned it into a dke Sadean explosion of corruption and vice, and was a word whispered by fearing mothers who tried to keep their sons clear from its moral taint. According to Livy, the Bacchanalia were banned by a senatorial decree in 186 BCE; they were hotbeds for political intrigue, and besides, leading members of the cult were – would the gods believe it! – women.

The spirit of the orgy was, however, resurrected by some of the most corrupt Emperors such as Caligula, to whom a taste for sexual excess was (so says the eternal gossip Suetonius) part of his nature.

The end of the Bacchanalia followed an investigation after a woman, Hispola, gave evidence as to the senate and a full account of the cult's activities were disclosed. Livy:

> The pleasures of wine and feasting were added to their religious rites, to entice more proselytes. After the wine, dirty talk, the dark night and intercourse between the sexes had drowned out every modicum of modesty, then debauchery of every variation were practised – everyone finding close at hand that sexual preference to which he was attracted by the predominant passion of his nature. But this one kind of vice – the promiscuous intercourse of free-born men and women – was not the sole mischief practised here; from this store-house of villainy proceeded false witnesses, counterfeit seals, false evidence, and pretended discoveries. From the same place, too, proceeded poison and secret murders, so that in some cases, not even the bodies could be found for burial. Many of their daring deeds were brought about by treachery, but most of them by force. The loud shouting and the noise of drums and cymbals, served to mask the violence as none of the cries uttered by the persons suffering attacks or murder could be heard outside.

Although the Bacchanalia was banned, there were many other avenues at which a youth could find safer sexual release. It was a matter of paternal pride for a young man to sow wild oats, and this could be done by slaking his sexual desires on slave-girls or daughters of the less well-to-do. There were of course always prostitutes in all the main thoroughfares of Rome, particularly around the Circus Maximus following the games or in the poorer districts. As Roman decadence grew, a man could even find comfort in the richer resorts outside the city, such as the baths of Baiae. It is interesting that the great Goddess of Love, Venus, herself was a patron of whores. A favourite tryst for clandestine lovers were the many baths of Rome; there were even separate baths for prostitutes; among the rich bathing was a pleasurable pastime and a taste for such luxury embodied the upper classes. As Martial said, 'Oppianus, if you have not bathed in Etruscus's baths you have not bathed.'

The national feeling towards libertinism was a conflicting one, and there is an obvious stand-off between the official stance of the government and everyday practice – at least among the rich. The Roman nation was a great one, and had a strict code of virtues to which all good men aspired, and there were even gods to represent them – piety, dignity, and so forth. But most men in the public eye took their cues from their Emperor – and, by and large, they were poor examples to follow for moralists. Many stories have come down from the ancient historians delighting in tales of debauchery and lubricity, and while many have been denounced as ranting rumour, it is hard to accept part of these tracts as genuine history while rejecting others on the grounds of taste. It is all too easy to accuse Heliogabalus of outrages, but then he did have many examples behind him. If the tales be true, then the Roman annals suggest that he was doing little more than following well-worn precedent.

If we stir the cauldron of dark whispers and stories dredged up in the old histories, we discover a horrifying list of dark deeds performed in the name of sex. Caesar's adulteries have already been mentioned, but it was said that the great Augustus himself, role model for so many future Emperors, hired procurers and was eminently fond of young virgins. In his island hideaway of Capri Tiberius indulged himself in wild orgies and the excesses of Caligula have become a by-word for incest and corruption. Claudius' wife Messalina was famed for her infidelities, and her name passed into the English language as the epitome of all female adulterers; while Nero's incestuous behaviour excited just as much comment from the annalists. While there were always moralists such as Cato to denounce these lewd practices, it has to be said that the catalogue of Roman leaders includes a formidable list of fornicators and debauchees.

The sexual licentiousness of the Romans was common knowledge, not only in Rome, but in the furthest-flung corners of the Empire. When Julia Domna visited Britain with her husband, it may have surprised her when a local lady told her: 'We answer the call of nature in a much better way than do you Roman women; we have sex openly with the best men, whereas you let yourselves be fucked secretly by the worst.'

There was another reason why Heliogabalus should have cultivated a more amiable rapport with the senate; he needed all the support he could get. He had further annoyed the government by his continued reckless spending. It had been expected that, on assuming the title of Emperor, he should distribute a certain sum of money in celebration; but he went further, and almost bankrupted the state in his zeal for spending. He was a boy, and given what seemed like a bottomless purse, he spent it on games and lavish spectacles – not to mention the ornate new Temple for the sun-god and his own statue of gold. Before long the privy purse was looking woefully depleted and the senators pointed the accusing finger at the Emperor.

Dark whispers began to be spread about Heliogabalus in those unwholesome corners where conspiracy thrives. Maesa's spies were everywhere, and soon they began to report areas of unrest and potential troublemakers. Criticism was widespread and Heliogabalus (or at least his family and advisors) knew that this was just a step away from revolution. To cultivate a more favourable opinion of the senate – and probably to mask his incipient homosexuality – the best thing for Heliogabalus to do was to make an alliance with a good family of Rome and to settle down in the honourable state of marriage. Although he was young – most men married when in their mid-twenties – the Emperor was no ordinary person and it was the norm for him to make a show of old-fashioned family virtues, even if only for outward appearances. It made political sense, and as such probably originated from Maesa. First of all it was necessary to find a suitable match from an appropriately distinguished ancestral line, and that was done with all expediency.

Now began his unfortunate and rather clumsy foray into the world of heterosexual sex. He began by marrying a widow – Anna Aurelia Faustina - whose husband Bassus had been killed in the first reprisals, as described earlier. Bassus's wife was 'both fair to look upon and of noble rank; for she was a descendant of Claudius Severus and of Marcus Antoninus'. Quite a pedigree; but there was some grumbling about the speed with which the marriage took place.

It seems that Heliogabalus had not even given her an appropriate time to mourn for her loss. This suggests a lack of sensitivity, although it could also point to impetuosity, or even a desire to put her under his own protection. At any rate, he seems to have been captivated by her beauty, unless this was just a blind to project his manhood. Whatever may have been the ulterior motive, the whirlwind marriage went ahead.

There was little that was complex in the marriage ceremony in the days of ancient Rome. There were some stipulations of course, many of which had been passed by that great proponent of marriage, Augustus Caesar. In his *lex Julia*, he allowed freed slaves to marry – but not to senators. It was also forbidden for men to marry prostitutes and actresses, whereas those stationed in the provinces were not allowed to wed local girls. There were conditions attached to the marriage of soldiers, and a connection between close relatives was taboo. A woman divorced for fornication could not marry again, whereas a woman divorced by mutual consent could do so.

No account of the wedding has been carried down to posterity, yet it is possible to deduce the activities from known precedents. Once Heliogabalus and his future wife had agreed to marry, they would have attended a ceremony known as the betrothal, at which the two families would have gathered, presents would have been exchanged and a dowry settled upon. In the case of the Emperor, of course, this would have been an elegant and sumptuous affair. A written agreement would have been produced and signed, the couple sealing their consent with a kiss. After these things were settled, the wedding day would have been set, in this case with remarkable abruptness. On the morning, the bride would have made herself as beautiful as possible, having a special hairdo for the occasion; then she would have dressed in her *tunica recta*, her white tunic tied with a belt done up in a 'knot of Hercules'. The veil – and shoes – were orange in colour. Heliogabalus would be at the head of a grand procession, leading his guests to the home of his fiancée. Now the wedding certificate would be signed, and the rest of the day would be spent in partying – and it is not hard to imagine the splendour of one of Heliogabalus's wedding feasts. Finally, everyone would have accompanied the couple to their new home in the Palace, and Heliogabalus would have carried his new wife over the threshold to avoid bad luck. It is impossible to imagine a wedding of Heliogabalus unaccompanied by exquisite shows and distributions of imperial gifts.

The hope of everyone, of course, was for a long and fruitful marriage. Heliogabalus's was destined to fail with spectacular abruptness; in no time at all they were divorced. Such an act was simplicity itself, because the marriage contract had no basis in law. It was simply a statement that the two parties were willing to live together; if they changed their minds, they would simply stop doing so. Bigamy did not exist, because if the couple were no longer living together, then a divorce was implied by that very fact. The wife was entitled to her dowry back, unless she had been found guilty of adultery in the special court known as the *quaestio*; in this case she was only entitled to half. Adultery did not apply to men.

The separation in Heliogabalus's case may have been due to his meeting with another lady of noble birth, one Cornelia Paula, whom he courted and married in January of 220. She had come from one of the highest families in Rome and so seemed a good match for the Emperor; perhaps, again, it had been arranged by his family; he himself declared that he had married early so that he soon might become a father, a feat which was held in doubt by many senators. Of this wedding ceremony we have at least more details; it was again a rich affair and once more large gifts were given out at the time; the people and soldiers feasted on public money, and grand gladiatorial games were announced. A record number of wild animals were killed for the entertainment of the crowds, including an elephant and fifty-one tigers. The Emperor watched the proceedings dressed in his purple robe of state. This marked another time of lavish donatives – as well as the people, the dignitaries also received a generous gift; 150 denares for all senators and knights, and 250 for the soldiers.

In keeping with Cornelia's lineage and his imperial status, Heliogabalus pronounced her 'Augusta', and it must have seemed that at last the wayward Emperor had settled down into a solid Roman marriage and was beginning to conform to Roman customs. Such opinions were short-lived; his wife quickly followed the path of Bassus's widow, and poor Augusta soon found herself as plain old Cornelia again. Apparently, Heliogabalus claimed to have found a blemish on her body. It may have been true: a boy as fastidious as Heliogabalus may well have been disgusted by a 'blemish', depending upon its size and unsightliness. These two divorces, however, were more than simple failed marriages; they were slights on a couple of the most eminent families in Rome. Whether these weddings were well-intentioned or not, the actions of the Emperor led to a further decrease in his popularity.

However, it was nothing compared to the furore which followed his next choice of bride. Surely not even his admitted inexperience in the ways of Roman customs and religion could excuse his actions; had he deliberately determined to cause as much havoc as he could he could hardly have done better. This time he chose a girl of noble birth – one Julia Aquilia Severa, connected to both the Julian and Severan houses – but there was a serious catch. She was a Vestal Virgin.

The Romans took the role of a Vestal Virgin very seriously indeed. The punishment for violating the vow of chastity was to be buried alive, as was the fate of one Clodia; this reflects the great solemnity of her position and the great esteem the nation held her in. It also reflects the fact that the Romans linked the well-being of Rome to that of the Virgins, so that any betrayal of vows was also a betrayal of the city. A betrayal was the most impious of blasphemies and so treated in the most savage manner. The power and prestige of the Vestal Virgins may be seen in the fact that the dictator Sulla spared the life of Julius Caesar after their intervention. In addition, they had seats of honour at the games, could pardon a condemned man simply their presence, they could vote, and nobody could attack them under pain of death. No-one could afford to ignore the priestesses of Vesta; and they were always mentioned by Augustus in his official prayers.

The Vestals were recruited from the best families in Rome, until such times as recruitment became difficult, when they were accepted from more plebeian backgrounds. They had to be virgins, of course, and they had to have no blemish on them; they must be born in Italy and have both parents living. These were the criteria for selection; and the successful candidate was inducted by the *pontifex maximus*, with the words:

'I take you, Amata, to be a Vestal priestess, who will carry out sacred rites which it is the law for a Vestal priestess to perform on behalf of the Roman people, on the same terms as her who was a Vestal on the best terms.'

The term of office for a Vestal Virgin was that of thirty years; ten as a student, ten as a servant, and ten as a teacher. Their main occupation was to keep the flame of Vesta burning; they were also used to discharge important tasks such as keeping important wills in their charge. They dressed simply, wearing a mantle or *palla* fastened with a broach called a *suffibulum*; on their heads they wore a covering called an *infula*.

It is a simple thing to envisage the outcry which followed this blatant sacrilege, one which not even the worst of the previous Emperors – not even Caligula himself – had dared to perpetrate. The senate were incensed, and seethed in rage as Heliogabalus took Julia from the House of the Vestals to be his bride. For him, the matter of marrying a high priestess of one of the most honoured goddesses in the Roman world was the most natural thing in the world; he may even have seen it as a compromise to the people. In his eyes, nothing could be more fitting than a wedding between the priest-king of the great sun-god and the priestess-queen of the honourable Vesta. It could be a joyous occasion, a marriage between the two cultures and an acknowledgement of the beliefs of the pious Romans. The marriage was made in Heaven, and their children would be as gods.

Hardly surprisingly, the senate did not see it like that at all; instead, it was a breach of one of the most revered protocols in the Empire. It is impossible to imagine that Maesa sat back and did nothing while this outrage was being perpetrated; and the only conclusion is that once again Heliogabalus asserted his authority and ignored her entreaties. In fact, it seems that the boy deliberately crossed his grandmother at every turn, something which must have infuriated her. Once again the imperial family must have feared for the continuous blunderings of their child, and doubtless under their instigation he sent a conciliatory letter to the senators, which did not appease them. He told them that a marriage between a priest and a priestess was backed by precedent and that he had thereby broken no holy laws. This might be the case in other scenarios, but certainly not for a Vestal Virgin. Seeming to realise this, he excused himself on the grounds that he had been carried away by the beauty of the maiden, and asked them to forgive his 'impious and adolescent transgression', thereby negating his previous argument and squarely blaming his lack of years and maturity. In a boy who wanted to offend no-one and yet offended everyone, there is a note of apology and a desire for reconciliation in his words. He also argued that his action was due to his overwhelming passion – a 'masculine failing'.

The senate, and especially Cassius Dio, were not fooled by the last argument, and suspected that this 'masculine failing' hid his innate lack of masculinity 'so that he may seem to be doing something manly'. His doubts seemed to be confirmed when the marriage went down the same forsaken road as the others, and he divorced his Vestal in favour of someone else. There is an outside possibility that if he had stayed faithful and built a solid marriage with Julia, the senate may eventually have come to terms with the matter, distasteful as it was; but Heliogabalus quickly closed the door on such a remote chance. His breaking with Julia only marked him as unreliable and unstable, adding extra fuel to the fire of discontent which was slowly rising high in the forum. It was said that he did return to Julia, but not before he had managed to steer his way through several other entanglements.

It is fascinating to watch the boy stumble from error to error with a kind of constancy which is amazing in its lack of reason or sense. Having failed in his own marriages, and having successfully enraged the senators at the same time, he still made efforts to promote the holy aspect of marriage while relentlessly forwarding the cause of his own native god. Throughout his reign he danced and officiated at the Temple and performed all the rites owed to the sun-god. His great aim seemed to be to attune the Roman people to the rituals of Elagabalus, and having failed in his intention by marrying a Vestal Virgin he turned his minds to the gods themselves. The senate had been stirred up by his option of two priests marrying – that of Vesta and that of the sun-god; but Vesta was the only Roman god with female priestesses, and so the only one to which he could ally himself in marriage. But if the Roman mythology could take the sun-god on board – if the god could be seen to marry a Roman deity

– then he could achieve a lasting place inside the pantheon. Following this twisted logic to its extreme conclusion, he decided to marry the god off.

Heliogabalus the Procurer now looked through the Roman catalogue of deities to find one suitable for his god, and with unfailing misprision he settled on Pallas Athena, the Greek equivalent of Minerva. Athena was the daughter of Zeus, born from his head, and so ranked as one of the highest of the deities appropriated by the Romans. She was also an ideal escort for a god, as she was chaste. This may have led to uncomfortable parallels with Heliogabalus and the Vestal. She was also the goddess of war, as well as having lesser functions; although a Greek borrowing, she was coupled with the ancient Etruscan goddes Menrva, and so enveloped the realms of poetry, wisdom, commerce, medicine and music.

Having found his choice, Heliogabalus next set out to view the goddess, and ordered her statue to be moved to his room. Once again, either purposefully or accidentally, he trampled on Roman sensibilities. The goddess was customarily worshipped unseen and hidden away in the Temple. Only once had this statue ever been moved, and that was when the House of the Vestals had burned down and it was moved for safety reasons; before that, it has remained with the Virgins since it was first shipped over from Troy, according to local beliefs. Not only was the Emperor planning a blasphemous parody of a marriage ceremony, he violated religious tradition by having it moved – simply because he wanted to peruse it.

To make matters worse, he did not think the goddess was an appropriate escort for his god, dressed as the statue showed in military armour. So, after such an act of gross sacrilege, he simply discarded the goddess.

Having perfunctorily dismissed Pallas, Heliogabalus now set his sights on one of the nine Muses, born to Zeus and Mnemosyne (Memory) – Urania, the goddess of astronomy, who was thought to have been born in Pieria, Thrace. This deity was more congenial to Heliogabalus as she was a great favourite of Arab tribes, particularly worshipped in Libya and Tunisia. The Phoenicians, to whom the Emperor had strong links, adored her as the goddess of the Moon, and this seemed eminently appropriate for the god of the sun. There was a statue in Rome of some antiquity; legend had it that Queen Dido herself constructed it at the time of the founding of Carthage. What could be better? In no time Heliogabalus had announced his decision to marry his native god to the Greek Muse in a wedding ceremony of extraordinary splendour.

The wedding day arrived and the Emperor had busied himself with all the preparations. Gifts were mandatory, and Heliogabalus even insisted on a large dowry to be sent from Carthage (two gold bulls – which, he later claimed, had been melted down). The statue of Urania had been placed in the Palace alongside the statue of the sun-god, and the bizarre ceremony was carried out. It was to be a day of great splendour, lavish feasts were given, and the whole country was invited – or ordered – to give themselves up to eating and merry-making. It is hardly necessary to add that it was also a day much anticipated by the common citizens of Rome; they had had experience of Heliogabalus's festivities before and their appetites must have been sharpened. The senate witnessed all the proceedings with a dour astonishment. Surely the gods could organise their own marriages? The pantomime played out before them was alien and irreverent; even symbolically it seemed foolish and shallow. Perhaps it would be more apt to say it was child-like; a game played by a young man who had not properly grown up and acted out his fantasies in the chair of the most powerful man on earth.

The real reasons for the discontent of the senate were the reckless expenditure and their unrelenting abhorrence of the Syrian sun-god, to whom they had been forced to appear as servants to the high-priest, and to whom all of their gods had been made subservient. A marriage between gods was not unheard of in Roman history, but this marriage would have seemed more blasphemous as it secured a place for El-Gabal even in the spinning mythos of the time. It was the obvious intention of Heliogabalus to have his god graciously accept the Roman religion; sadly, its only outcome was to distance himself even further from the political powers in the senate-house. In some ways, Heliogabalus saw the wisdom of at least partially accepting the old tenets, and his marriages may have been an attempt to placate an already disgruntled senate.

But as far as these marriages went, they seem to have been little else than a show for the people. As well as his numerous wives (six in all), he was known to have had many affairs out of wedlock, and this was surely for the same purpose. He had married Cornelia with the idea of becoming a father, and he had wedded a Vestal Virgin to become the father of god-like children. These children never materialised and gives rise to the question of his potency. As a boy with a serious gender identity problem, it also begs the question whether Heliogabalus was bisexual or not. The mist of almost two millennia shrouds such queries and the only clues are the hints given by the ancient histories. It is certain that he had problems with his sexual orientation, and that his sexual pleasures constituted not only the sexual partner but on occasion the sexual aim. His only love seemed to be a homosexual one, and he had a strong effeminacy which grew as he left puberty and entered adolescence. From a female point of view, the sexual act with a woman may well have been repulsive to Heliogabalus; and his boredom with each one of his women is reflected in the dizzying changes in partner he went through. However, more of Heliogabalus's complex *vita sexualis* in the next chapter.

   Was this claim of his – this wish to be a father – merely a blind for the people? Perhaps. But it must be remembered that at the centre of his religion – the rites to the sun-god – was the recurrent theme of fertility. His worship involved sacrifices for the sake of the perpetuation of the circle of life, and the orgiastic nature of the worship clearly demonstrates the major importance of procreation. That his religion was dear to him cannot be doubted, and if the effeminate Emperor felt it a religious duty to preserve the ring of life and give the world children of his own, he would find himself in an unenviable quandary. It is very likely that this was another reason for these imprudent marriages; that Heliogabalus was duty-bound to fulfil his destiny.

That his sexual problems were in direct conflict with his religious beliefs was no doubt a cause for great concern to the Emperor. But while these needs, urgent as they were, knocked at his door, he was beset by other urges, stronger and more powerful. Urges that would cause his name to be one of the blackest in the whole history of the Roman Empire, and which would rock the nation with scandal.

Chapter 8: Heliogabalus Heliogabala

If Heliogabalus had managed to estrange himself from the people and senate of Rome by his past actions, his latest behaviour would both shock and disgust an entire nation. Today, nothing that remains of the history of the Emperor escapes the taint of outrage, hatred and disdain. His memory is even more blackened than that of his most cruel and unjust predecessors, and some ancient biographers bluntly stated that they would rather not have the job of describing the details of his disgusting habits. Practically, Heliogabalus had done little to deserve such censure. His real crime was to offend the sensibilities of the time. Then again, in all honesty, his actions would excite a good deal of comment today, let alone in the world of ancient Rome.

It is time to deal with the question of Heliogabalus's sexuality. It was a matter which coloured much of his past life and was to have an all-embracing effect on the rest of his short existence on earth. It was also a subject which was to appal the senate and was to be a happy hunting-ground for his few later biographers who would use his gender problem to colour every aspect of his life from the cradle to the grave. An understanding of the driving forces inside the young man is imperative if we are to give an accurate and honest account of his behaviour in the coming months ahead.

It may be argued that such a task is impossible, that after the dust has settled over two millennia no-one can uncover the truth behind his mentality. Yet we have a number of concrete facts which are corroborated by the biographers whose works are still extant. Those facts, when examined in order, point to an unmistakable progression in the way Heliogabalus acted and behaved. This progression leads inexorably to a development of his personality which is both comprehensible and in a way unavoidable. Heliogabalus was the victim of a sexual predilection over which he had no control and which would drive him to seek satisfaction in whatever appropriate avenue was open to him.

It is plain from the very onset that Heliogabalus began life at a big disadvantage. Whether or not there was a hereditary psychological taint is questionable, although the parricidal tendencies of Antoninus and his personality may make one wonder. There was, however, an overpowering female influence in his earliest years, in the form of Soaemias, and later through Maesa, Mamaea and probably Domna. In infancy his mother dominated his little life, and was the voice of authority around him. His father was away much and died soon after, leaving no role model of masculinity around him. Throughout his young life, the female was the symbol of strength and discipline, and few men affected his life. At a young age, when he learned the duties of the priest, he was taught and aided by his mother.

Whatever the results of the influences of Maesa and Soaemas, if one is to study the driving forces in Heliogabalus's mind, it would be helpful to consider his own Oedipus Complex, a complex which, since Freud's discovery, still remains a vital component of present-day psychoanalysis. The classical description is one of a hatred directed towards the father, often ending in death-wishes, and a love for the mother, which needs to be resolved for mental health. Argument still rages over whether the converse is true; that an inverse complex can exist by which the attachment is made to the father and an equivalent death-wish towards the mother. Should the father be the centre of infant love fantasies, then the male may become the cherished object later, as can be demonstrated by many memories of father-attraction in the memories of adult homosexuals. The question of whether or not this constitutes a *normal* mental state is a matter of hot debate, and the yeas and nays still face up to each other in the psychoanalytic arena.

This is not the place to become embroiled in a psychoanalytical argument, and whatever the merits of both points of view it does seem that Heliogabalus experienced an inverted Oedipus complex. Later in life, the object-choice of his desires was exclusively male and so based on the experiences of his infancy. Later, he would resolve his complex completely, and this phase of his life will be discussed in the next chapter – but at the point when he was bundled off to a new life in Syria, the female side had begun to claim dominance over him.

It is not difficult to see how the jigsaw pieces fell into place when the young Varius was inducted into the new way of life as the high priest; when he was given sumptuous gowns of silk to wear and make-up applied to his eyes and lips. As the high priest heir apparent, Heliogabalus played an important role from the very beginning. Although other officials at the temple had some sort of authority, he was recognised as the future leader. Men became minions, praying to the sun-god. He travelled in lavish processions in gorgeous robes which were almost feminine in their richness; he wore necklaces and bracelets, and he danced. The only role-model for a father was the symbolic father of the skies – Heliogabalus the sun-god. On earth, he was growing up in an all-female environment where the women were the mistresses. It is hardly surprising that he was a candidate for sexual confusion; in Rome, where women were thought of as inferior and kept under male control, things must have seemed strange to him.

To begin with, there is strong evidence that Heliogabalus had a fetish for certain cloths, and loved the feel of fine fabrics – especially silks – against his skin. It is likely that, at an early age, these materials were substitutes for his female self, especially as these were delicate and his clothing preferences leaned towards the feminine. Such longings stretch back to early infancy and may be a soothing replacement for a lost or misplaced affection, a repressed sexual urge, or a symptom of latent feminism. Interestingly, late in his life, Freud equated every case of fetishism with a phallic root cause, and phallic symbolism played a prominent part in Heliogabalus's life.

The resolution of Heliogabalus's psychology is not easy; he never sat on a psychologist's couch and no-one would have been able to elucidate the complications in his mind. But should his conflict not be resolved, this could lead to a return to an earlier stage of development, a regression. As a baby, our first experiences are to do with ourselves; the sucking of the nipple, the feeding, the sensations of pleasure; it is the 'narcissistic' phase. Later comes the acknowledgement that something exists apart from oneself – the 'not-me'. A regression back to that state leads to narcissism, and certainly Heliogabalus displayed much of that, not least in his preoccupation with a search for pleasure, his constant desire for games and play, even his amusement at the expense of others, almost a failure to realise at these times that this 'not-me' world exists.

Effeminacy and narcissism were the two major facets of Varius's personality. This narcissism does not mean that the Emperor Heliogabalus was a true megalomaniac, in that he never used his absolute power for his own ends; the lavish spending he was guilty of may have been the result of a childish desire to spend, but it was all geared towards the aggrandizement of Rome. He himself did not victimise his fellow man in any way, in fact he was the model of consideration and generosity.

After the Year of the Five Emperors, and the plotting of the Bassiani for the imperial chair, it was the narcissism of Heliogabalus which reared its head. The women and their colleagues played on his innocence and feelings of grandeur and like a child actor he donned a soldier's uniform and won the Empire. It was a new conquering Caesar who made a triumphal entrance into the capital of the world. But once safely ensconced on the throne of Rome, Heliogabalus slipped back into his old desires and looked to satisfy his sexual needs. The girl in him reared her head once more.

At first his actions seem senseless and incomprehensible. He knew that effeminacy was distasteful to the muscular macho image of the Romans. He knew that he had to play the part of the mighty Caesar and yet he insisted on wearing effeminate clothing when on official duties despite the fact that it enraged the senate. Moreover, we know that he knew of this, because the historians keep reminding us that Maesa and the rest of her family continually advised him to step back in line and follow the customs of Rome. Why then did he flout their sensibilities and ignore the counsel of his family when he knew well that his course of action was unacceptable to his government? To Lampridius, the answer was simple – he was an 'empty-minded idiot'.

But at this stage of his life Heliogabalus's confusion over gender was not an idle fancy; at times he demonstrated a strong urge to be female, at first concealed behind religious extremes. He had himself circumcised, explaining this as a necessary part of his beliefs, and even this would have seemed peculiar to the Romans. They found much amusement in this trait of the Jews, and would mock them for this strange self-mutilation. But Heliogabalus left no doubt that this was based on sexual urges; he even expressed a desire for castration, and this wish for demasculination can admit of no other explanation than a fervent wish to change his sex. Although hidden behind religious zeal, this belies a powerful need to express his female nature.

If any shadow of doubt was to remain, the Emperor made his desires known without equivocation when he consulted the physicians and plainly expressed his wish to have a sex-change operation, then researched the possibility of having a vagina cut into him. This not only proves the inner conflict inside him, but suggests that the same conflict had been growing in his mind for some time. The strength of his desires is obvious in the extreme danger of the proposal in a time when anaesthetics were unknown and sex-change surgery was unheard-of; the sheer agony of such an operation would have been excruciating. Perhaps he made the suggestion in a climax of ritual orgasmic excitement. It is even doubtful whether he could survive such an ordeal, as the chance of infection were almost inevitable, and the results probably fatal. No doubt all of this was explained to him, and he did not go ahead with the proposal, but the fact that he did seriously consider such a course merely proves the desperation to which his sexual orientation had driven him. He could no longer brook being trapped in a male body.

In short, Heliogabalus had a core gender identity problem. In the twenty-first century, as public opinion becomes more lax, there has been a growing opportunity to study such a mental state, even if opinions vary. Gender identification disorder – now relabelled 'gender dysphoria' – has been written about and agonised over for many decades and several markers have been noted: a boy's inner insistence that he belongs to the opposite sex and a need to cross dress; play or fantasy in which the boy is a girl; an intense dislike of primary or secondary sexual characteristics and the desire for those of the female. Moreover, as the boy grows he develops a keen desire to be accepted as a member of the opposite sex and to live as one.

As far as Heliogabalus is concerned, there is little doubt that his mental processes were predominantly, if not exclusively, female. This core problem should be carefully dissociated from his other mental idiosyncrasies; a distinction has to be made between what is normal sexuality and what is abnormal psychology. Should we assume that Heliogabalus had a perfectly female mind, it follows that a lot of his preferences for the remainder of his life (although not all) become quite normal – even heterosexual. His choice of partner, his penchant for dressing in female attire – both of these are quite acceptable, provided the subject is a woman. Heliogabalus, then, was predominantly female – no easy thing in the Rome of the third century.

He was therefore left with the only option open to him; to accept his fate and somehow come to terms with his femininity. But his actions plainly show how powerful were the driving forces within him. It is all but impossible to imagine that he could continue with a normal masculine life; yet what could he do? He was hemmed in by the dictates of society, which gave strict guidelines on the rules of etiquette and 'normal' behaviour. These strictures should not be underestimated as they were of immense importance in the development of his conflicts.

The impossibility of living out his desires and obeying the regulations of ancient Rome produces a strong conflict in

Heliogabalus, but often the wish to feel release grew until it could no longer be borne. Like a drug addict, Heliogabalus felt the need for the drug rise up inexorably until he must feel satisfaction. This satisfaction was felt when an appropriate compromise was reached; and after the need had passed it was replaced with a feeling of terrible shame; and the need for degradation and punishment achieved in the real risk he ran during his actions.

In effect, Heliogabalus did little physical harm. All of the executions carried out in his reign may easily be put down to political expediency, and his role in them is not clear, although as head of the state the blame was put down to him. He did have many animals killed, but again this was the norm for his time and a common form of entertainment, however barbaric it may appear to modern eyes; often his only fault was one of excess. But not even the historians, so hostile to him, could find evidence of sadism in him. Nero enjoyed watching Christians hung up in wax suits and burned alive in his garden; Caligula's atrocities were notorious, and even Claudius had an unfortunate taste for torture. Nothing like that could be laid at the door of the boy whose real fault simply lay with his struggles against his own sexuality.

This was almost peculiar in a time when sadism was almost the norm. It was a time of master and slave, and more often than not the slaves were savagely treated. When the Bacchanalia was active, the Greek celebration of sex was distorted and the rites became perverse and twisted, with scenes of flagellation and total abandon. Cruelty filtered through Roman life even down to the household, and was not limited to the men. Juvenal, in his Satires, attacks the sadistic housewives, as in this example, where the mistress of the house punishes the slave Psecas for a hairdressing fault:

The house looks like Phalaris' court,
All bustle, gloom and tears.
The wretched Psecas, for the whip prepared,
With locks dishevelled, and with shoulders bared,
Attempts her hair; fire flashes from her eyes,
And 'Wretch! why this curl so high?' she cries.
Instant the lash, without remorse, is plied,
And the blood stains her bosom, back and side…

Male slaves are treated with even more severity:

'Go crucify that slave!' 'For what offence?
Who's the accuser? Where's the evidence?
Hear it all! no time, whatever time we take
To sift the charges, when man's life's at stake,
Can ever be long: hear it all, then, I advise!'-
'You wimp! is a slave a man?' she cries:
'He's innocent? – very well, - it's my command,
My will: let that, sir, for a reason stand.'

With such examples of sadism being apparent in the social structure of Rome (even though Juvenal exaggerated to make his point), Heliogabalus was marked more by his leniency than his harshness, even more strange when one considers that he was a mere boy and may perhaps have been expected to display a child-like cruelty. It would seem that his passive nature had little relish in acts of sadism and perhaps even here a strain of effeminacy can be detected.

Heliogabalus's impossible dilemma – how to give release to his female side and still remain within the dictates of Roman society – was at first answered in his native garb, and by wearing that he could hide behind his foreign background. Eschewing the manly Roman toga, Heliogabalus donned his native costume of expensive material and, his ear-rings and jewellery tinkling, danced into the senate-house. The material of his dress he excused on the grounds of a skin allergy, and his entire costume on Syrian preference, but there is no doubt that he knew his appearance would be offensive to the eyes of the senators. He refused the advice of his family and advisors, surely because he was well aware that his appearance was effeminate, and although he made cogent excuses for this display it was no more or less than an act of transvestism and exhibitionism. Moreover, the senate knew it too, and did not appreciate it.

Even Heliogabalus's colour preferences were odious to the eyes of the grave senate; white had been and still was the representation of aesthetic good taste and its solemn simplicity was admired by the Romans. Instead, in keeping with the tastes of the East, the Emperor took to wearing colours of remarkable brilliancy, scarlet and gold and deep azure. Not only did this seem unseemly to the people, it smacked of degeneracy and depravity.

As they became more and more aware of Heliogabalus's feminine nature, every extravagance in his mannerisms was interpreted in this light. Wherever he went he insisted that flowers of all hues should be strewn in his path – Hay mentions lilies, violets, and narcissus. Moreover, he had a positive passion for fragrances, which, as with everything he did, erred on the side of excess. Of course, Lampridius condemns the Emperor for his dissolution, but conveniently forgets that many Emperors before him – Caligula and Nero, for example - also shared this passion for perfumes and would spend extortionate sums on the rarest and most exotic unguents they could buy. This was simply an extreme extension of a habit which pervaded throughout Rome; it was commonplace for men to perfume their tunics, togas, horses, rooms – even the streets. It becomes apparent that far from suggesting a covert femininity, a penchant for perfumery merely represented the prevailing fashion of the day. What became objectionable to the people was the Emperor's obsession with these fine fragrances, an obsession which came to suggest abnormal lusts.

A fondness of scents and aromatics was not limited to the Romans, like many other things, they copied the fashion from their neighbours. Cheap scents were easy enough to obtain, but the rarest and most exotic were greatly sought after by the affluent. It is a sign of the great respect the Magi had for the infant Jesus that they brought him gifts of the most expensive kind; gold, yes, but also the most envied of perfumes, myrrh and frankincense. The ancient Egyptians were noted for their expertise in perfume manufacture and honed the process to a fine art; Dioscorides (the Greek botanist) claimed that Egyptian unguents were the finest in the world. Apart from the wish to smell good, people used perfumes for medicinal and religious practices, certain perfumes being recognised as efficacious in the repulsion of demons – and, of course, incense was burned for the delectation of the gods.

Looking through the testimonies of ancient historians, it is clear that Heliogabalus was effeminate in almost every aspect of his life. His obsession with fashion, his love of cookery, his fanaticism for costly perfumes and flowers, all point to a female character, especially for the time. Added to this are his penchant for helping out at market stalls, like a waiting girl, his need to wear feminine clothes, his sensitivity and his general demeanour, all suggesting a female constitution. Even his love of gladiatorial contests was probably based on his love of seeing his male heroes in action like the sighing girls of Pompeii.

The behaviour of Heliogabalus would have been unfavourably compared to that of Greeks, and everyone knew that Greece was the heart of depravity – especially when it came to sexuality. Men there were expected to groom themselves well – those not doing so could even be punished – and the latest fashions would be posted at the door of the temples. Men would wear make-up, and even paint their nails with henna; they would perfume various parts of their bodies with the customary scents; baccaris for the feet, ivy for legs, mint for the arms and marjoram for the hair. Such behaviour repelled the Romans – but then, everyone knew what sort of people the Greeks were…! Such was the Roman attitude.

Heliogabalus, with his background of pomp and magnificence, went to extremes, and poured mountains of aromatics on the altar of his god. He used the most expensive of them to heat his bathrooms; he banked up the fires with Indian perfumes, and burned precious balms in his oil-lamps. The sheer scale of his excess beggars belief. Myrrh, cinnamon, saffron and aloes were burned away twenty-four hours a day. It is hard to even imagine the fortunes that were squandered in his reckless insistence on living a life-style beyond that of the most fabulous of kings; and the senate gossiped about the dissipated life led by this most effeminate of Emperors.

The boy also made use of his religious practices and delighted in wearing the luxurious robes of office and ornamentation in his rituals, to which the most noble gentlemen of Rome were invited – and dared not refuse. There, flaunting himself in his feminine clothes, dancing for the edification of the watching audience, whipping himself into an orgiastic delight as he celebrated strange fertility rites, Heliogabalus exhibited himself to the whole of Rome, who witnessed the affair with barely-concealed disdain. True, the Emperor wished to promote his beloved sun-god, but adoration of the Heavenly Father certainly went hand in hand with a blatant form of exhibitionism which he felt impelled to enact.

The scandal-loving Lampridius would have us believe that Heliogabalus loved to put on private shows in which he played the part of a woman. Although the account cannot be accepted at face value, such sentiments would not have been out of character:

> ...He used to have the story of Paris played in his house, and he himself would take the rôle of Venus, and suddenly drop his clothing to the ground and fall naked on his knees, one hand on his breast, the other before his genitals, his buttocks projecting out and thrust back in front of his partner in depravity. He would likewise model the expression of his face on that with which Venus is usually painted, and he had his whole body depilated, judging it the greatest enjoyment of his life to look fit and worthy so that he might arouse the lusts of the greatest number of people.

The goddess Venus seems to have been a particular favourite of Heliogabalus, putting aside for one moment his obvious commitment to the sun-god. Venus was widely revered among the Romans, and judging by her countless epithets covered a wide range of functions – she was known as 'the Armed', 'the Victor', 'the Celestial', 'the Friend', 'the Golden One', 'The Changer of Hearts', 'the Indulgent', 'the Lucky' and 'the Purifier', among others. But Heliogabalus was probably drawn to the goddess for other reasons. She had a conflicting role as patron of prostitutes and defender of virtue, so such a mixture may have been attractive to someone of Heliogabalus's mental make-up, as will soon be demonstrated. Moreover, she was the goddess of love and so depicted as a being of supernatural loveliness, and what better role-model for an imperial transvestite?

The reason for this public scarcely hidden show of femininity is not difficult to determine and was bound up with the need for punishment and derision. He would have seen the contempt in the eyes of the senate and have been assured of it when his family tried to control his actions. But Heliogabalus was hell-bent on a path from which he could not veer, even if he tried. The satisfaction – the sexual pleasure – of seeming feminine and the scorn it drew was a drug which, it seems, drove him on. The suggestion that he acted the way he did simply because he was the Emperor and so all-powerful, that he had no need for self-abasement when he was in ultimate control, does not fit in with his actions. They betray a consistent wish for humiliation and punishment. Social taboos, both Arabic and Roman, taught him shame, even at the top of the world, and his inner conflict could not be resolved by the administration of power; on the contrary, one could argue that his standing in the world only increased his feelings of worthlessness and insufficiency.

Given some small satisfaction in the fulfilment of his sexual desires, it only led to more. Gradually he became more audacious. As the senate became accustomed to his appearance, he managed to keep himself in the glare of contempt by adopting stronger and stronger measures; if the titillation caused by his exhibitionism began to waver, he spiced things up by ensuring that no-one could mistake his intentions. He took to wearing mascara, and then rouge on his cheeks. One can only imagine the tremulous anticipation he felt when he first walked through the door of the *curia* and appeared before his ministers, now undeniably feminine. More is never enough. As he became more and more effeminate, the senators became more and more appalled and, accordingly, he felt the desire to go even further.

It is important to note that up to this point Heliogabalus had never settled on the idea of a perfect partner. It is likely that he did not even consider the matter, and more than likely that he was unaware of the full ramifications of the sexual orientation he had. He was a man, albeit a very effeminate one, and age-old custom dictated that he should have a female partner. His sad fumbling in the realms of wedlock have already been discussed, but what seems strange is the amount of fumbling he perpetrated. If he really wanted to fit in with the Roman ways, why did he not simply settle on one choice and leave it at that?

The only feasible answer is that Heliogabalus was seriously and intently looking for an ideal partner. It would seem that the choice of a male partner had not entered his head, or if it had, it was quickly repressed. He may well have been confused when the unions did not go to plan and desperately hunted around for someone who could satisfy him as a loving partner. There is no reason to doubt that he was serious when he talked of a man's weakness when picking a bride which did not suit the senate. In all likelihood, he still felt that he was, or should be, a man, and one can only be left to speculate over the futility of any sexual activity which may have occurred between him and his wives. The impression is of a confused adolescent who is searching for a dream he doesn't quite understand. In the end, he simply gave up.

As Heliogabalus became more embroiled in his mental problems, he began to consider his own masturbation fantasies, at the centre of which were his fantasies of being a girl. Moreover, for the first time the misty idea of a homosexual relationship stirred in his mind. This may well have given him feelings of great shame and he shut out the possibility with as much force as he could. This is evident from the fact that the first leanings towards homosexuality blossomed not with tentative attempts to nurture relationships of that kind, but with hidden fancies which distorted his leanings and developed into neurotic punishment-fantasies.

His official functions took him to many areas of the city and on occasion he would pass through the poorer areas where he would sometimes notice the prostitutes soliciting in the dirty streets and around the 'taverns' (*stabulae*). He would also see them outside the Circus Maximus, where they would gather to pick up men coming from the games, whose lust had been stoked by the gladiatorial shows and animal fights they'd witnessed there. The favourite dens here were underneath the arches, and this was so well known that everyone knew where to find them. The sight of provocative women flaunting themselves at hot-blooded muscular young men fired his imagination, and one can imagine the envy he felt and the wish that he himself took take their place.

The fulfilment of such a strange ambition was not impossible, after all. The Palace had many exits and entrances, and it would not be difficult to sneak away unseen and do whatever his heart desired. Such a course was fraught with danger, but such risk may have lent spice to the venture. In the end, he decided to follow his whim, and, dressing like a common street slut, he made his way to the dark unsavoury streets were the ladies of the night plied their trade. Outside the dingy, dirty old inns Heliogabalus stood among the others, dressed as a young coquette, luring the common man towards him.

Despite the fact that coins from his reign were roughly cut and depict a head with rather coarse features, Heliogabalus was an attractive youth. So much can be seen from the surviving bust which is on display in the Capitoline Museums, a rounded, slightly female face and unmistakably good-looking. Even his contemporaries could not deny this; earlier it was noted that, in the account of Herodian, it was Heliogabalus's beauty which attracted the attention of the soldiers billeted in Emesa - and while abhorring the Emperor's appearance in the senate, even Dio had to admit it:

He didn't wish to sin secretly, but appeared publicly with eyes painted and cheeks rouged; these cosmetics spoiled a face which was naturally handsome.

It takes little imagination to see that, with fine wig, jewelry and make-up, Heliogabalus could have made a convincing – even an attractive – girl. No doubt he knew it well enough. One is left to imagine the thrill he must have felt when he first took up his place among the whores of the street, or the titillation when approached by would-be clients. Sexual excitement and shame mixed together in one moment. He would have known that he could not stay incognito for long, and part of the thrill was possibly in that feeling of danger, in the probable wish to be caught out and punished. As well as gratifying his need to express his femininity, he was also punishing himself by his public humiliation and abasement which he thought he deserved according to the morals of the day. There he was, the Emperor of Rome, the most powerful man in the world, standing in the street as a common hooker, the lowest of the low.

The manner in which Heliogabalus strove to convince the passing men that he was a female was a fixed tradition among the transvestite homosexuals (*molles*) of Rome. The Stoic philosopher Epictetus claimed that as all men are naturally hairy, depilation of body hair is a sure sign that a man wanted to be female, so it is certain that this is what Heliogabalus did – especially the legs and buttocks. Eyebrows would be plucked and painted and make-up applied; he would also perfume himself – balsam was the commonest perfume, but someone as extravagant as Heliogabalus might well have used the most expensive varieties. His clothing would be see-through, and made of fine silk of saffron or green colour. As for his gait, he would practise the feminine manner, and walk as naturally as he could; no doubt he had practised this in the privacy of the Palace.

The scandal which accompanied Heliogabalus's forays into the twilight world of prostitution can only be appreciated given a better understanding of the disgust with which the oldest profession was held at that time. The opinion towards prostitutes in ancient Rome was more odious than it is now, and a hooker was classed as a woman of infamy, someone who could not even give evidence in court or file a complaint against rape. A girl had to register to solicit, and the official would strenuously try to dissuade the girl if she was from a decent background. Once registered on the official role there was no turning back; the procedure was irreversible and the girl would be classed as a whore for the rest of her life, closing off any avenue for reform or respectability. A prostitute was aware that any client had the right to abuse her, or to beat and flog her if his tastes so dictated; moreover, Heliogabalus knew that too.

He would also have noted the customary practices of prostitution. If the prostitute was in a tavern, waiting for a client, on the door of her cell would be written her name, to indicate that she was available for sex. When she had been chosen, and the price agreed, the client would enter and the prostitute would turn the sign so that it indicated OCCUPATA. The room was usually quite bare, apart from some kind of lamp and a makeshift bed or cot covered with a blanket which could also serve as a curtain. This world of closed doors, darkened alleys and dark deeds became the chosen milieu of the world's most powerful man.

Some professions were inextricably linked with the stain of prostitution, especially the theatre and girl dancers; in fact a female dancer was immediately classed as a whore, as were many musicians and theatrical types - *mimae* (mime artists), *cymbalistriae* (cymbal players), *ambubiae* (singing girls) and *citharistriae* (harpists). The only reason they did not avail themselves of the chance to enrol on the register of prostitutes was that under their thin guise they could hang onto some degree of respectability, although everyone knew that, in reality, it was practically non-existent. This connection was clear from the scandal which broke out when the Emperor freely danced around the Temple under the disguise of a priest, or when he ended his spectacles with a dancing performance of his own, dressed in the most effeminate of clothing. Few people could help comparing their ruler with the commonest of *meretrices*. It did little for his reputation that he consorted with the theatrical performers, either.

The whole subject of whoring in ancient Rome strikes at the heart of the hypocrisy which was so rampant in all classes of life, but more especially in the top echelons. It is clear that although prostitution was deplored by the sensibilities of ancient Rome, they were also used, and commonly, too. Laws against visiting brothels were so useless as to be worthless. As Cicero himself declared:

> If there is anyone who thinks that young men should be banned from having sex with the whores of the town, he is really austere! That, ethically, he is in the right, I can't deny: but nevertheless, he is at odds not only with the sexuality of the modern times, but even with the habits of our ancestors and what they permitted themselves. For when was this *not* done? When was it ever punished? When was it ever even *criticised*?

Dio, with some acuteness, guessed that the only reasons Heliogabalus had put on such a show of heterosexuality in his many entanglements was simply a means of investigating the art of sex from a woman's point of view. How could he be a woman and play the woman's part when he knew nothing of sexual matters? Given that the six marriages he had were not bisexual flings – and no-one can be totally certain – then these shams might have been by the way of experimentation, an examination of the female body and an education into how they are satisfied and aroused. It would also be necessary, as a latent homosexual, for him to have some idea of male desire too, although all of this might have been outside the grasp of his as yet unformed personality.

The knowledge that his whoring antics must become common gossip was soon realised, and before long the senators had wind of the newest outrages perpetrated by their Emperor. Their revulsion can easily be imagined. No-one knows how long he had spent in these disgusting pastimes, but soon even that was not enough to slake the Emperor's appetite. His activities were repeated and exaggerated in street talk, and later reports are possibly coloured by stories coined to amaze and astound the credulous. But there is little doubt his behaviour was enough to repulse his contemporaries. It was reported that he took to emptying brothels of their women, and taking his place as the sole prostitute, making lewd suggestions and beckoning to the customers as they came in. Despite all this, the Emperor was in a strong political position, all his adversaries having been dealt with, so there was little the senate could even say, let alone do. And their impotence only egged on the boy to more and more outrages.

Now that his deviation was an open secret, and everyone knew the hidden life he led, he went further and further. He taunted even the nobles with his fantasies and allowed his self-humiliation to spread to them. He chose a room in the Palace and turned it into a brothel, where he would appear as the common harlot, decked out in finery and soliciting custom even in the heart of his royal residence. For flattery's sake – or for sycophancy – some of high rank accepted his advances and took advantage of his offers. Of course, the senate was disgusted, and Dio noted:

He used his body both for doing and allowing many strange things, which no one could endure to tell or hear of; but his most obvious acts, which it would be impossible to hide, were the following. He would go to the taverns

by night, wearing a wig, and there ply the trade of a female whore. He went to the most notorious brothels, kicked out the prostitutes, and acted the prostitute himself. Finally, he set aside a room in the palace and there committed his indecencies, always standing nude at the door of the room, as the prostitutes do, and shaking the curtain which hung from gold rings, while in a soft and melting voice he solicited the passers-by. There were, of course, men who had been specially instructed to play their part. As in other matters, so in this business, too, he had many agents who searched for those who could best please him by their dirtiness. He would collect money from his johns and pride himself on his profits; he would also argue with his fellow sluts, claiming that he had more lovers than they and made more money.

Now the Emperor's family and advisors knew that Heliogabalus was going to take no heed of them but was determined to continue his dangerous course towards destruction. As the voices of reason and persuasion died slowly away, Heliogabalus began to lose all sense of propriety, and openly affected his femininity wherever he went. He did make one concession, however, and that was when his state duties demanded that he act in the role of judge; during that time he would appear and act as became a man. At all other times, he followed his own inclinations.

When trying someone in court he really had more or less the appearance of a man, but everywhere else he showed affectations in his actions and in the quality of his voice. For instance, he used to dance, not only in the orchestra, but also, in a way, even while walking, performing sacrifices, receiving salutations, or delivering a speech.

This was not to say that Heliogabalus lost that sense of shame or degradation he felt during these times. He had a need to be punished which increased as his sexual leanings became more apparent. As a female, the obvious target of his affections were male, and this was again against the moral codes he had been brought up with. To punish himself and give the veneer of righteous indignation, he dreamed up another psycho-drama which obviously stemmed from a masturbation fantasy. He would choose a couple, of which the male was the object of his desire, but who was married. He would then seduce the wife and plan the timing so that he was caught *in flagrante delecto*.

Again, fantasy became reality, and he acted out in real life the fantasies which had haunted him. He would visit the home of the couple and set about the seduction just as the man returned home. Then he would offer no defence but stand passively as the man beat him and thrashed him. The unholy desire he had for the man would be punished, and the avenger would be the man in person; Heliogabalus himself would gain the dubious pleasure of the masochistic beating. Sometimes he would be thrown out of the house, his face black and blue after repeated blows. Of course, the outraged husband would soon spread the gossip, and again the bizarre antics of the Emperor would reach the ears of the senate.

…..He would often let himself to be caught in the very act, as a result of which he used to be violently insulted by his 'husband' and beaten, until he had black eyes. His affection for this 'husband' was no flirtation, but an ardent and firmly fixed passion, so much so that he not only did he not

become enraged at any such harsh treatment, but on the contrary loved him the more for it and actually wished to make him Caesar; he even threatened his grandmother when she opposed him in this matter, and he became at odds with the soldiers largely on this man's account. This was one of the things that was destined to lead to his destruction.

Strange as it seems to us now, the formulation of bizarre and peculiar drama-fantasies is not unusual in masochism. Indeed it is a key feature. Today, brothels dealing with this particular type of sexual inclination often contain rooms which pander to the willing victim's tastes. Dungeons await the prisoner, equipped with the rack, with whips and assorted instruments of torture. Whipping-posts and benches wait ready for use. There may be school-rooms, in which the adult schoolboy takes his lessons and is inevitably caned by his stern schoolmistress. Prostitutes may be asked to dress up as nazis. Slaves may be harnessed to chariots and traps to act as pony-boys and pull the mistress or master around a field. Fettered victims may be forced to enter a boxing ring to be pummelled by the object of his desire. There seems to be never-ending potential in these fantasies designed to humiliate or punish, physically and mentally, leading even to a wish for castration and death.

Why did Heliogabalus need punishment and self-abasement? As described earlier, much of the reason may have had a lot to do with a feeling of worthlessness, but it may also have gone deeper than that. Strange as it may seem, research has shown that it is usually the 'important' members of society – including judges, attorneys, policemen, celebrities – who bow to this sort of inclination. It is not difficult to see how a period of release, of total surrender – may be craved by such people, and Heliogabalus would fit into the category. One psychoanalytic theory is that an infant forges a 'false self' to ensure parental love, and that masochism is an attempt to break away the scaffolding that supports this self and tries to find its 'true self'. Whether this is so or not, the ideal of the masochist is to be deprived of the sexual object, and the pleasure is increased when that object is in reality inferior. It is self-denial for one's own projected inadequacies, and the reason for the need for punishment lies in the mind of the subject.

The background of many masochists often contains evidence of a domineering woman, most often the mother. The early life of Heliogabalus fits well with such infantile influences. Even without other adverse influences, this can often produce an early feminisation, the earliest sexual conflict, possibly brought about unconsciously by the mother's desire for a son to be a girl. The early dawning of the idea of masculinity can therefore not only intensify this conflict, but also a sense of humiliation, especially if the infant feels ridiculed by the woman due to his sexuality. One psychotherapist expressed a clear conviction to me that Heliogabalus may have been teased as a young infant because he had a penis. The earliest feelings of sexual humiliation can be powerful and enduring, and if the continual sexual life of the boy is consistently negative, it can lead for a wish to return – to regress – back to those original states of comfort in the arms of the mother and humiliation at his 'inverted' sexuality.

The Oedipus complex, already described, takes place in (according to Freud) a phase in infantile development known as the 'phallic' phase, when stimulation is directed to the genitals rather than, say, the mouth. The awareness that a woman lacks a penis can lead to terror, in that the little boy fears that some people have lost their phallus – have been castrated. This 'castration complex' can be of enormous importance in the development of varying psychoneuroses. To complicate matters, the dominant mother takes on many forms of the masculine, father-image – the strength, the dominance, and the moral standards normally given to the male. In such a mind-set the individual can allay his fears by imaging that the mother has a penis after all – and so is born the idea of the 'phallic woman', who plays such an important role in heterosexual masochism.

Meanwhile, it is pertinent to consider the role of Heliogabalus's father. It does not mean that if a boy is brought up in a single-parent environment that he cannot have normal resolution of the Oedipus complex; the father-figure remains as an unconscious element in his make-up. What may complicate matters is if the mother takes on his role to an alarming degree. In the mind of someone like Heliogabalus, the father-image is transferred to his phallic religion – El-Gabal – the sun-god and father of mankind; it is hardly surprising that a fertility-based religion with a high phallic content should attract a boy like him, onto which he could transfer his pent-up needs. But in the normal family background, the father-figure becomes demoted as secondary to the intense domineering characteristics of the woman. This may not be a decisive factor in his choice of partner, but certainly the negative Oedipus complex –

father-love and mother-hate – was of great importance to his development.

Humiliation and love were inextricably bound up in his earliest memories when he reached a more objective stage in his development and first fumbled with that idea of 'not-me'. They were to remain that way with Heliogabalus for most of his life. Being hunted by the enduring memories of lost childhood – the need to find love in that earliest of all relations – drives the masochist to re-enact those lost feelings of thwarted desire. All the cravings for humiliation, self-abasement and punishment stem from this, and are always accompanied with a sense of shame and worthlessness. As the complex begins with a desire for abasement, it dovetails neatly into the social and cultural demands of the day – that men should be men, and that perversion is a taboo against society. This leads to a secondary appeal for the masochist – not only can he feel satisfaction in his re-enacted humiliation, he can achieve further punishment by popular censure.

There were further stimuli for the acting-out of masochistic fantasy-dramas for someone like Heliogabalus. First, it could produce an environment in which he achieved total release in the climax of the drama, at which point the craving for punishment becomes intense, the love-object is magnified out of all proportion as a figure of divine sexual appeal, and conversely the victim is belittled to an infinitesimal degree - the epitome of insignificance. The conditions for humiliation are heightened to the level of the sublime. Most importantly, for once the masochist can control his addiction, can set limits on his suffering, and can gain a powerful release from his oppressive longings, which act like a drug and force him to find relief at any cost. This strange paradoxical balance between control and surrender is a crucial part of the mechanics of masochism.

One thing stands out in all of Heliogabalus's fantasy-dramas, and that is the need to be beaten or abused, not by homosexual men, but exclusively by heterosexual men. This leads to an apparent contradiction, as one may well assume that his love-object should be the avenger, punishing him for his debased desires. Yet in all the scenarios we see the opposite. Heliogabalus purposely chose a married man – a heterosexual man – to be his tormentor after pretending to seduce his wife. As a prostitute, he is at the mercy of purely heterosexual men, who at the time were legally allowed to beat or whip the whore if she didn't please him (as Heliogabalus obviously wouldn't). In parading before Rome as a girl Heliogabalus invited abuse, not by homosexuals, but by the powers-that-be, the heterosexual masculine community in which he lived. On two levels we can see the attempted resolution of the Oedipus complex; the revenge of the father for the seduction of the mother (positive complex) and the punishment because Heliogabalus is inadequate and so unable to satisfy the sexual desires of his father, who has become the true object of his affections (negative complex).

But things are not as simple as that. The husband bursting in through the door, the client selecting him in the street, the punisher, may well represent a father-figure, but that figure is entrenched with the infantile projection of the phallic woman, an early resolution of the castration complex. In his little fantasies he was not only being punished for being an inadequate love-partner for his desired father, but was also reliving his earliest humiliation at the hands of his mother and grandmother. This repeated attempt to relive and somehow undo those infantile traumas lies hidden in the core of most masochistic acts. It is hardly surprising that Heliogabalus was a psychological mess.

As stated earlier, many masochists come from a line of successful men in their working lives. No-one could be more successful than Heliogabalus. From the heights of his status as Emesan high priest to the dizzy Olympian levels of being the most powerful man on earth, Heliogabalus held in his small hands the fate of the entire Empire. It is interesting to see what he did with that power. He gave it away, both psychologically and consciously. Objectively, he gave away – without stint – the physical benefits of his power, his wealth, to all and sundry. Mentally, he abdicated his grandeur by parading himself before the heterosexual public as a man of no worth, a pervert, someone to be despised. Linked closely with his self-abasement was an overwhelming need to love and to be loved, showing themselves in his need to allay suffering and his own intense urge to please all of his people. On an unconscious level, he would be aware of the disdain in which he was held, and yet consciously there were times when he seemed blissfully ignorant, believing his own wish to be a beloved father to his nation. This need for love and humiliation is, as already noted, a driving and primitive force in the mechanics of masochism, the need to assuage feelings of love through re-enactment of his debasement and shame.

More is never enough. Despite his increasing dissipation, he was not taken to task seriously by anyone, so that his transvestism in the senate became increasingly obvious. His next step was to alienate the senate and the state even further. He had shown an increasing tendency to flaunt his sexuality in public and even in the core of government, but now he decided to exhibit himself before the whole world. He began to receive foreign dignitaries and ambassadors dressed as a girl. As they entered his apartments, they would look wide-eyed at the coquette lounging before them, fully made up and dressed in female garments. It is impossible to imagine a western leader in the twenty-first century appearing at an official meeting dressed in drag, let alone at a time when transvestism was thought of as a disgusting aberration. None of this discouraged Heliogabalus, who probably found more satisfaction in putting himself to the global pillory, degrading himself before the whole world.

One of the tragedies of Heliogabalus's short life is that no-one recognised these actions for what they were - abortive attempts of an adolescent to find a solution away from the derailed path of homosexuality. These episodes of masochism were desperate attempts to come to terms with a sexuality which was growing and which he repeatedly tried to deny. This denial of his homosexual character brought him great pain and suffering, as well as a measure of sexual release. Unfortunately, these months of development, which were shortly to be straightened out, took place not in a boy's backyard but on the centre stage of the entire world, under the floodlights of the whole Empire.

It would seem that Heliogabalus's masochistic fantasy-dramas began at quite a young age. Almost certainly they were in evidence almost as soon as he arrived in Rome, and were running in tandem with his ineffectual attempts at marriage, which fits in with the fact that both were attempts at dealing with the strange impulses which were dogging him. As far back as the attempt by Bassus and Messala to oust him as Emperor, the activities in the royal palace were common gossip throughout the capital. What his several wives thought of his bizarre pursuits can only be imagined, but it is certain that they were instrumental in tarnishing his name among the respected citizens of Rome. They merged with the obvious outward trappings of his femininity to strengthen the view that he was perverse in body and mind.

At the same time, there is no doubt that the Emperor enjoyed his new-found freedom, even at the risk of making implacable enemies, but yet more clouds were gathering. The army was furious at seeing their leader running around as a girl and would not put up for long with the degrading of their homeland. Politicians gathered in clandestine groups to talk of the future. The hostile feelings against Heliogabalus were rising slowly but surely towards a crescendo, but Heliogabalus had not finished. If the senate was wondering what this crazy mixed-up kid would do next, they would soon find out.

Chapter 9: How The Assyrian Became Tiberianus

Even the gods showed their disapproval with several omens. The Goddess Isis, astride her dog at the entrance to her Temple, was seen to turn her head and peek inside; no-one seems certain exactly what the inquisitive Egyptian was peering at, but it was a bad omen by anybody's standards. Rome held its breath and everyone knew that some disaster awaited the state.

So far, no disaster had happened; in fact, on the international front, all seemed quiet and peaceful. With increasing eccentricity, Heliogabalus continued to perform his imperial functions although he was mostly driven by his personal tastes and desires. As far as entertainment went, he still took especial pleasure in the games, as they afforded a glimpse of men showing off their prowess and their muscles. So enthusiastic was the boy for the games that he held them at every given opportunity, thereby depleting even further the national coffers; but a boy is exactly what he was, wanting more, more, more, regardless of cost.

One of Heliogabalus's heroes was the acclaimed wrestler Aurelius Helix, who was a formidable athlete who also specialised in *pancratium*, a Roman form of *pankration*, which was a Greek martial art combining boxing and wrestling together. His fame spread far and wide, and he was so feared that he applied to participate in both wrestling and *pankriation* at the ancient Olympics, but the jealous lowlanders – or Eleans, on whose land the games were held – refused to permit him to do so. There were no such discriminations in Rome, however, and in front of Heliogabalus Helix triumphed in both, something no-one had ever done before. The admiration of the Emperor rose accordingly.

The Emperor was also fond of charioteering, as described earlier, when he would ride around the palace in his carriage drawn by fantastic beasts. He also imagined himself in the role of a great sportsman, the fantasy growing when he attended the games and would eagerly watch the races in the Circus Maximus. He would try to emulate the sportsmen himself:

He also used to drive a chariot, wearing the Green uniform, privately and at home - if one can call that place home where the judges were the foremost men of his suite, both knights and imperial freedmen, and the very prefects, together with his grandmother, his mother and the women, and likewise various members of the senate, including Leo, the city prefect - and where they watched him playing charioteer and begging gold coins like any ordinary contestant and saluting the presidents of the games and the members of his entourage.

Looking beneath the cover of Dio's withering scorn, here is a pleasant picture of a boy at play, albeit in magnificent surroundings. The lad had never had much time for play, having divided his little life into learning priestly rites and how to rule, and we can see his excitement and pleasure at pretending to be a great charioteer, waving to his family from his carriage, and living out his childish fantasies. Despite the incongruity of an Emperor at play, this is probably the only picture we have of Heliogabalus in a healthy pastime, regaining his lost childhood.

It is true that Heliogabalus had a boyish side and delighted in play, but he was also growing up. Although he would never lose that childlike love of play he was casting off the cloak of infancy and becoming a man in all senses of the word. On his other, adult, side he was becoming more and more *au fait* with his responsibilities as an emperor, building the fine temples and embellishing his city with statues and ornate structures to keep it an awe-inspiring example to the civilised world. Moreover, Heliogabalus, even in times of peace, had given thought to his city's defences, and even constructed a huge wall which engirdled it. He had also learned how to keep the senate in its place and while they gnashed their teeth at his odd follies. They towed the line and bowed beneath him. Foolishly, however, he became complacent in his position of power, a weakness shared by many emperors before him; and this was to prove his undoing.

If the person of Heliogabalus seems incomprehensible in his apparent inconsistencies it is because he was, at this point, two people in one, the child and the man. While acting the king satisfied his childish lusts, he also learned how to act as a judicious leader of men. While enjoying the cut and thrust of gladiatorial contests and the exuberance of his shows, he also realised that he was gaining the love of the common people. And while careering around the palace grounds on a chariot he was not only enjoying the play of a lost boy but was also learning a manly skill.

But as Maesa stood smiling and waving at the young Emperor, her mind of wheels and plots were turning. There was good reason for her to be worried. That Heliogabalus was headed down the road to death and destruction was obvious to her – but then, what would happen to the Bassiani? She could hear the secret whispers, and went to countless meetings with her advisors, and it was obvious that the disaffected soldiers were on the point of mutiny. The boy, head full of his own importance and his apparent invulnerability, would no longer listen to her at all. Her pleas that he should adopt Roman clothing, that he should temper his sexual desires, that he should nurture a feeling of devotion in the eyes of the senate, had all fallen on waste ground. There was no more that she could do for him, but it was crucial for her family that the name of Bassianus be preserved, and that she should assure her own safety in the political circus. To do that, Heliogabalus must appoint a successor, and one which would be favourable both to herself and the Roman people. There was only one choice – Alexianus, Mamaea's son. Since the Emperor had ascended the throne on the assumption that he was the true son of Antoninus, Alexianus was looked upon as Heliogabalus's younger brother.

Alexianus had none of his cousin's eccentricities, and as the blood relation of Severus and Antoninus he was qualified enough to claim inheritance to the royal seat. The bubbling unrest would before long have damaging repercussions on the boy Emperor, and ultimately on the fate of her entire family, over which Maesa had held sway and an invisible but powerful position in national affairs. From the moment Heliogabalus turned against her she had been considering the future and the best course of action for her family's well-being. But her main problem was that, to the public eye, a woman could not be seen to rule the state, and the only two possibilities were uncomfortably young. It was imperative, however, to keep Alexianus in the forefront of the people's eye, so that his accession may be as seamless as possible.

To safeguard Alexianus's claim to the Empire, it was necessary that Heliogabalus should adopt him as his own son, a suggestion which was itself fraught with difficulties. After all, he was only four years junior to him, and how the senate would view the proposal was a matter of conjecture. Besides this, should she broach the subject with the Emperor, it may well arouse his suspicions, and he would want to know why he should appoint a successor at all. It was a hand she would have to play with extreme caution, or all would be lost – but Maesa was well versed in political intrigue, and more than capable in the arts of diplomacy.

She was clever. She bemoaned the overwhelming workload which had been placed on Heliogabalus's shoulders – how could he expect to fulfil his function as high priest of the sun-god, with all the ritual and time-consuming rites that involved, and still manage to run the affairs of state? This argument suited Maesa as the damage had already been done, and should he concentrate his efforts on his sun-god that would only serve to accentuate his peculiarities. Moreover, she was well aware that, if given more leisure time, his pursuits would be towards more gratification of his sexual desires, which would continue to disgust the senate. Meanwhile, Alexianus could be groomed in statesmanship; he was a much better raw material anyway, and lacked the perversions of his so-called brother, in reality his cousin.

If her machinations worked, Alexianus would slowly rise in the popular estimation while Heliogabalus would continue to fall. But the timing was crucial. Heliogabalus was in decline and sooner or later would be victim to assassination, but so far there was no-one courageous or powerful enough to commit the deed; the family's past manoeuvring had accomplished that. Maesa needed time to groom the emperor elect and to gain the approbation of the Roman people. When Heliogabalus was gone, the senate must be convinced that not only was Alexianus the natural successor, he was also the most able to perform that function. She had to act immediately.

As she expected, Heliogabalus was open to her entreaties. 'There should be another person responsible for human affairs, to give you leisure and freedom from the cares of the Empire. It's unnecessary for you to look for a stranger or someone not related to you; you should entrust these duties to your own cousin.'

The unsuspecting Emperor eagerly accepted his grandmother's proposal. A family ally could help him promote his own views and be a boost to his evangelical programme, a prop to support him in his quest to convert the nation to his religion. This was still at the top of his agenda. Besides, his tasks of office swayed him from his private interests, and an assistant may deflect some of the public gaze and scrutiny under which he was constantly subject. He held no animosity towards anyone, least of all his cousin, and his mind was so far removed from intrigue that he suspected none himself. The suggestion was a no-lose situation which attracted him, and of course he was more than happy to promote the interests of his own family which could do no worse than to strengthen his own position. Perhaps he even welcomed the opportunity to be reconciled with his grandmother, after the continual aggravation he had received from her; although seemingly omnipotent, he did not undervalue Maesa's influence and importance in the Empire. He well knew who was responsible for pushing him to the ultimate seat of power, and who had wiped clear any possible future annoyance; so to have her as friend was both politic and wise.

Having successfully dealt with Heliogabalus, Maesa had tougher adversaries in the form of the senators, who had spent a good deal of time condemning the Emperor and who were tiring of being asked to concede to the whims of the Bassianus family. They were well aware that their voices had counted for little over the years of the supremacy of the Severan Dynasty, and had become skeptical about their roles in the new order, but Maesa had two strong weapons at her disposal – strength and fear; she also knew how to manipulate the Preatorian Guard, as had been amply demonstrated in the past. Although she was aware that she could push through her plans with bare-faced might, in the long term this was not a satisfactory arrangement, as it was never a good idea to alienate oneself from the government completely – there was no better goad for insurrection and revolt. So she outwardly sought the approbation of the senate-house, although she also made sure her point was made for her in the strongest possible terms. The appointment of Alexianus as heir apparent was something which was forcefully and enthusiastically advanced.

The senate were less enthusiastic – the idea of a boy of sixteen adopting a boy of twelve! 'Ridiculous!' But despite their misgivings they unanimously voted for the procedure, and Alexianus was made the son of the Emperor and named 'Caesar' – next in line to the succession. Maesa had acted wisely, going through the proper channels and gaining the approval of the senate before going any further. She was determined to assure the senators that Heliogabalus was a rotten branch of what was otherwise a sound tree, and her official methods were calculated to gain respect from the government. At the instigation of Maesa, Heliogabalus visited the senate to formalise the adoption and to accept Alexianus as his co-consul for the forthcoming year. He asked Maesa and Soaemias to take their places at either side of him, and then went through the adoption procedure, as set down by precedent. Here we get a rare glimpse of the young man's playful sense of humour; in what might have been a comic attempt to lighten matters, he congratulated himself for having become the father of 'such a big boy'; he did not doubt that his heir would 'keep his house free from despondency'. In keeping with his role as priest of the head god – his own – he went on to state that this path he had chosen. He declared the adoption was dictated to him by the god, and that from thenceforward he should be known as Alexander.

Why was Heliogabalus so unsuspecting, so naïve? Because although he had many gifts, not least compassion and a sense of justice, he had not inherited the cold calculating craftiness which had been handed down directly through the line of Severus as far as Mamaea. Maesa had always kept her cards very close to her chest, and the secret conspiracy with Mamaea had been handled with her usual circumspection. It is likely that Soaemias suspected nothing either, although she would have been worried about the influence of her great relatives. The whole plot to supplant Macrinus before had been carried out with one object in mind – to elevate the house of Bassianus – and now that the project had come to fruition, Heliogabalus saw no reason for betrayal. After all, his grandmother and aunt still had eminent status in Rome and as far as he knew had what they were angling for. He may have had his spats with Maesa, but that did not seem a reason to suspect treason from her; besides, he was still under the delusion that he had the full support of the senate and the army – the same people Maesa and Mamaea were surreptitiously encouraging to turn against their Emperor.

The argument that Maesa and Mamaea expected Heliogabalus to hand over imperial power to his cousin does not bear examination, nor does the story that Maesa was driven to fear for her safety when he did not. Both are extremely unlikely. When push came to shove, he accepted his cousin as Caesar all right, but his title was that of *imperatorii heres*, not of *imperatorii consors*. His grandmother could not seriously have expected much else, certainly not the last of these, as it would have given him equal power with Heliogabalus and made him virtually co-ruler; the first simply made him his hereditary heir. Heliogabalus had only raised Alexianus's profile enough to allow him to take on some administrative duties which was, after all, what Maesa had suggested. She was not so stupid as to think that Heliogabalus would simply hand over half of his Empire on request; his whole behaviour had proven that he saw his mission as a divine right granted from El Gabal, and in his disagreements with Maesa had shown that he wanted to use his regal power. Any suggestion that he give up that power would certainly have alarmed him.

Maesa knew that Heliogabalus's end would come sooner or later; with her machinations, it could come soon. After his fall it was imperative to have someone legally recognised as his heir. This is what she wanted – and this is what she achieved. Not long after, she achieved more; as Alexander was now in the public eye and had administrative duties, it would be in his interests to have him as co-consul the following year. Again, Heliogabalus did not see his danger and, seeing the advantages to his family of having his cousin as his colleague, he acquiesced. At the time he had no idea how perilous the decision was.

In this way, Heliogabalus unwittingly played into the hands of his grandmother and ultimately his enemies. At first, this did not occur to him, and he took to his role of surrogate father with relish; it was a new experience for him and he was as delighted and as keen as the boy he was. It was the first time he had been given the responsibility for the grooming and education of a son, so he was determined to make a good job of it, intending to elucidate all the mysteries of El-Gabal as well as what he considered to be the most important factors in the running of Rome – winning the favour of the people through games and shows, as well as his past ideas of lotteries and splendid feasts.

At this time the only one of his family who had any real feelings for Heliogabalus at all was his mother Soaemias, but not even her motherly attempts could persuade Heliogabalus to take a more respectable life. Although not as experienced as Maesa, this did not mean she was blind to her aims, and she could see as well as anyone how the chessboard was stacked up against her son, how ill-prepared he was for subtle ingenuity and plot. But perhaps all was not lost. Despite the fears of her own mother and sister, she still had hopes for him, and perhaps the introduction of an heir may be of use to him after all. To begin with, it was apparent that the boy enjoyed having a protégé and took pleasure in acting as his mentor. But instead of assigning him the role of administrator, and giving him that office which would have freed him from damaging himself in the eyes of the senators, he did the exact opposite. With an unerring ability to court disaster, he began his tuition by indoctrination into the very activities for which he himself had been censured. Firstly he enrolled him as an official priest of the sun-god and then began to show him his duties, teaching him how to dance and to perform the rites necessary for his vocation.

   This is exactly what Maesa had feared. As soon as she learned what Heliogabalus was up to – degrading the youngster in the eyes of the Romans – she took him away. Alexander was not going to follow the same path as the Emperor, who had made his ignominious start by dressing in votive robes and prancing before the sneering senate; it was imperative that he be seen as one in sympathy with the Roman way of life and worship. Instead, she employed teachers to instruct the lad in those subjects fitting for a Roman boy and would-be Emperor – in Greek and Roman government, in wrestling and physical exercise, and above all in self-discipline. Lampridius names his tutors as the grammarian Scaurinus and the rhetoricians Julius Frontinus, Baebius Macrianus, and the celebrated Julius Granianus. In short, she began to instil the Roman virtues into him.

It did not take long for Heliogabalus to discover what was going on behind his back. All of a sudden Alexander was no longer available to him; and after some inquiries he found out that he had been taken in hand by his grandmother and her advisors. In a direct affront to him, he was not allowed to teach his own heir, but instead he was being taught everything contradictory to what he had worked towards and treasured. It was a betrayal made even worse by the knowledge that it had been engineered by his own family, people he would have assumed he could trust. At once he knew that his own decisions and even the core of his reign had come under a surreptitious attack, and that, if allowed to continue, his rule could be threatened.

Heliogabalus was aghast, and his anger had much to do with jealousy as well as anything else. Now it was obvious that he had been tricked into accepting Alexander as his heir because he was being groomed for the highest position, and would eventually topple him from the empery. In a paranoid fit of pique, he saw the whole rabble of teachers as part of a larger conspiracy and accused them of treason. But this was only the tip of the iceberg; Heliogabalus had a strong belief in what he had been doing and saw his religious role as that of educator. Assured that the Romans were erring in their beliefs, he had tried to give them a better alternative, a religion by which they could achieve inner greatness and strive for the betterment of their souls. Such a task had been a noble one, and had taken a predominant role in his purpose as head of the Empire. If people argued against his religion on theological grounds, there could still be no mistaking the purity of his intentions – rightly or wrongly he was working for what he considered to be the welfare of the Roman spirit.

Now all of his efforts seemed to be crashing about his ears. At last, the quiet conspiracy was burst open and everything was clear to him; that the arguments of his grandmother had been decoys, that he had walked into the trap which had been laid for him. Not being perfidious himself, he did not expect perfidy from others, least of all those he had relied upon for his own protection and support. At long last his own very real danger became apparent, and he had no choice but to assess the forces arrayed against him. It was a staggering total; not only his powerful family but the senators and even the army. In a moment he realised how precarious his own position had become, how easy it would be to shake him and how difficult it was becoming to fight back. Maesa had been crafty and intelligent; wherever he looked around the Empire he could see her pawns, ready to back her at the slightest command. It seemed to be a hopeless situation – he was in check and in serious danger of losing the game on the next move. That move was born of sheer desperation.

He did have friends, and that was an important bonus, albeit they were friends he had made through play and through his pastimes. He gathered together all he could trust, and then looked at the rest, who now had their masks pulled away and were revealed as potential threats. There was one other advantage, and that was he was still the

Emperor, and could use his status to command. Alexander was still only a small child. As yet the Praetorian Guard were not completely against him; and to the senate he was their Emperor, for good or bad. It was crucial that he acted. There was not a second to lose, or the title of Emperor – even his life – would be lost to him.

First of all he turned his attention to those who were educating his heir, under the guise of teaching virtues. This was not how Heliogabalus saw things; he was being brainwashed into rejecting his innovations, and into being his enemy. It was clear that those people were in the pay of Maesa, and were plotting his own downfall. To some extent, this was true. Heliogabalus had to demonstrate that he was yet strong, strong enough to deal summarily with such acts of treason. Some of them were banished to other countries, while others were executed. This act of aggression, so unlike the Emperor, was born out of necessity, and appalled the senate.

It also pointed to something else which again has been missed by the old biographers and historians. Heliogabalus was growing up more and more. He was no longer just a boy who allowed the machinery of government to turn above his head while he indulged in his childish whims. The precedents of recent history had not been lost on him and at this point he proved that he could act like a powerful emperor should to protect his position and, to his mind, the Empire. Far from being the imbecile he was later described as, he proved that he had watched through the reprisals following his inauguration and ad learned several lessons which he had kept to heart. No doubt his presence of mind and tough determination shocked Maesa and Mamaea, who little expected such prompt and decisive action. It was a pity Heliogabalus had not shown such a steel will against his true enemies, but by now it was too late. His reputation went before him, and besides, Maesa and the rest of his family had been shown to be guilty of plots against him. He had waded so far in the mire that at this time there was no turning back; the possibilities and qualities in Heliogabalus that could have been transformed into a model emperor had been too badly tainted by scandal and disgrace. The only option now was to show the actions of Heliogabalus in the worst possible light.

Like Maesa, who no doubt made her own feelings known to the senate, the senators put the reprisal down to their Emperor's mental instability. In their eyes, the heir had simply been groomed for the post of Emperor, and had simply been taught all things pertaining to that great task. They remonstrated with him, arguing that his policy was uncalled for and brutal. Heliogabalus explained everything to the senate as eloquently as he could, arguing that they were misled; that Alexander had been taken from him, but not to learn the art of being an Emperor; this he himself had been trying to do until he had been removed. Now the boy was being contaminated and corrupted against him; the whole affair had been engineered as part of a bigger plot to overthrow him. But Heliogabalus was no match for the rhetoric of his enemies, and Cassius Dio put a different caste upon his actions: 'The emperor offered the most absurd excuses for doing this, claiming that these men, by teaching Alexander self-control, educating him in human affairs, and refusing to allow him to dance and take part in the frenzied orgies, would corrupt his adopted son.'

Heliogabalus was furious, and saw how dangerous things had become. Although his main adversaries had been dealt with in Rome, he had to consider his safety both at home and abroad. The agents of Maesa were everywhere, each one posing a significant threat. It is very likely that Heliogabalus's friends were quick to point that out, and to suggest that until he corrected this state of affairs he would not be safe; these were the same sycophants and flatterers who had so easily wormed their way into his affections. In fact, Heliogabalus's nodding friends were more than likely more concerned with their own welfare. Now, having seen the reactions of the senate to his excuses, it was obvious that Heliogabalus had become aware that he had enemies in all corners of the Empire - which must have come as quite a shock to someone who had believed himself to be universally loved. The mature side of the Emperor knew that something had to be done – and speedily.

So the Emperor once again proved to an amazed Rome that he was more than capable of acting on his own initiative to prevent strife. Heliogabalus took action to remove anyone who posed a danger to him; in this he had had a good example in the person of Maesa, who had acted in the same way when Heliogabalus first came to the throne. Now he would use her own tactics against her, and supplant the agents she had placed in strategic points throughout Rome and the Empire.

The first priorities were his own personal safety, and the backing of the Praetorian Guard. He therefore promoted his friend Publius Valerius Comazon to the rank of Praetorian Prefect. Having secured their leadership, Heliogabalus, along with his new advisors, began a campaign of replacing suspect officials with his acquaintances. Unfortunately, his leisure time had been filled with games and sports, not with anyone of senatorial rank, so the only people he felt he could trust (no doubt encouraged by themselves) were those same flatterers. Stage actors were given important roles and, if it can be believed, he bestowed governorships on slaves and freedmen. If true, then this was an ill-advised - and suicidal - kick in the teeth to the Roman senate. Heliogabalus had tried his best to secure his position, but all his efforts had resulted in important posts being given to the undeserved and that the senate could not stomach. It was construed as a personal uprising against Rome, and was a direct insult to all it stood for.

It goes without saying that Lampridius rubbed his hands at another chance to take a swipe at the maligned Emperor. This writer, who did not even shrink from inventing an Emperor for his history book, cleverly mixes undoubted fact with undoubted fiction as he describes the acquaintances of Heliogabalus who reached high rank simply because of their friendship with him. He includes the charioteers Protogenes and Cordius, the latter of whom became the Prefect of the Watch; a barber called Claudius who became Prefect of the grain supply, and a mule-driver, a courier, a cook and a locksmith as tax-collectors. He asserts that men reached eminent positions through the size of their penises, that he appointed 'low-born profligates', and that he made his freedmen 'governors, legates, generals and consuls'. Moreover, he states that Heliogabalus placed the task of selling posts in the hands of his slaves or his sexual partners, and that these would simply go to the highest bidder.

Heliogabalus had been at the centre of the political forum on his succession, and had noticed the machinery in operation; how Maesa had effectively removed his enemies and opposition from the senate, and placed those she held in esteem in places of authority and trust. Now sensing an imminent uprising, the Emperor continued to follow the same example himself, realizing that he would not feel secure while those sympathetic to Alexander were in positions of great power; led by example, he had them removed and sought to replace them with his own friends. More and more of Maesa's friends were discovered and rooted out. The difficulty lay in the fact that he knew few people of proven political worth, so again trusting to amity rather than competence he selected those of his own acquaintance. This concern worried him little, as he had already noticed how impotent an organ the senate-house had become; but if his friends in power – and the army – stayed true to him, his position would remain secure. Or so he thought.

Heliogabalus was neither as insane or foolish as his biographers would have us believe. He realized full well that this was a time of crisis, and that he was facing a power struggle which would determine his future. Also that he was lined up against two very powerful enemies; his grandmother, and the Roman senate. For the sake of his own security it was essential that he once again placed himself in an unassailable position; this he attempted to do by removing any obstacles in the form of those of his family's allies who held positions of great rank. Although his actions may have given him a feeling of security, they were received with disdain by the senators.

The madness of Heliogabalus reached such a point that he appointed all the actors from the stage and the public theatres to the most important posts in the empire, selecting as his praetorian prefect a man who had from childhood danced publicly in the Roman theatre.

Unfortunately, although his actions were unavoidable they were hollow, and Maesa would have known it. Weak administrators were easy to supplant, and as Maesa's agents were lined up waiting to fill all the posts, she only had to wait for the right moment. She knew she couldn't wait too long; there was always the danger that in remote provinces, the appointment of an unsuitable governor might be the catalyst for civil war. They would have to be uprooted and replaced before they did any real damage to the area they had been given by their inexperience. She may have been surprised at her grandson's tenacity, but she remained firm and determined.

As the game was played in the centre of Rome, the Emperor's worst enemy – his gender crisis – reared its head again, arguably at the worst possible time. The next phase of his life would be a happy one for him, but unknown to him it would mark the end of his reign and his life. He was slowly maturing and making international decisions as befitted an Emperor, but they were too little too late and dismissed as the lunatic whims of a madman. He was also maturing sexually and this necessary development marched alongside his new-found maturity in the political jungle. Sadly for him, instead of recognising that he was beginning to bloom into full-grown maturity, all of his actions were compounded into a single opinion – they were the behaviour of a fool.

It was at this time Heliogabalus gave way to all his sexual inclinations, and became openly homosexual. As has been described, this was odious to the Romans, but not so to the Greeks, with whom Heliogabalus may have felt a greater affinity. Yet it is important to realise that homosexuality was not accepted *in toto* in Greece at the time; instead it was bound within rigid codes of etiquette and social rank. The usual form of homosexuality was pederasty, in which an older man (the *erastes*) would couple with a younger partner (the *eromenos*), and the elder man was normally of higher social status and play the active, or penetrating role, whereas the youth would necessarily play the passive, or penetrated role. It would be completely against moral behaviour for the older man to take the passive position, and a peculiar addendum was that the younger man should respect his seducer, but not desire him sexually. An episode of pederasty was one which was almost the norm for any up-and-coming young adolescent of the time, but not everyone agreed with this form of love; Plato described it as unnatural, favouring what became known as the 'Platonic' relationship.

Sometimes it was considered useful for the bond of affection between homosexual partners to be used in times of warfare; such as the famous example of the Theban 'Sacred Band', who used their affections to form a strong united, self-protecting – and powerful – fighting force. Valerius Maximus went even further, suggesting that Greek love could harness a strength which led to a toughness, in contrast to the weakness of the eastern races. It had produced a mentality which served 'to strengthen hardihood, to breed a contempt for death, to overcome the sweet desire for life, to humanise cruelty, to which powers almost as much veneration is due as to the cult of the Immortal Gods.'

This is not to say that approved homosexual activities did not take place in Rome; but the practice was much frowned upon and used only on persons who did not matter, such as slaves, who were thought of as not even human beings, or non-Romans. As with the Greeks, the most shameful position was that of the penetrated; but under certain circumstances, an active participation was condoned. But despite the official speeches and writings of the day, a subculture did emerge, and many of the Emperors such as Nero showed a taste for males. Taking a passive, penetrated role was looked down upon, and Nero aroused disgust when he would play the passive role and imitate the moans and whimpers of a female.

Although several writers described the existence of homosexual activity in Rome itself, it was more of a secretive cult than a norm. It is said that public baths were an ideal place for men to search out consenting partners, and Juvenal suggest that a willing partner would express himself by scratching his head. As in modern times, the harbours and docks were common places to find same-sex partners, especially among sailors from the newly-arrived ships. There is evidence that fellatio was practised; a piece of graffiti from Pompeii states: 'Secundus is a great cock-sucker.' Of course, this may have been a gibe or practical joke; but it does suggest that the practice was well-known even then. On the other hand, female homosexuality was always seen in a worse light. Only with the advent of

Christianity, in the fourth century, was the practice of homosexuality absolutely taboo.

As manhood began to dawn on the Emperor, the sexual objects of his desires became clearer and clearer. It has already been shown that he had experienced a 'inverted' Oedipus complex, in that the boy attached his love-object to the father and built up a resentment of his mother, rather than the other way around. This usually occurs at around the age of four, but some modern researchers suggest that this may not be the end of the matter.

In a healthy individual the positive Oedipus complex is resolved in boys after the age of four, when a period of latency kicks in. For a long time that was thought to be the end of the matter and any abnormal sexual inclinations could be traced to a hang-up or 'fixation' during that time. A normal expression of the admiration for the father-figure often is represented by hero-worship; for example, leading sports figures – this was certainly the case for Heliogabalus, as it is for boys of today. Recent research, however, suggests a second mechanism, which occurs towards the end of adolescence; the very point at which Heliogabalus now found himself. In this phase, the hidden negative complex comes back to the fore and its resolution marks the end of true childhood. Should the complex not be satisfactorily dealt with, a father-fixation easily leads to the male figure being the love-object for the young man. If we accept that Heliogabalus had a female mind – was, in all but body, a woman – it was simply a matter of course that he should choose a male partner. In the time leading up to his decision, he was obviously toying with his choice, and this led to much soul-searching and perhaps guilt, whether neurotic or not. But in the end, Heliogabalus was male in body and when the decision was made was therefore described as homosexual in the eyes of Rome.

The Romans, priding themselves on their masculinity, spurned the idea of homosexuality as foreign to natural instinct and therefore classed it as a perversion. Hence their disapproval of Heliogabalus and his apparent emasculation, as well as his open transvestism. This culmination of his sexual development happened at a moment of crucial importance to his life, and would once again cause his name to be one of universal repulsion and contempt. It took place during a chariot race attended by the Emperor, the source of it beneath his very feet.

One of the competitors was a Carian slave by the name of Hieracles, a powerful athlete with curly fair hair. He was well-known as a master of the sport, and the story went that he was taught the arts of charioteering by no less a personage than Gordius himself. Although if this was true then it must have been a different man to the one who aided Pontian Mithadates and died three centuries before. At any rate this Hierocles was racing in the heat of the event when his chariot upturned and he was thrown out before the Emperor himself. As he tumbled, his helmet fell from his head and revealed his luxuriant hair and shaven face, one which immediately attracted the young Emperor. Heliogabalus straight away ordered that he athlete be carried to his Palace for attention, and as soon as possible he made the acquaintance of the charioteer who had made such a favourable impression upon him.

Their meeting was the seed of the first flower of real love the Emperor had known, and he became besotted with his patient. It was, to admit a cliché, love at first sight. The two became inseparable, and, whether for reasons of ambition or true love, Hieracles returned his Emperor's affections. Before long they were lovers, Heliogabalus playing the passive role of *eromenos*, a role which would have been condemned by the Greeks on the grounds of social status. Before long no-one could doubt that the pair were an item, and Heliogabalus openly played the part of wife to Hieracles and gave himself up completely to his femininity. It was a role in which he felt absolutely comfortable.

It was now that Heliogabalus finally resolved his identity problem. In retrospect, it becomes clear that during his early life he was in the throes of a gender issue which dominated and tormented him. During puberty, he battled against these impulses with little success, and the struggle between sexual orientation and social expectation was an agonising one, during which he toyed with heterosexual sex. This did not work and men continued to fuel his sexual desires, so at this point guilt and a powerful need for satisfaction – Heliogabalus had a volcanic sexual libido – led him to masochistic homosexual fantasies which united his need for punishment, sexuality and release. Such fantasies were unhelpful and damaging in that they represented a pathetic attempt to deny his inclinations even to the extent of humiliating himself and putting himself in the public pillory. It was a case of 'I am attracted to men; this is forbidden; I am unworthy and deserve to be immolated.' Only now did he find that he was wrong; the key to his future happiness lay in accepting his sexuality and following it to its inevitable conclusion. His mistake lay in thinking that Rome would understand or at least accept it.

The important difference between the Heliogabalus unchained and the Heliogabalus of the brothels was one of fulfilment. It is not known whether Heliogabalus had sexual encounters before Hieracles – the picture of the palace brothel may have been a fiction similar to the uncertain gossip of Suetonius – but it is likely, and if it did occur it was as part of his masochistic punishment fantasy as if the submissive role was shame enough to beat himself for his own degradation. Now, things were different. The neurotic gave way to the normal; at least, normal for Heliogabalus's psychological make-up. In historical terms, this could not have come at a worse time, but it may be argued that for the sake of Heliogabalus's peace of mind it was Elagabalus-sent.

The months ahead were arguably the happiest time of Heliogabalus's whole life. He doted on his partner, and lavished such shows of favour upon him that he rapidly rose to become one of the most powerful men in the Empire; indeed, Heliogabalus wished to depose Alexander and set up Hieracles as Caesar himself. The senate gnashed their teeth as they watched a mere slave – and homosexual – rise above them, and his mother, who was also a slave, be conveyed to Rome under royal guard to participate in functions alongside the wives of eminent men and consuls. This was the ultimate insult – respected dignified public figures forced to bow before the lowest of the low – slaves and homosexuals. The depths to which Heliogabalus had fallen beggared belief.

Public disgust was mirrored later in Lampridius's fantasies, when he declared that the Emperor used to kiss his lover on the groin in public.

In some ways, Heliogabalus began to move into adulthood and cast off some of the dreadful adolescent neuroses which had dogged him. He no longer felt the need to hide his transvestism away, or use it as a stick to beat himself with. Nor did he feel the need to flaunt himself in palatial or downtown brothels. He settled into the life which suited him best – that of a woman, the wife to a loving husband. At once he became known as queen, mistress and wife. It became a matter of everyday routine for him to wear make up and become employed in womanly tasks such as weaving; to enhance his femininity he had himself depilated and kept his face closely shaven. To all intents and purposes he was a complete woman, and would appear as such whenever his duties demanded that he visit the *curia* and face the senate. He would recline before the men there, splendid in his female attire, his eyes daubed and painted with make-up.

No-one can know just how devoted Hieracles was to his 'mistress' and how much he played a game for political gain, but he does seem to have been proud of his relationship, jealous of potential rivals, and loving to his partner. As the Emperor's consort, he became a powerful man, and many would flatter him as well as the Emperor to win his confidence and to enhance their social standing. His flatterers, of course, would hardly have objected, although there may have been some consternation in that Hieracles was wiser and more worldly-wise than his partner, and may have been able to see through some of them. Hieracles was to prove a good lover and a good son, always looking out for his mother and bursting with pride when she stood alongside all the other ladies of aristocratic origin; in many ways he was a settling influence on the young Emperor whose waywardness may just have been an expression of a tortuous search for happiness.

Heliogabalus's love remained intact, although he was a fickle youth, and still had an eye for other men. In many ways he was now fair game for any young lusty adventurer who took it in his head to make a play for him. There were times when he would seem to give way to his impulses – always a time of great anxiety for his partner – but Hieracles was to remain the main object of Heliogabalus's desire right until his death. He did have a naughty lascivious nature, and seemed to derive a secret pleasure from teasing and tormenting his lover, but these actions were those of a young man in the flower of his youth who found it hard to resist the pleasures tempting him.

It was said that among those he raised to public office in his cleansing after the actions of his family, were those with whom he had committed adultery. It is difficult to assess how many of these tales are true, coloured as they are by the prejudices with which they were originally written; it was said that Heliogabalus had a passion for well-endowed men, and was always on the lookout for a man with a suitably large penis – in fact, it is charged that he made official searches for just such men. It is always a possibility that, in his exaggerated desire for womanhood, that he should develop an obsession with such things; an abnormally large penis becoming synonymous with a corresponding degree of masculinity.

Such an obsession would not be out of place in Heliogabalus's mental make-up. A sexual obsession with all things masculine could encourage it; what's more, he had had to negotiate the 'phallic phase' in his psychological trials, and a fixation at that stage could easily lead to just such an obsession. It must be remembered, too, that the phallic symbol had a great importance for Heliogabalus, being central to his religion as well as to many of those of the east. It was also symbolic of the father-figure to which Heliogabalus was constantly drawn, and an obsession with the penis for a youth whose idiosyncrasies suggest a fixation in the phallic stage of his development would not be unexpected. It was also a fact that that the possession of a large penis was thought to be an attractive thing and a sign of manly beauty.

After some time Hieracles had cause for worry, in the form of a native of Smyrna by the name of Aurelius Zoticus, a fellow athlete who was nicknamed the Cook – because that had been the trade of his father. This athlete was famed for his personal beauty, so much so that as soon as Heliogabalus had seen him he could not wait to meet him, and desired an immediate audience. So Aurelius was ordered to come to Rome for a royal interview and so determined was the Emperor to impress the young man that he arranged a gigantic escort; of course, Heliogabaus was accustomed to such extravagances, but this one surpassed anything he had ever organised; the dismayed Aurelius found himself led up to the imperial palace and escorted to the presence of Heliogabalus himself, as described by Dio:

This Aurelius had a body that was beautiful all over, as if prepared for a gymnastic contest, and he towered over everyone in the size of his penis. This fact had been reported to the emperor by those who were on the lookout for such features and the man was suddenly snatched away from the games and taken to Rome, accompanied by a huge procession, larger than Abgarus had in the reign of Severus or Tiridates in that of Nero. He was appointed *cubicularius* before he had been even seen by the Emperor, was honoured by the name of his grandfather, Avitus, was adorned with garlands as if at a festival, then he entered the palace the centre of which was a great glare of lights.

Heliogabalus was dressed in his finery and at his most feminine. The astonished Aurelius bowed to his Emperor, crying:

'Hail, Emperor, my Lord!'

Heliogabalus titled his head back and adopted his most seductive pose; then faced him coquettishly.

'Don't call me 'Lord'. I am a Lady!'

There need be no doubt that Heliogabalus meant every word he said. He was no longer hiding behind half-truths and subterfuge; the Heliogabalus new-born was exactly what he had come to believe he was – a lady in everything but genitalia.

Aurelius became a guest in the Palace; and as he reclined in the bath Heliogabalus came to join him. It had been stated that Aurelius was famed for the size of his penis, and Dio suggests that he joined him in the bath so that he might judge for himself and did not find Aurelius wanting in that department. Soon they were lovers, and Heliogabalus heaped honours on his new inamoratus. The relationship was a very physical one, Heliogabalus experiencing special delight in sex; he had not studied the ways and the bodies of women for nothing and prided himself on his female abilities to arouse and excite.

He was still young and fickle, although as stated still very much in love with his partner Hieracles, and prey to good-looking, over-ambitious men. In a rare passage from the *Historia Augusta* which smacks of some truth it is suggested that Aurelius made much political mileage out of his situation, as lovers of high-ranking statesmen often do; that he amassed quite a fortune from Heliogabalus and would sell his secrets for coin. Immersed in his passions, the Emperor would often wonder whether this overwhelming need for homosexual sex was normal, and would even ask contemporary philosophers about it, asking if they had ever felt the same way. Although misinterpreted as a passion for depraved talk, it was simply the case of an adolescent exploring his own emotions.

There is no validity in the suggestion, from the same work, that Heliogabalus underwent a marriage ceremony with Aurelius and, leaping into bed, ordered: 'Go to it, Cook!' Grotesque and amusing though the story is, it only puts in doubt the true worth of the *Historia* even more.

Hierocles was a worried man. Should this new entanglement prosper, his own ambitions and standing in Roman society were in danger; and he knew well enough how unpopular he was with the senate and the relatives of the Emperor. Stung by jealousy and a gnawing doubt, he began to conspire against his rival. Having acquaintance with the cup-bearers, he persuaded them to be a party to his plots, and he spiked Aurelius's wine with a preparation designed to rob him of his potency. It is not known how many times Hieracles sabotaged Aurelius, but the outcome was everything he had desired. Finding Aurelius incapable of raising an erection despite all of his ministrations, Heliogabalus grew angry, concluding that either Aurelius had another lover or his affections had waned. As a result, he denounced his lover, and removed him from the Palace. Hieracles once again became the husband and the object of all his partner's desires.

Although Heliogabalus was happy enough in his role as a woman, the nagging need to go further haunted him, and he still yearned to have a sex-change operation, even offering large sums to anyone who could affect this safely. The surgeons would hardly have agreed to so dangerous an operation, knowing that if things went badly – as they almost certainly would – they would be blamed for high treason.

The peace in which the Roman world found itself suited Heliogabalus admirably as he had little taste for warfare. The tale – Lampridius again – that he was planning to go to war against the Marcomanni, the tribe defeated by Marcus Antoninus, is nonsense. Lampridius repeats a rumour that the Marcomanni were forced into obedience and perpetual amity by the dealings of magicians, who had used a secret rite for this reason. Heliogabalus, Lampridius claims, wanted to break the formula and instigate a new war because a portent had claimed that the war would finally be ended by an Antoninus, and as such he wanted to take all the glory. The whole idea is ludicrous. Not only were the Romans basking in a rare period of peace, but the thought of warfare and battle was completely at variance with everything known about Heliogabalus. It is simply another Lampridian fantasy; besides, if such a prophecy were current, it had already been fulfilled by Marcus.

Heliogabalus's main preoccupation – apart from his sexual needs – was with his religion and with keeping the peace. As he once said to the senators; 'I do not want titles derived from war and bloodshed. It is enough for me that you call me Pius and Felix.' At the same time, he went to great lengths to secure the loyalty of the soldiers, knowing that in them lay his security; but the fickleness of the Praetorian Guard troubled him. Naturally he kept them well-paid, as they had a reputation for selling their allegiance, but the possibility that they could be bought by his enemies was ever on his mind. One day the senate flattered him, and in reply he said:

'Yes, you love me, and so, by Jupiter, do the people, and the legions abroad; but I don't please the Praetorians, even though I keep giving them so much.'

The words betray the illusion he lived under; that the Roman nation had accepted him for what he was, and that despite his actions he had managed to retain the affection of the people. No doubt it was under these beliefs that he had felt confident enough to carry out his cleansing programme to root out anyone whose sympathies were suspect. This reflects the position he had found himself in, and the fact that no-one dare disillusion the Emperor, spending their time in flattery and nodding agreement rather than warn him of imminent dangers. It was not in their interest to do so; better to allow the Emperor to destroy himself by continuing his self-destructive course of life. It is hardly worthy of Cassius Dio that he should strenuously attack every aspect of Heliogabalus while freely admitting that he was willing to flatter the Emperor in public. That said, there was little else he could do.

Heliogabalus's words leave us in no doubt that the Praetorians were getting restless. It is simple enough to understand. This crack group of soldiers had always prided themselves on their prowess in all things military, and ever since the Year of the Five Emperors had prided themselves on being emperor-makers as well as protectors. True, their status had been curtailed by the expediency and machinations of Heliogabalus's predecessors, but by now they had regained their position of power and knew themselves to be the strong arm of Rome. They also knew that Heliogabalus knew it too, and played on his dependency. Once again the Guard was rising in arrogance and pride, and were well aware that a change in ruler would do little to change their station, as they themselves would steer the situation as suited best their own inclinations. There is a suggestion that they were becoming complacent and did not even bother to hide their dislike of the transvestite Emperor whose reign reflected on them and their reputation. From above there was an obstinate silence from the senate and the imperial officials, discontented whispers had risen from the Praetorian Guard, and such grumbles could only have disturbed the Emperor. As he himself said, he had kept them sweet for long enough, but despite that fact these soldiers had made it apparent that they had no liking for their figurehead. The dangers of a wavering Praetorian Guard were obvious to Heliogabalus. The possibility of using the Guard against him was very real.

What Heliogabalus did not know was that there were already plots afoot and they sprang from the very centre of his family. There was another reason that the Guard seemed indifferent to Heliogabalus, and that was that Maesa had already begun spinning her plots and almost certainly had already approached the Praetorians, seeking their help. This was no precipitate step – nothing Maesa did was hurried – but was part of a conspiracy which had possibly been taking root in her mind since the beginning of her grandson's reign.

But the biggest mistake Heliogabalus made was to misjudge the views of his government and his people. By this time, Heliogabalus had lost all grasp of the situation. He had no reason to doubt the love of the senate and the people, because nothing to the contrary had been reported to him; certainly, his flatterers would have fared worse had they made any effort to convince him that he was mistaken. A change in lifestyle, however unlikely, would undo all the privileges they had carefully garnered; so they kept silent. The senate had always resented Heliogabalus as being a shameful representative of the Empire; mostly they were prejudiced by his transvestism and insistence on accentuating his femininity, even on state visits. The people by now were aware of the eccentricities of their Emperor, and were equally mortified by stories of his sexually perverse exploits, although they weren't likely to show their displeasure at the lavish games they loved to attend. Heliogabalus imagined that the senate thought he was doing a good job by appeasing the people and carrying out religious reforms; and that the people reciprocated the love he bore them.

Hay strenuously argues that Heliogabalus had done nothing to incite the odium of the people, arguing that prejudice of his psychopathology fails to recognise Roman susceptibilities and antedates common prejudices. Pleasing as such a theory may be it is unfortunately a simple case of wishful thinking. The senators and people of Rome had strong prejudices at the time against certain forms of homosexuality, as we have seen, particularly against passive sex or against whatever feminizes a man, especially transvestism. It was also a shameful thing for a man to accept sex from an inferior - which, in Heliogabalus's case, was everyone. Although the people certainly appreciated the care their Emperor showered upon them, his shameful appearance and his role in his last marriage would indeed have shocked their sensibilities. People have changed little, even in the twenty-first century, and although in Heliogabalus's day there was some official leeway in the act of pederasty, having an Emperor who insisted on appearing in public dressed in drag would not have been appreciated. Among certain subcultures of the time he may have been idolised, but in the mainstream he would have been an object of shame. Admittedly, Nero married a man and aped a woman, but this was seen as a foible in an otherwise imperial reign. In fact, if anything, attitudes became more hardened as the Empire ran on its lumbering course.

What happened next is told in a confusing record of conflicting stories, but the basic sequence of events would seem to be as follows.

The situation Heliogabalus was in became more and more precarious, and in the chess game which was Roman politics, his pawns were weak. His recent purges in Rome and outside seemed to have been successful, and Maesa had wisely kept silent on the matter. It was politic to have her grandson believe he had been victorious and so she could connive and plot in secret. But behind the scenes, his grandmother and his aunt Mamaea were busy, no longer trusting in his mother Soaemias who retained a maternal affection for her son. Such sentimentality was of no use in the science of power; but as things reached a head Soaemias must have been a worried woman, well aware that Heliogabalus's latest actions had been enough to enrage and completely alienate her sister and her mother. She could admit to an unsavoury love affair to help her son achieve world greatness, but it was a different thing to disown or plot the downfall of her son.

Maesa had no such principles. Her single worry was for the safety of Alexander, and she kept him away as far as was possible, privately continuing his education. The Emperor's latest exploits with Hieracles and characters such as the Cook had alienated him even more from the people, but Maesa knew that the main pieces in the game were the Praetorian Guard and the army. There was one way – and one only – of achieving their loyalty, a way which had been successfully repeated countless times. She would buy it. Slowly but surely they bought the service of the soldiery and even the Praetorians by money and by rumour and insinuation; if Heliogabalus had been made aware of the wavering of the Praetorians then certainly Maesa knew of it, and made capital from it. In fact, the Guard may already have been in Maesa's pay. But the Bassiani needed time; Alexander was no more than a child and it was important that he should reach some degree of manhood – at least putting on his *toga virilis* – before they could have the confidence to openly revolt against the Emperor. Maesa used her past experience well and carefully positioned her pieces on the board, while Heliogabalus tried his best to use the little resources he had.

At least Heliogabalus was no real danger to Maesa; she realised that the puppet administrators set up by Heliogabalus were woefully weak and could hardly stand up against a full-scale *coup d'état*, especially when they controlled the military. At this juncture it was wise to allow the Emperor his hollow victories, just so long as Alexander remained safe. There would be no need for action unless his safety was threatened – and there was little need to muddy the waters by blackening Heliogabalus's name. He was doing that very well on his own. So the priority was to control the senate and the army and that could be done in deals behind doors and covert negotiation – not that they even needed much in the way of bribery; the Emperor had engendered such a hostile feeling among the people that they would be all too willing to support a revolt. The Praetorians were another matter, led as they were by the love of gold – readily supplied by Maesa.

There was another reason for Maesa to act carefully. The preservation of Alexander was precious to her, and the whole future of the Bassianus family; this was the reason Maesa and her advisors did nothing. Further actions against the Emperor may lead him to see Alexander as a threat, and may lead his flatterers to suggest his murder. After all, she had what she wanted – Alexander was the official Caesar, and he was gaining a reputation as a sober, intelligent and respectable boy. All she needed was time for her grandson to mature.

Trouble reared its head when Alexander started his term as consul along with Heliogabalus. Up to this point, his cousin had entered little into his thoughts; his enemies had taken him from him, and Heliogabalus may have thought that this was done against his will, which may or may not have been the truth. There is no evidence that he thought of Alexander anything but kindly. All of that changed when some advocates were in conversation with him, and remarked how fortunate he was that he should have a fellow-consul as his son. The comment jarred Heliogabalus, who assumed that he alone was pre-eminent in the thoughts and loves of the people; after all he had done for them, it seemed to be the natural assumption. Now he realised that Alexander had become a great favourite; the comment made was not that Alexander should be fortunate for having Heliogabalus as a colleague, but the other way round. The insinuation was that Alexander was thought more able than he, and the idea played on his mind.

The Emperor was piqued, and did not relish the state of affairs, claiming that things would improve in the following year, when his consul would be his real son. Whatever he meant by this cryptic remark, many saw it as a suggestion that Alexander was out of favour with his cousin and that Heliogabalus was plotting how he could remove the boy who was fast becoming his greatest rival.

Alexander was not simply a rival to Heliogabalus; if he came to power following an insurrection all of his friends would be in danger too. For them, the only safe way to be rid of the threat of Alexander was by his assassination; but it is uncertain whether or not Heliogabalus began to consider the idea. In any case such a course was most difficult; Maesa and Mamaea had taken alarm from the utterances of the Emperor and took strong steps to guard him, employing bodyguards from the army and the Praetorian Guard. His mother Mamaea was especially solicitous and, worried in case Heliogabalus should attempt to poison her son, she would not allow his food or drink to be prepared by the palace staff, but only by servants she deemed trustworthy. The Praetorian Guard kept a close eye on things too.

Despite such strong precautions, Heliogabalus was determined to end his doubts and fears and set a plot in motion to demote his rival; the first thing he did was to take away the title of 'Caesar' from Alexander, thereby disinheriting him. The youth no longer appeared in any official capacity, either at festivals or in the *curia*. Not only did all this come to nothing, it led to a near riot, and marked the moment at which his fate hung in the balance. The senate listened carefully to Heliogabalus's speech, in which he stated that he now regretted the adoption and wished to refute it, demanding that Alexander be stripped of his title. But Maesa's work had not gone for nothing; the government and the army both loved him and did not appreciate such a wrong done to a pleasing and promising member of the royal family. The senate said nothing, although their stony silence gave their message as clearly as any words could have done; they sat waiting to see from which direction the wind would blow. To accentuate this breach with his cousin, Heliogabalus refused to appear with him as co-consul at official engagements, which stressed his disaffection. This was also a clever move; by refusing to participate in official functions he brought the civil duties of government to a standstill, and until they disinherited his cousin he would not allow the proper running of the state to continue.

This obvious snub made it very clear to Alexander's supporters that he was no longer in favour and therefore in danger. He needed protection. Worse, Heliogabalus had unwisely declared that the soldiers must deface any statue of Alexander and erase the title of 'Severus' which had been placed there – unwise, as these were the properties of the army. As Alexander was a favourite of the soldiers, they made a great hue and cry over the matter, their anger fuelled by the urging of Maesa and Mamaea.

The reaction of the senate and the army to his decisions may have shocked Heliogabalus, as he had no reason to believe that they held him any animosity. Whether these incidents changed his mind or not, it had become clear that Alexander was becoming more and more popular in Rome.

A story told in the *Historia Augusta* - which must be treated with caution – suggests that Heliogabalus plotted Alexander's assassination in the Garden of Spes Vetus, and smeared mud over his inscription on his statues; but the attempt was never made. Whether any of this bears any truth at all, certainly the army was rumbling its discontent, and, as the outcry rose in violence, Heliogabalus knew that if he did nothing he was doomed. He was losing control.

Among those baying for his blood were the army and the Praetorians, and if he allowed the rising discontent to continue then he would be signing his own death warrant. Perhaps he had not realised the enormous affection in which the people and the army held Alexander, an affection nurtured and cultivated by his grandmother and aunt. According to Herodian, The Emperor, in his usual blunt way, decided to gauge the popularity of Alexander for himself, and decided upon a dubious plan; he put out the news that his cousin was dying, and awaited the general reaction.

The ruse did not succeed, and Heliogabalus's vanity almost proved his downfall. The Praetorians, guessing at foul play, were incensed, and refused to leave their camp unless given sure proofs that Alexander was alive and well. Seeing that he was backed into a corner, Heliogabalus ordered the imperial litter to be sent for, and, with his cousin by his side, rode out to the Praetorian camp. It was a courageous step to voluntarily ride into the lions' den. The guards opened the door to them and led them both up to the Temple. They cheered Alexander enthusiastically, but pointedly ignored their Emperor.

Only now did Heliogabalus fully realise that his lifestyle had not been accepted by the people. It was a soul-destroying revelation to him, but as well as that he realised that he was the victim of a long-planned conspiracy. He had to do something to save his reputation, and the situation; if his subjects were allowed to voice their disapproval whenever he appeared in public, he would be beaten. Then he considered that a number of paid servants had been planted among the crowds; if he could eliminate them, it could prove that the

Alexandrian faction were a small minority. In a rash moment of pique, he decided to regain respect and authority by demanding the arrest and punishment of those who had cheered the loudest for his cousin, thinking by this measure to quell what appeared to be a rising rebellion. Things turned ugly. The soldiers became incensed when they heard their hated Emperor, and only did not kill him because he at least seemed to be on amiable terms with his successor. But their mood was unforgiving, and now that matters had reached a head they were set upon putting things to rights and insisted upon a scouring of the palace. They demanded that all those who had been given promotions by the Emperor because of his aesthetic tastes should be handed over for execution – especially those known to have the same sexual orientation as he. In other words, there was to be a cleansing of homosexuals from the heart of Rome.

In the face of the military might displayed against him, the appalled Heliogabalus had no choice but to surrender to the will of the soldiers, but not before having begged them for clemency. It was of no use. The summary executions began. But when they came to Hieracles, it was too much for the grieving boy, whose love for his consort was real and deep. He supplicated himself before them and pleaded for them to be merciful, and even offered his own life in exchange for his safety.

'Grant me this one man, whatever you may have been pleased to suspect about him - or else kill me.'

For the time being Heliogabalus was spared, and his show of courage before the soldiers had not failed to impress them – so

Hieracles was spared too. But at last Heliogabalus realised the extreme peril he was in, at the mercy of the army and the Praetorian Guard who, he now knew, were affiliated to his enemies. Now he fully understood the political manoeuvrings which had been going on behind his back. That he had been outplayed and outfoxed by his wily grandmother. He had no means to fight against the ranged might of the armed forces, and there was one way – and one only – of returning to his past status. It was obvious that his aunt and grandmother had huge ambitions and at all costs wanted to remain in the seat of power, wielding it behind a figurehead from their family. After Heliogabalus, there was only one heir apparent, and that was Alexander. It was clear how far down the imperial path the boy had already walked, and how he had been groomed as the most acceptable successor after he had gone; it was also clear that his own usefulness was drawing to a close. Alexander had to be eliminated. If that could be achieved then he would be the sole man with the right to the Empire, and the only one on which Maesa could pin her hopes. At the death of Alexander, Maesa would be trapped; to cling to power she would have to change her allegiance. That was what Heliogabalus was banking on.

Although Hay tries hard to exculpate Heliogabalus from the taint of planning to murder his cousin, it is difficult to escape that conclusion. Although a kind boy with many good points, he was not the saint Hay would like us to believe, and all of the histories agree on this particular episode. Besides, Heliogabalus would now have known for certain that Alexander was on his grandmother's side, and a proven enemy. It was either his or his cousin's death.

It was a strategy of enormous risk, but the Emperor had nothing to lose, as his own death was staring him in the face. Once again he began to conspire against his cousin, gambling everything on one fate-defining blow. One account suggests that Heliogabalus was also worried that, after the death of Alexander, the senate may appoint someone else in his place, so he banished them from the city to pave the way for his plan. This is extremely unlikely, but his enemies were on their guard against an assassination attempt on their Caesar, and the plot was stifled almost as soon as it was born; again the Praetorians gave rise to such an outcry that Heliogabalus had to look for a way of escape. Last time he had managed to survive by demonstrating that he had been misjudged and that, despite appearances, he held Alexander in great affection. Then, he had been forced to surrender his friends to the executioner's sword. Now he had little to surrender. So again he made his way to the soldier's camp in the company of his cousin, a ruse which reflected sheer desperation.

The army, stirred by Maesa and Mamaea, had had enough, and wanted no more danger from their Emperor; so hardly had Heliogabalus walked in the camp than he found himself under an armed guard. The two women began to excite the army and to incite them to assassinate their Emperor; the only voice sounding in his favour was that of Soaemias, his mother. But she too had been dismissed by the grandmother and aunt, and found herself utterly alone. In some terror she ran to her son's tent and told him of the plans to have him killed. Frantically they sought some way of saving him. Then they formed a plan of escape - Heliogabalus would hide in a convenient chest and be carried away unseen past the soldiers. It was a plan born from utter desperation, but, seeing nothing better, the boy clambered into the chest and waited.

Meanwhile, the soldiers had been exacting summary justice on the Emperor's entourage, blaming them for plans to assassinate the heir apparent. According to Lampridius, some were disembowelled while others were pierced through the anus –impaled. When the soldiers discovered that Heliogabalus was missing, a search was instigated throughout the camp. In his room, they found the terrified Soaemias, who told them she had not seen her son. As they wandered about the tent, Soaemias's heart was in her mouth, and her one hope was that he would be overlooked. Then, what she feared came to pass. One of the soldiers noticed the chest. They opened it up and discovered him.

Here, knowing that he was facing death, Heliogabalus the man lost his composure and again became a child looking to the protection of his parent. The frightened boy ran to his mother, who hugged him tightly for the last time as the men drew their swords and approached. As they embraced each other, they were cut down and died together, and so it was that Heliogabalus found the end of his life just as he had found its beginning – in the arms of his mother.

Upon hearing of their Emperor's death, the army rejoiced and, not content with killing him and his mother, they proceeded to cut the heads from the corpses. Soaemias's body was thrown away, but that of Heliogabalus was carried off, dragged through the streets, and then, according to most accounts, thrown unceremoniously into the sewer which flowed into the Tiber river. In *Forum Romanum*,

Sextus Aurelius Victor describes the scene; although written in the fourth century, it reflects well the more contemporary accounts:

> **His body was dragged through the streets of the city just like the corpse of a dog, while the people, like soldiers, joked that he was a young bitch of uncontrolled and mad lusts. Finally, since the body wouldn't fit through the narrow opening of a sewer, it was dragged all the way to the Tiber and, after a weight was attached to prevent it from rising, was thrown into the River. He lived sixteen years [*sic*] and from what had happened was called … Tractitius ["the dragged man"].**

Whether he fitted into the sewer or not, this was the ignoble end of the boy Emperor Heliogabalus. He had been given several other names – Sardanapolis, Avitus, Antoninus, Marcus Antoninus, the False Antoninus, the Assyrian – but now was added a grimly ironic title. As his headless body floated down the river, he was named 'Tiberianus' – the man of the Tiber.

Chapter 10: The Fall Of The House Of Bassianus

It was now a matter of tradition for there to be reprisals after the death of an Emperor, and even more so in the case of one so universally detested as Heliogabalus. Now that he was out of the way, there was no bolting-hole for Hieracles and he was sought out and executed. Aurelius Eubulus, who had hidden beneath the coat-tails of his native countryman and Emperor, was also bereft of any protection and stood at the mercy of the soldiers and the people. They showed him little. Instead, they tore him apart for the vices and corruption he had been so plainly guilty of. Fulvius, the ex-city prefect, also perished. Now the soldiers rampaged in the city, and effectively eliminated any residue of Heliogabalus's former appointments. Everything was cleaned out, leaving no obstacle to Alexander's succession.

The blood-letting was savage even by the standards of the day. Virtually all of Heliogabalus's friends and acquaintances were rooted out and killed, the innocent as well as the guilty. Many had feathered their nests by the grace of the young Emperor's innocence and credulity; now these were left with no way to escape from the oncoming onslaught. Those undeserved who had been given eminent positions during Heliogabalus's desperate attempt to control his Empire were mercilessly weeded out and disposed of.

So venomous was the hatred directed towards Heliogabalus that after his death a concerted effort was made to erase his name from history. Clerks were engaged to go through official papers and records and erase his name from them, even when referred to as 'Antoninus'. The royal family, and the senate, were desperate in their effort to wipe away this shame from their blood, as if Heliogabalus's entire reign could simply be swept under the carpet of Roman annals. The fine Elagabalum was pulled down stone by stone and the holy meteorite packed away back to Emesa, to the rejoicing of its inhabitants. The young boy had been a stain on the character of the house of Bassianus, and as such his own kin decided to do whatever they could to eradicate his memory in favour of his successor.

It would perhaps have been better if they had succeeded. Instead, Heliogabalus would become famous in the worst possible way, as a pariah and a misfit. Cassius Dio and Herodian were already gathering their notes, and made a concerted effort to renounce him and present him in the blackest possible light. Thanks to their efforts, and those of the later Lampridius, Heliogabalus's character would be transformed from a well-meaning, kind-hearted boy, with a different sexual orientation but with a passion for religion, to a perverse imbecile with traits of insanity and immorality. To a large extent, they succeeded in their plan, and this is how Heliogabalus was remembered for almost two millennia.

An example of this systematic attempt at befouling the name of Heliogabalus may be seen in Lampridius's account of the senate's speech to Alexander at the time of his succession:

> 'The gods have rescued you from the hands of that evil man, may the gods keep you always! You suffered the foul despot as well, and you also have reason to lament the existence of that dirty and foul person. The gods have got rid of him, all of him, and have preserved you. The notorious Emperor has been rightly condemned. We and the state are happy in your rule! The notorious Emperor has been dragged off as an example of that which man should fear – the lascivious Emperor has been rightly punished, he who

dirtied the public honour. The divine gods allow Alexander a long life! This is how the gods show their rulings to us…'

Maesa and Mamaea had won the day by virtue of superior experience and devious conspiracy. Maesa had triumphed and emerged as the mentor of a new Emperor who was amenable and obedient, while Mamaea's dreams for her only son had at last come true. Finally, after being sidelined for three reigns of their Dynasty, they had achieved the positions of power they had lusted after for so long. The threat of Heliogabalus's scandals had been eliminated and the stage set for a smooth rise at the helm of the Empire.

The fruit of the Avetan branch of the tree of Bassianus had now been tested, and had proven to taste different from the Severan side. Whereas Severus and Antoninus had been marked by cruelty and wanton lusts, the two boys, Heliogabalus and Alexander, were gentle by nature and virtuous in their intentions, even if Heliogabalus's idiosyncrasies worked against him. Alexander was a noble youth who had not inherited any of his cousin's sexual preferences, nor his religious fervour; as such, he was in an enviable position to resurrect his family honour and be a credit to his imperial role. At his succession, he was given the honorary title of Augustus, as well as *pater patriae* and *pontifex maximus*. His mother Julia Mamaea became Augusta.

Cassius Dio believed that his succession had already been foretold, and in his histories writes a peculiar account of this portent; it may be of interest to quote it in full:

And I, for my part, am persuaded that all this did come about truly by some divine plan; though I infer this, not from what he said, but from the statement made to him by someone else, to the effect that an Alexander should come from Emesa to succeed him, and again from what happened in Upper Moesia and in Thrace. For shortly before this time a spirit, claiming to be the famous Alexander of Macedon, and resembling him in looks and general appearance, set out from the regions along the Ister, after first appearing there in some way or other, and proceeded through Moesia and Thrace, revelling in company with four hundred male attendants, who were equipped with thyrsi and fawn skins and did no harm. It was admitted by all those who were in Thrace at the time that lodgings and all provisions for the spirit were donated at public expense, and none — whether magistrate, soldier, procurator, or the governors of the provinces — dared to oppose the spirit either by word or deed, but it proceeded in broad daylight, as if in a solemn procession, as far as Byzantium, as it had foretold. Then taking ship, it landed in the territory of Chalcedon, and there, after performing some sacred rites by night and burying a wooden horse, it vanished. These facts I ascertained while still in Asia, as I have stated, before anything had been done at all about Bassianus at Rome.

Whether or not the shade of Alexander had hand-picked a band of companions and made this fantastic journey is open to debate; at any rate, the first priority for the new Emperor was to clean up the mess left by his predecessor and to give proof to the senate that he was a potentially capable and upright ruler. Under the direction of his grandmother and mother, he followed the book in everything he did, and the first thing he turned his mind to was a responsible man to lead the Praetorian Guard; the choice fell to Domitius Ulpian, a dedicated and able jurist and commander who soon set about tidying things up. Sadly, he was not fated to last very long. After the executions of the former Praetorian chiefs Flavanius and Chrestus, he found himself out of favour with the Praetorians themselves, who may have felt at risk after they had witnessed these deaths.

The Praetorian Guard itself had, as usual in such times of crisis, risen in power and showed a disposition to use or abuse it. Once again they had proven that they were the real power in Rome and could make or break an Emperor. The peaceful reign of Heliogabalus had suited them well; they had been well paid to keep faith with the imperial family and had had little to do to earn their money. Maesa's bribes were tantamount to a confession that the Guard held the ultimate power, and now that a young and inexperienced Emperor had taken up the diadem, they decided to make even more of their privileged position.

This pride led them to make attempts to rule the people, who were incensed and protested against their pretensions. Soon the cries of rebel discontents led to a full-scale riot. The mob angrily attacked the guard for three days, and even though they were not equipped for warfare, bearing only rude arms such as sticks and clubs, they beat down all defences and started to get the better of the soldiers. Angered by such a show of force – and the fact that they had been bettered – the Praetorians took to a dubious course of action. They set light to the houses. As the populace watched their homes burn they realised that soon the whole city would be swallowed in a mighty conflagration, so they had no choice but to capitulate with the worst possible grace.

Having put down this rebellion, the Praetorians turned their attention to Ulpian. Seeing himself in danger of his life he fled to the

Palace for the protection of the new Emperor and his grandmother, but not even they could avail against the fury of the guards, who, led by Epagathus, slew him anyhow. In this they over-reached themselves, and in the aftermath of so much bloodshed the senate felt that an example should be made. They were determined that the sting should be taken from the Paraetorian tail. Accordingly, they sent Epagathus to Egypt to govern the province, which to all intents and purposes seemed like a grand promotion but was really done to get him out of the way. They realised that if he were punished openly in Rome the Guard, sensing that their authority was being questioned, would offer reprisals; so he was despatched to the end of the Empire, from where he was secretly taken off to Crete and executed.

As so often is the case in times of insurrection, there was discontent both at home and abroad, men of power jostling for position when they assumed the government to be in a state of weakness. While those uprisings were quickly quashed in Rome, it was more difficult to stretch an arm to the extremes of the Empire, and in Mesopotamia things were reaching dangerous levels. At this point Rome needed a great commander, but unfortunately Alexander had had no experience of war. To make matters worse, his grandmother Julia Maesa, the Godmother of the Empire and a lady endowed with huge experience of Roman politics in peace and in war, finally died. A scheming, ambitious woman, she nevertheless had a flair for the politics which her grandson desperately needed, now more than ever. Despite her obvious thirst for eminence, she was realistic and forward-thinking, and was one of the prime instigators in the deposition of Heliogabalus when she saw that his course of action was not becoming to an Emperor of Rome. The first lady of the imperial family, her political acumen would be sorely missed.

Alexander had the potential of becoming a great Emperor, and restored the dignity of the senate as well as putting right many of the unfortunate misdoings of his dead cousin. He sorely missed Maesa, but his mother Mamaea, although less experienced, was a good influence on him and all his secret grooming paid off. A naturally kind and noble boy, his single aim seems to have been to win back the affection of the people for the role of Emperor.

Despite the differences between the reigns of Heliogabalus and Alexander, their kinship within the Avitan branch of the family gave them certain similarities. They had taken office at a very young age – Heliogabalus at fourteen and Alexander at thirteen. Both had a generous nature and neither had a penchant for cruelty or double-dealing. They each had a love for their people and an ability to cross the boundaries of class and communicate with all levels of Roman society. Neither of them tried to abuse the power which had been entrusted to them. Not least, both were ruled to a large extent by women, Alexander to such an extent that he was often known as Alexander Mamaeae – Mamaea's Alexander. Mamaea's influence was all-invasive. She even had apartments in the Royal Palace, and various public buildings were named after her.

On the other hand, there were several notable differences between the two. Alexander had little time for pomp and circumstance, and the extravagance of Heliogabalus was uncongenial to him. Instead of imperial Syrian robes, Alexander preferred to walk around wearing a plain white robe devoid of ornamentation, as well as ordinary cloaks and Roman togas. He did not believe in divine right, and did much to restore power to the senate. He was frugal to the point of miserliness, and although this can be seen as a backlash from Heliogabalus's reckless spending, in the end it also brought him some criticism. He became involved in the decision-making machinery of the state, and worked hard to achieve financial stability. He also looked masculine and prided himself on the martial arts. All of these things made a favourable impression on the senate and the people, and were probably engineered to do so.

Because we have little data, there has been some contention as to who directed Alexander in the first years of his reign. Most sources suggest Maesa and, after her, Mamaea. But the workings of state policy and the sheer size of the Empire suggest that others must have been involved. It is commonly stated that Ulpian acted as a kind of regent, but as he was killed a year into Alexander's reign his influence must have been short-lived. The most reasonable assumption is that he was advised by the tried and trusted cabinet which had been assembled by Maesa and Mamaea prior to Heliogabalus's death, and whose names have not been transmitted to posterity.

It was important for Alexander to ally himself in a good marriage. There is a suspicion that the first lady Alexander married drove Mamaea to a jealous rage. She is named by Lampridius as Memmia, the daughter of Sulpicius, and the event seems to be confirmed by Herodian. He suggests that her father was condemned on a charge of conspiracy and that she herself was banished to Africa. Herodian remarks that the father's name was Macrinus, but there is no further evidence on the matter.

He did marry one Sallustia Orbiana in 225, who received the official title of Sallustia Barbia Orbiana Augusta; she was the daughter of an eminent statesman called L Seius Sallustius. Now in a respectable and honourable marriage, he restored the religious traditions so respected of the Romans, and paid homage to all the gods in the Pantheon – even, it is said, Jesus Christ (which bought him approbation from later historians). He embarked on a practical and ambitious building programme, erecting the last great aqueduct in 226 – the Aqua Alexandrina – and other projects including a set of apartments for his mother known as the Diaetae Mamaeae. There is no doubt that, if he had enjoyed the same period of peace as that of Heliogabalus, he would have restored dignity to the house of Bassianus.

There were two domestic uprisings at home in his lifetime, one engineered by his father-in-law Sallustius, who let himself to ruled by ambition once he had been exalted to the position of 'Caesar'. His attempt on the life of Alexander failed in 227, and as a result his daughter was held in suspicion. Alexander had no choice but to divorce her, which he did, and exiled her to Libya. There is a suspicion that Herodian and Lampridius may have been confusing Memmia with Sallustia.

The only other uprising was by a man named Taurinus, who was even hailed as Augustus; but after the failure he committed suicide, drowning himself in the waters of the Euphrates.

The rest of Alexander's thirteen-year reign may be summed up as follows.

A foreign threat came in the form of a man named Artaxerxes. Artaxerxes was ambitious. A Persian, it was his burning ambition to resurrect the glory days of his country's old Empire, and during the peaceful years of Heliogabalus he had been marshalling his troops, expanding them and preparing them for war. Now that Rome seemed to be in turmoil, he took his chance. First of all he attacked the Parathians, who put up some resistance in three hard-fought battles; but in the end Artaxerxes was triumphant and killed the Parthian King, Artabanus. To enhance his position, he decided to invade the country of the Medes, which he did with remarkable success, apportioning a good part of the land. Having seen little warfare for some time, the Medes were no match for the ravaging Persians, and Artaxerxes controlled his newly-acquired territory by menace and show of arms. So far, his campaigns had been a great success, and the next step was to attack Armenia. But this attempt ended in failure, and some Medes in his troops ran off, possibly to regroup and prepare a large force with which to defend themselves. So Artaxerxes experienced his first serious reversal; but his troops were still fearsome and a force to be reckoned with. Worryingly, he even boasted that he would invade Syria and so become a serious threat to Roman interests in the region.

In contrast, the Roman forces had become stagnant and idle, not relishing the idea of a return to war. Discipline had reached rock bottom. In the Mesopotamian legions, the commander Falvius Heracleo had tried to muster his men and been murdered for the attempt, a gross act of mutiny which shocked the nation. It seems that the army was not prepared to fight unless it was to protect the idleness which had been instilled in them during the years of peace. They even went so far as to threaten any commander who had had a reputation for severity, in the fear that such an example may serve as a precedent for others in charge. The historian Cassius Dio was singled out, as he says that he ruled the Pannonian legions with a strong hand; and the soldiers insisted that he be arrested and surrendered up to them. In fact, at this point the future historian was in grave danger.

Dio found an ally in the shape of his new Emperor, Alexander, who not only took little heed of the threats but went as far as to appoint him consul with him, and to pay his expenses out of his own pocket. Although obviously moved by his Emperor's faith and generosity, this did not lessen the risk to Dio himself, and as the threats escalated Alexander considered it best that Dio spent the remainder of his consulship outside Rome for his own safety. So Dio went into retirement and settled down to write his valuable history without which most of the events in the life of Heliogabalus would remain hidden.

The affairs in the east were now becoming serious, and the Emperor decided to go to war himself, visiting the region in the company of his officers and his mother. Local discontent had been quashed and the soldiers were delighted to see their Emperor taking an active interest in the situation. It gave them a new determination and lease of life. They took to battle with vigour and their old experience soon told; before long the advances of Artaxerxes were checked and the Romans took the upper hand. But as the war progressed the Germanic tribes, hearing of the disputes in Parthia, took advantage of the situation and began their own uprising. On the horns of a hostile dilemma the only solution was to close with Artaxerxes and turn to the suppression of Germany. A pact was therefore concluded, and after peace had been restored Alexander and the troops headed off to deal with the new threat.

Although Alexander himself did not participate in the fighting, his presence was a definite fillip to the army's confidence. Alexander arrived in the German capital of Mogunticaum (present-day Mains) and immediately morale improved. The main action was taking place (as it usually did) on the banks of the Rhine, so first of all the soldiers built a bridge over which they could attack. Bridge-building was an art which had been adopted and perfected by the Romans. Many times had Julius Caesar resorted to it in his dealings with the hostile Germanic tribes. Until the arrival of the Emperor, the troops were under the command of Caius Julius Verus Maximinus, a tough, Thracian, no-nonsense soldier who was one of the men responsible for the tight discipline among his men. In return, his soldiers loved him and gave him unquestioning loyalty. Under the command of such a man, and with the presence of their Emperor, success was assured.

However, Alexander preferred peace at all costs, so he negotiated with the enemy and bought their loyalty. The soldiers were not pleased at the outcome, as they were geared up for war and eager to fight. To pay off the enemy seemed base to them and tarnished the honour of the fighting troops. Discontent took over, and thinking their Emperor to be afraid and spineless, they mutinied under the directions of Maximinus. The result was that the soldiers forced an entry into Alexander's quarters, and, in a scenario painfully reminiscent of Heliogabalus's end, both he and his mother were butchered by their own men.

Maximinus took over command, and led several brutal punitive expeditions over the Rhine. Soon after, he was chosen as Emperor, although there were a number of grumblings about that; two uprisings against him were ruthlessly quashed, and Maximinus became the first of a line of soldier-emperors of the third century. It had become increasingly obvious that the soldiery were no longer prepared to be ruled by an aristocrat, and only a tough military commander could control them. The bluff, uneducated Thracian commander – nicknamed Thrax because of his provincial origins – became the Empire's leader in a move which changed the face of the imperial family.

With the demise of Alexander and his mother Mamaea, the Bassiani dynasty foundered. The legacy of intrigue, murder and ambition which had marred the family's destiny was left to posterity in the writings of the contemporary historians; the only saving grace being the leadership of the last, Alexander. Taking over from his cousin as a boy, he had grown to manhood and did much to restore the prestige so carelessly thrown away by many of his predecessors. But his military inexperience, and desire for peace, led him in conflict with a changing world where tough military prowess was to replace the aristocratic preference of the past.

The demise of Alexander was the catalyst for the Third Century Crisis during which the Roman Empire almost foundered. The battles for the imperial diadem, coupled with insurgencies throughout the Empire, led to a state of anarchy which lasted for half a century and was marked by bloodshed on an unprecedented scale. Eventually the Empire was split into three; the western Gallic and the eastern Palmyrene with the remnants between them. This violent period was marked with war, disease and economic disaster, and finally ended with the coming of the Emperor Diocletian in 264 AD. A far cry from the peaceful reign of Varius Avitus Bassianus.

If history denounced many of the actions of his forebears, it reserved its odium for the boy-Emperor Heliogabalus. As the most vilified emperor in the history of ancient Rome, he was also surely the most tragic, and the least fitted to live in the public glare. Inured to humility by a childhood seeped in extravagance and excess, tormented with the confusion of his sexuality, and passionate only in his belief in his one god, Heliogabalus trod a narrow rocky path which was strewn with disaster. The seed of his own destruction lay in his tortured mind, and the only outlet for his frustrations and needs was a public display of his own neuroses. The wonder of his reign was that it lasted as long as it did. A boy elevated to the top of the world, he flaunted his omnipotence with ill-advised grandeur, while pinning up his demons for public display. His reign was a pitiful helter-skelter leading to shame and death, as irresistible as it was destructive.

But surely there was more to the Emperor Heliogabalus than just that. In the dim corridors of history, from the beacons of the towering figures of the great Caesars who had built and moulded that greatest of Empires, certainly at least some light flickered over the face of the boy who was cut down almost before he had reached manhood. If he was the most controversial Emperor of the Severan Dynasty, there is little doubt that he was the grandest. What an impressive figure he must have cut, dressed in his sumptuous robes of office riding in a cortege of 600 chariots, the most regal and imperial of all the emperors who had gone before him! And what a rare combination, the matchless extravagance married to a compassionate nature, a boy who would give away fortunes at a meal-table and then weep for the oppressed! Of all emperors before and after, no-one had given his people such a spectacle of richness and grandeur, and no-one had been so recklessly destroyed by his personal inclinations. If thought of as the strangest, he was at least the most flamboyant and the most striking of all the Bassiani.

In the final analysis, Heliogabalus was killed not out of wrath but out of fear, not for what he was but what he appeared to be. *Monstrum in fronte, monstrum in animo.* It is simple to see a physical affliction – to sympathise and even empathise – but the dark mansion where mental problems lie is like a haunted castle people veer away from; that ghosts exist is a nonsense yet no-one wants to confront them. The natural aversion someone may feel when they see a natural bodily blemish is valid enough, but any pity often disappears and is transformed into revulsion when one is confronted by someone possessed by demons. Heliogabalus was beset with sexual forces which pushed him down a path which he was powerless to resist, and the majority of his contemporaries were repelled by the result. His oddities estranged him from his powerful enemies, and despite his good nature and sweet disposition he appeared alien and therefore someone to be avoided. In the end, he was put down just as one might destroy a sick beast.

He and his family are long gone now, only dimly lit in the pages of history with their ancient taint of immorality. The Temple in Rome with its fantastic trappings was stripped bare soon after the boy-Emperor died with his mother on the edge of a sword, and with him his dreams of the great god he had worshipped to such disdain in the public temples of Rome. But still the Temple of Emesa stood, oblivious to the passing time, its stones glistening in the Syrian sun.

Printed in Poland
by Amazon Fulfillment
Poland Sp. z o.o., Wrocław